ISRAELI FA

ISRAELI FAMILY
AND COMMUNITY
Women's Time

Editor

HANNAH NAVEH
Tel Aviv University

VALLENTINE MITCHELL
LONDON • PORTLAND, OR

First Published in 2003 in Great Britain by
VALLENTINE MITCHELL
Crown House, 47 Chase Side
London N14 5BP

and in the United States of America by
VALLENTINE MITCHELL
c/o ISBS, 920 NE 58th Avenue, Suite 300
Portland, Oregon, 97213-3786

Website: www.vmbooks.com

British Library Cataloguing in Publication Data

Israeli family and community: women's time
  1. Women – Israel – Social conditions 2. Family – Israel
  3. Feminism – Israel
  I. Naveh, Hannah
  305.4'2'095694
                ISBN 0 85303 506 7 (cloth)
                ISBN 0 8 5303 505 9 (paper)

Library of Congress Cataloging-in-Publication Data

Israeli family and community : women's time / editor Hannah Naveh.–1st
ed.
    p. cm.
Includes bibliographical references and index.
First published as a special issue of: The Journal of Israeli History
(ISSN 0952-3367), Vol. 21, No. 1/2, Spring/Autumn 2002."
  ISBN 0-85303-506-7 (cloth) – ISBN 0-85303-505-9 (pbk.)
  1. Women–Israel. 2. Sexism–Israel. 3.Sex role–Israel. 4.
Family–Israel. I. Naveh, Hannah. II. Journal of Israeli History.
  HQ1728.5.I874 2003
  305.42'095694–dc21   2003014724

This group of studies first appeared as a special issue of
The Journal of Israeli History (ISSN 0952-3367), Vol. 21, No.1/2,
Spring/Autumn 2002, published by Frank Cass

Printed in Great Britain by Antony Rowe Ltd., Chippenham, Wiltshire

Contents

Contributors   vii

Introduction   **Hannah Naveh**   xi

The Politics of Honor: Patriarchy, the State and
the Murder of Women in the Name of Family
Honor   **Manar Hasan**   1

Familism, Postmodernity and the State:
The Case of Israel   **Sylvie Fogiel-Bijaoui**   38

Women and the Changing Israeli Kibbutz:
A Preliminary Three-Stage Theory   **Amia Lieblich**   63

"Career Women" or "Working Women"?
Change versus Stability for Young
Palestinian Women in Israel   **Khawla Abu Baker**   85

Normalizing Inequality:
Portrayals of Women in the Israeli Media   **Dafna Lemish**   110

Women of the Wall: Radical Feminism as
an Opportunity for a New Discourse in Israel   **Leah Shakdiel**   126

"Gone to Soldiers": Feminism and the
Military in Israel   **Orly Lubin**   164

Index   193

Contributors

HANNAH NAVEH. Professor of Hebrew Literature and Chair of the NCJW Women and Gender Studies Program, Tel Aviv University. Her recent publications include *Min, migdar, politikah* (Sex, Gender, Politics: Women in Israel) (Tel Aviv, 1999) (co-author); and *Nosim ve-nosot: Sipurei masa ba-sifrut ha-ivrit ha-hadashah* (Women and Men Travellers: The Travel Narrative in Hebrew Literature) (Tel Aviv, 2002).

MANAR HASAN. PhD student in the Department of Sociology and Anthropology at Tel Aviv University. She has published articles on Palestinian women in Israel and was among the founders, in 1991, of Al-Fanar, the Palestinian Feminist Organization.

SYLVIE FOGIEL-BIJAOUI. Senior Lecturer in Sociology at the New School of Journalism, College of Management, Tel Aviv, and the Head of the Gender Studies Center, Beit-Berl College, where she teaches Political Sociology. Her current research focuses on citizenship; women and the trade union movement in Israel; and "Gendering the Kibbutz: Utopia in a Post-Utopian Era."

AMIA LIEBLICH. Professor of Psychology, Hebrew University of Jerusalem. Her work on the Israeli kibbutz was published in *Kibbutz Makom* (New York, 1981), and more recently in *Gilgulo shel Makom* (The Metamorphosis of Makom) (Tel Aviv, 2000).

KHAWLA ABU BAKER. Senior Lecturer in the Department of Behavioral Science, Emek Yezreel College, Israel, and Director of "Mar'ah" Institute for Middle Eastern Women Studies. Her recent publications include: *Ha-dor ha-zakuf* (The Stand Tall Generation: The Palestinian Citizens of Israel Today) (Jerusalem, 2002) (with D. Rabinowitz); *Mediniyut ha-revahah ha-hevratit veha-hinukhit bekerev ha-okhlusiyah ha-aravit be-Yisrael* (The Social and Educational Welfare Policies towards the Arab Citizens of Israel) (Jerusalem, 2001); and *Be-derekh lo slulah: Nashim araviyot ke-manhigot politiyot be-Yisrael* (A Rocky Road: Arab Women as Political Leaders in Israel) (Ra'anana, 1998).

DAFNA LEMISH. Associate Professor and Chair of the Department of Communication, Tel Aviv University, Israel. Her research and teaching interests include gender-related issues of media representations and consumption; the role of the media in the construction of gender identity; as well as children, media and leisure. She has published many scholarly articles and book chapters on these topics, in both English and Hebrew.

LEAH SHAKDIEL. Teacher and educator, social activist in the areas of Jewish education, social justice, civil and human rights, peace and feminism. In 1988 she became Israel's first female member of a local Religious Council following a successful struggle that ended with a landmark Supreme Court decision. Most recently she has worked in teacher training at Ben Gurion University, and gender equity programs for the Ministry of Education, and has taught Jewish feminism in The Shechter Institute in Jerusalem. She currently heads "Be'er" (a well), a new program for women which combines Torah study with community work, in Yeruham.

ORLY LUBIN. Head of the Department of Poetics and Comparative Literature at Tel Aviv University, where she also teaches in the Department of Film and Television, and a founding member and head advisor of the NCJW Gender and Women Interdisciplinary Program. Her recent book, *Women Reading Women* (Haifa, 2003), is a critique of reader/spectator response theories.

"How can we reveal our place, first as it is bequeathed to us by tradition, and then as we want to transform it?"

Julia Kristeva, "Women's Time"
New Maladies of the Soul

Introduction

Hannah Naveh

This is the second of a set of two interconnected volumes devoted to exploring women's time in two modes: that of recounting stories and histories of women, along with other marginalized groups, categories and classes, and placing them back into history; and that of applying a feminist gaze to the dominant order and reason to expose its policies of inclusion/exclusion. Feminist criticism often turns to the public sphere for detecting discrimination and disentitlement — this aspect was the main theme of *Gender and Israeli Society: Women's Time*. This volume begins with examinations of the same policies in the "natural" sphere of women's experience, that is, the private sphere — that of the family and the home.

Manar Hasan examines the phenomenon of the murder of women in the name of "family honor" within Palestinian society in Israel to detect not merely a case of brutality against women but a well-orchestrated and tightly supervised institution designed to maintain patriarchal order on the part of the family and the state. Hasan questions the understanding of women-murders as inherent to cultural factors within Palestinian society, without due consideration to the role played by the state in perpetuating the practice. She argues that the politics of the patriarchal family and the politics of the state coincide in their combined interests to uphold the structure of Palestinian society and to turn a blind eye to its practices in return for so-called stability and self-governing. By supposedly maintaining a policy of minimal intervention in the name of multiculturalism and cultural autonomy, the state thus supports violence against women. Hasan goes further to suggest that the practice of these women-murders is based on the economy of the patriarchal family, and that murdering women in the name of family honor, when the real trespassers in the cases at hand are men, proves to be "cheaper" for the *hamula* than the murder of men. She even goes on to consider the economic basis for the fact that a woman, even after marriage, continues to bear in her body and behavior the honor of those men who are her patrilineal kin rather than that of her husband and his male kin. Hasan deals here not only with the symbolics of the female body, as it is dealt with in several papers in this volume, which leads to marginalization and oppression. She deals with the actual corporeality of being female in an androcentric and patriarchal order, which leads to the endorsement of her physical annihilation.

Sylvie Fogiel-Bijaoui turns to the results of the predominant concept of familism in Israeli society, as it is upheld in its main ethno-religious groups: Israeli Jews and Israeli Palestinians (Muslims, Christians and Druze). Familism — the centrality of "the family" as a private and collective institution — has become a dominant value in Israel because it is institutionalized through the religious laws of all these groups and serves as a common norm in a country where two national collectives are in conflict, whether open or latent. And so, although post-industrialist societies, Israel included, have seen a diversity of family forms and mutations, familism in its traditional form still has a strong hold on Israeli society and shapes the limits of its accommodation of deep change. While the force of capitalism and its processes of individualization and privatization are evident in the postmodern, multifaceted practice of familism in Israel, the different forms of Israeli families today still continue to reflect and perpetuate the gender, class and ethno-religious stratification of Israeli society. The concept of familism, therefore, the base of which is grounded in religious patriarchal systems, eventually forecloses any attempt to change the status of women and of other minorities in Israel.

The family form offered by the kibbutz in Israel ever since its establishment in the Second and Third *Aliyah* has recently suffered a major value shift. From being valorized, among other reasons, for its supposed gender egalitarianism, it has come into disrepute as an assault against women, motherhood and femininity. Amia Lieblich offers a three-stage study of kibbutz women's perception of their role in the creation and maintenance of norms and practices regarding family life and childcare arrangements. Lieblich's research defines an initial subordination of women's positions to the egalitarian discourse of the kibbutz, in the name of which women supported and adhered to the kibbutz family and childcare institutions as prescribed by the ideology of collectivity and communality. They entertained a belief in the power of these new institutions to de-patriarchalize the former social order and to authentically liberate women. The second stage — titled "the feminine revolution" — brought on a dramatic change, when women reconsidered their roles and demanded their reversal, thereby effecting a strong impact on kibbutz history. It was women who led the change in the common education system and abolished the overnight sleeping in children's homes, which was so distinctive of kibbutz life and family arrangement till then. This change in gender politics reflects the shift from first wave to second wave feminism and rejects a liberal politics of (so-called) equality for a politics of significant and relevant difference. Nevertheless it introduced kibbutz women to the "double-shift" working world and could not possibly operate for equality without a deeper systemic change. The third stage Lieblich finds — titled "the masculine revolution" — is indeed a type of backlash, so typical of the history of women's movements and achievements. In this stage, currently in process, drastic changes in the basic assumptions that invented the kibbutz lead to new organizational and economic arrangements. Privatization here, as already shown in Fogiel-Bijaoui's work, may support diversifying of institutions but it rarely equalizes a stratified society. The complexity of women's position vis-à-vis family and childcare is most evident in Lieblich's conclusion that women play a minor role in the transition the kibbutz is undergoing today and more than men show an interest in preserving the "old kibbutz."

Khawla Abu Baker's study provides valuable insight into the question of women's options in the labor/work/career world. Interestingly enough, her research corresponds with some of the problems kibbutz women claim to have experienced in their struggle for normalizing their working life. Abu Baker shows how attitudes to family, marriage, divorce and other political, social and cultural norms control the freedom of an Arab woman to develop a career, and how she is usually constrained, in cases of relative freedom, to merely "go to work." Within the changing Arab world, including that of the Palestinians in Israel, young career women place themselves in direct confrontation with traditional social norms by introducing modern concepts of women's duties and lifestyle. Based on her long and intensive social work in a family therapy clinic which she founded, Abu Baker closely examines discussions between Palestinian spouses who sought therapy for reasons of contention over the woman's wish to work and to develop a career. The uncensored and authentic nature of clinical sessions offers a rare opportunity to view attempts to bring about social change in the face of the forces of social stability and traditional values in the life of Palestinian families and individuals in Israel. Although the exposure to Jewish and Americanized (and globalized) values and lifestyle in Israel is part of these young Palestinians experience, they find in themselves a strong loyalty to their ethno-religious values. So, even women who have their husband's and family's consent to seeking work outside of the home rarely find they are permitted to develop a career in the full sense. Again, this paper emphasizes not only the diversity of the women's agenda in Israel, and not only the need to personalize and contextualize the concept of "women," but also the persistent inability to find political time and cultural space for women within the grid of patriarchal societies.

Dafna Lemish studies the portrayal of women in Israeli print and broadcast media to demonstrate the marginality of women in Israeli society. Fundamental principles of patriarchal thought are revealed in her analysis. Most significant are those of relegating the female subject to the private sphere, restricting the representation of females to the physical functions of sex and reproduction, and placing women in the realm of emotions, irrationality and uncultivated behavior. The exclusion of women from forums of political, cultural and economic power as disseminated by various media is achieved by negation of their agentic subjectivity and repression of their rights for representation. Women's achievements in all realms of life are ignored or overshadowed in the media by a stereotypically limited range of traditional roles. In the present context of Israeli society, dominated as it is by a national discourse of (male) security and militarism, the media portrayals of women serve as a socializing mechanism for maintaining discrimination against women and for normalizing their inequality in the public gaze.

Leah Shakdiel offers a radical feminist critique of the activity of the Women of the Wall group (WoW), a group of Orthodox women who seek to give women an active role in public prayer within the limits of Orthodox policies forbidding mixed-sex prayer. She exposes the shortcomings of Israeli liberal discourse to come to terms with the radical subjectivity of WoW and with the challenge it posited for both secular and religious political bodies. The cultural split between women and nation, as it is conceptualized in the discourse of modern nationality, is brought forth with great force in WoW's reception both in Israel and in America. Shakdiel argues that relegating it to the arena of the chasms between the religious parties demotes the understanding of WoW's activism, whereas it is actually a thrust at redefining the role and rights of (all) women to participate bodily in the body of the nation on their own terms. WoW thus suggests what verges on the incomprehensible: Orthodox feminism, in which women conceptualize and practice their equality within religious discourse.

Much in the same line of radical feminism, Orly Lubin concludes this volume with an illuminating analysis of a gallery of visual representations of military Palmah women in pre-state Israel and in Israel today. She compounds theories of sexual difference with theories of sexual performativity to expose the egalitarian principle of drafting Jewish women to the Israeli army as a state apparatus designed to include and exclude women from the national project at one and the same time. What is included in the military role women enact, so the visuals suggest, is a representation of life and vitality, which the presence of the female body (whether as mother or as lover) seems to promise, and thus to assuage and deny peril of death for the national subject, i.e. the man in arms. In this role women are recruited not for executing military feats on an equal standing with men, a belief that political discourse in Israel seems to advocate, but rather to enable men to execute their life-risking tasks of violence with greater relative compliance and enthusiasm. Moreover, the (at times) overtly sexual implications of the visuals seem to serve as a reminder of the heterosexual commitment the men are called upon to uphold, and to balance off the homosocial aspects which military societies and fraternities cultivate. On the other hand, women are never included in the visual representations as an oppositional option, which may set off militarism with a discourse of pacifism and nonviolence. Proper and "correct" Israel womanhood is thus constructed under a strict policy of subservience to the maintenance of militarism and violence. Lubin's conclusions support Lemish's work on Israeli media and offer yet another case for observing the subservient role of the images of femaleness and femininity.

The preceding volume to this one (*Gender and Israeli Society: Women's Time*) included seven studies, which the editors hope may broaden the readers' exposure to contemporary Israeli research engaging in women, feminist criticism and minority discourse. The readers may find in that volume Hanna Herzog's study of the *Yishuv* (pre-state) historiography, where she exposes the fundamentals of feminist criticism by introducing non-conventional critical parameters to cultural research, showing how the production of scientific data when adhering to institutional paradigms is designed to exclude women's significance and achievements in the political sphere. Rachel Rojanski also examines women within political organizations and enters an ongoing debate within the feminist agenda: should women apply their political weight to women's organizations and thus consolidate their power to create significant social change, or should they work from within existing (men's) organizations and political parties and gain access to the public arena with the endorsement of established (male) leaders? Rojanski studies the case of Esther Mintz-Aberson who chose to act in the Poalei Zion party. Billie Melman argues that history and collective memory are gendered and tightly supervised by androcentric interests. Her paper calls on historians to employ gender as a critical tool and category and she focuses on the case of Sarah Aaronsohn. Judith Tydor Baumel studies gendered collective memory by examining the continuous yet changing representation of women in Israeli military memorials since the establishment of the state. She proposes a typology of various gender motifs, which are prominent in a range of military memorials, and discusses the generational dynamics of their development within the context of commemoration discourse in Israel.

Michael Feige's work also examines gendered aspects of national commemoration. Feige reflects on changes in the social, political and religious status of religious women in Israel by examining the case of the settlement Rehelim, which was established in 1992 by a group of religious women settlers to commemorate Rachel Druk of Shilo, who was killed in a Palestinian attack. Tsila Abramovitz Ratner focuses on the representation of women in the contemporary literary works of Israeli women authors who come from an Orthodox background and whose oeuvre centers on depicting religious social and familial life. The recent upsurge in Israel of writing by these women has evoked great public interest and fascination in the secular reading public, for whom the Orthodox world is usually inaccessible especially in matters concerning women, whose political and sexual invisibility nurtures mystification of their otherness. The review essay by Tova Cohen, which addresses Iris Parush's recent book, *Reading Women: The Benefit of Marginality in Nineteenth Century Eastern European Jewish Society*, closes the first volume. It affords a special opportunity to glimpse at a dialogue between two of the most prominent researchers of women's culture in the *Haskalah* (Enlightenment) period. Readers of this volume therefore are urged to seek the first one as well.

It is the editors' hope that these two multidisciplinary volumes of recent work from Israel do indeed create some women's time. Women's time is based on a procedure of resistance to self-evident truths and knowledge, which are too often constructed within the terms of androcentrism and patriarchy. Women's time decenters dominant narratives and releases gazes, problematics and interests, which have been systematically refused time. The concept of women's time serves also as a model for further investigation of other obliterated narratives, and therefore serves the well-being of all human beings, in Israel and outside.

The Politics of Honor:
Patriarchy, the State and the Murder of Women in the Name of Family Honor*

Manar Hasan

On 19 August 1994, the journalist Shaul Adar published an article in a local Jerusalem paper, *Kol ha-Ir*, on the work of Herut Lapid, who is involved in obtaining the release of Israelis from prisons around the world and their rehabilitation in Israel. Lapid, who usually deals only with Israeli Jews behind bars, decided this time to address the case of an Arab man from the Galilee village of Tor'an who had murdered his daughter for the sake of family honor. As Lapid commented, "he did a terrible thing, but for him, not to kill his daughter is like for the Chief Rabbi to eat pork." Lapid went on:

> He was obliged to kill his daughter just as the rabbi cannot eat pork. This a part of the culture of a people, a nation and religion, and if someone is a believer, he acts in accordance with his faith.... If he were a young man, I wouldn't be getting involved in his case.... But because he's old and in poor health, he has to be released for humanitarian reasons and allowed to return home.

In July 1994, a young woman from the village of Ramah was murdered by her brother, 17 years her junior. Ikhlas, who had spent many years in the United States, had returned to Israel to set up relief institutions for children and the elderly in her community. Deputy Commander Victor Ma'or, head of the local police in Carmiel, said after the murder that Ikhlas was doomed to die, "because that's their mentality."[1]

This "Orientalist" approach — "Arabist" in its local version, which attributes various social practices of the Arab Middle East, among them the practice of murder of women for the sake of family honor, to inherent and axiomatic cultural factors, while ignoring almost entirely the political factors that influence the stabilization and even the shaping of these practices — is neither new nor rare among sociologists and anthropologists.[2] For them, such things as the apparatus of the state are virtually invisible; the object pulled out of thin air and brought into the research "laboratories" is some sort of independent, resistant and unchanging "creature."

This approach is prevalent in much of the literature that treats social issues in Arab societies in general and in Palestinian society in particular. It is predominant in the small amount of material dealing directly with the practice of murder of women for the sake of "family honor." The outstanding representatives of this approach are Gideon Kressel and Joseph Ginat.[3] Ginat's research and theses are of special importance: both as a scholar and former government "advisor for Arab affairs"— an institution that determines the policy of control over the Palestinian population in Israel — he illustrates the double-faced character of the Orientalist investigator. First he injects and implements government policy within the society under investigation, shaping it along the lines of the state's agenda, then he studies that same society, only to contend in the end that his "research findings" spring from *fixed and unchanging* cultural or religious elements. In such sociological sleight-of-hand, the researcher behaves like an expert in legerdemain: in one hand he hides his object while in the other he discloses it, inviting his audience to gaze in rapturous wonder with him at his "discovery."

This article interrogates this approach, pointing to factors and mechanisms acting to maintain the phenomenon of the murder of women in the context of what patriarchal discourse terms "family honor," thus exploring the "politics of honor" bound up with interests of the state. But before doing that, I wish to examine several questions that have not been adequately answered in the literature, such as: why is it that women are murdered for the sake of "family honor" and not the "strangers" and "trespassers" who are the real desecrators of the women's family honor? Kressel, who answers this question by saying that this is because of custom, conceals more than he reveals. This article intends to analyze and interpret such "crimes of honor" (sororicide and filiacide), contending that women in the patriarchal family are sacrificed on the altar of "honor" because that has a cheaper social price tag for the family.

On the other hand, I also attempt to explain the patriarchal politics of honor — i.e. why the honor of the men who are the woman's patrilineal kin resides in the bodies of their female relatives, while revealing the economic basis for the control of women's bodies by their male family members. The article likewise explores how further fortifications have been built around the barricade of "honor" in a changing honor system ideology, becoming prime points of confrontation in the struggle for women's liberation. Initially I define the concepts of honor and shame and provide some answer to the question: what is "family honor"? The article's focus is thus the encounter between patriarchal and state politics, the consequences of that encounter and its implications for the continuance of the practice of "honor killings" in Palestinian society within Israel.

Honor and Shame — What is Family Honor?

It is useful to state from the outset that we are speaking here about the honor of the family as a patriarchal unit.[4] Thus, honor refers chiefly to the honor of males in the family. The maintenance of honor is the perpetuation of male control; an assault on that honor undermines that system of domination. Its perpetuation is made possible by utilizing the politics of honor, i.e. implementing the codex of laws binding chiefly on women and determining their behavior, actions, desires and even their thoughts. The form of that behavior, termed in Arabic *ihtisham* or *hishma*, is explained by Lila Abu-Lughod as the shame and embarrassment felt by a subjugated individual — i.e. the woman (whose moral values are regarded as inferior) — and the expression of this shame and embarrassment, in addition to voluntary submissiveness, in the presence of her male masters. *Hishma* in its original form was connected only with the sexual behavior of the woman.[5] Today, given the changes in Arab society generally and Palestinian society more specifically now buffeting the structures of the family, this concept has become more inclusive, along with the expansion of the codex of honor (*i'rd*), to include other new forms of behavior perceived as a threat to male domination.

Some scholars use the concept "family honor" in dealing with the question of preserving the virginity of the unwed woman.[6] It is true that the Arabic term also refers to the question of virginity, but not exclusively. Aside from the demand that the unmarried woman remain a virgin, and that the married woman remain faithful to her husband, the term also serves public consciousness which demands that the Arab woman, like the wife of a king, should be above all suspicion in the eyes of the relevant community.[7] One of the interviewees (Nasra) defined what proper behavior is for the woman by stating that "a good woman, a respected woman, gives no one cause to speak about her or spread rumors."[8]

It is important to note that in popular usage, the term "family honor" is sometimes replaced by "woman's honor," where the absence of honor is understood to be the loss of virginity. That is clear from responses to a questionnaire administered to Arab high school students where one of the questions included the term "women's honor" precisely in the sense of what I term "family honor."[9] But if one regards the Arabic *i'rd* as equivalent to "honor" and its opposite *'aib* as equivalent to "shame," it becomes clear that the concept of "family honor" is very broad and inclusive, actually expressing an entire codex of concepts and behaviors incumbent in the main on females.[10] As stated earlier, that codex determines the behavior, actions, desires and even thoughts when a woman moves in the fragile territory between honor and its desecration. The apparatus of control over proper female behavior is gossip as exercised by public opinion;[11] the relevant social group — the *hamula* (clan), the extended family, the village — decides if the rules of *i'rd* were breached. Violation merits punishment, which may be isolation, imprisonment, a ban on study or work, beating and even death.

Abu-Zeid distinguishes between two types of shame, the first called *'aib* and the second *'aar* in Arabic. In his view, *'aib* only influences and shames the doer of the deed, without affecting the members of his or her family. Thus, it is not connected with family honor, and punishment is light, such as open accusation of the man or woman, or subjecting the person to ridicule. As an example, he mentions a woman who decides to wear an immodest dress. *'Aar*, by contrast, as in a case of adultery, shames not only the doer of the deed but their family as well, thus requiring severe punishment, even death. For Abu-Zeid, only this second type of shame, *'aar*, is connected with the concept of family honor, *i'rd*.[12]

To me, however, this separation of two concepts that can both be translated as "shame" is problematic. In Arab society, "from a very early age, girls learn what is *'aib* and what is not"; otherwise they are liable to cause a family scandal during their adolescence, a scandal that would be *'aar* — the great shame, which, according to the ideology of family honor, only blood can vindicate.[13] One of the interviewees stated: "In our society, everything is *'aib*, to love, to choose a potential husband is *'aib*, even to laugh in a loud voice is *'aib*" (Jamalat). The *'aib* caused by a young girl or woman who wears immodest clothing or even who speaks or laughs in a loud voice is certainly connected with honor (*i'rd*), because this *'aib* is liable to put the *i'rd* of the family at risk. Thus, immodest clothing worn by a woman can shame not only her but her relatives as well, since people who see her are likely to project their antipathy towards her brothers or male cousins and thereby shame them as well. Fathiya, a 40-year-old woman interviewed, recounted the following:

> Around the age of 15, after I left school, I started to work together with other girls from the village in a textile factory in the nearby Jewish town. A few young men were also working with us. At work we usually wore dresses or long skirts. One day I and another one of my friends bought some slacks that were a bit tight in the fit. The next morning we put them on and went to work. A young man from the neighborhood who was a friend of my brother's and also worked at the factory saw me. He ran to tell my brother and asked him how I wasn't ashamed to dress like that. My brother came, started screaming at me and beating me, saying I'd caused a him scandal. He forbade me to ever wear the slacks again.

It is true that the punishment for someone who commits *'aib* is usually less than for someone guilty of *'aar*, but it is difficult to view the two types of shame as totally separate, with one supposedly harming and shaming only the individual while the other harming his/her family members as well, and thereby violating family honor. In my view, this distinction is unfounded, arbitrary, and not helpful for explaining the matter. It appears Abu-Zeid is even trying here to put forward a basis for some kind of "objective" criterion for punishing the woman. Actual cases prove how arbitrary and even inconsistent punishment is. For example, Ikhlas Kana'an from Rama in Galilee was murdered in July 1994 by her 21-year-old brother because he and family members believed she had desecrated the family's honor by her alleged misconduct. The act which caused her brother and family dishonor, it was later argued, was her decision to wear a mini-skirt — an act usually subsumed solely under the category of 'aib.[14]

It is important to note that the "value" of 'aib (as associated with the concept of family honor) within Palestinian society itself is not consistent, i.e. an act committed by a woman may lead to 'aib within a specific group or a specific place, but not necessarily in another group or locality. Things change from hamula to hamula or family to family within the same community and even the same village. Um Aiman relates:

> One day my daughter came and told me a young man had approached her and told her he'd like to get to know her better. My daughter was 25 at the time. So my husband and I said OK, why not. If she wants she can meet him in a public place and if she likes him, he may come to us to request her hand in marriage. After that I told this to my sister, who's married and lives in another village. She attacked me, saying that was not right, it was 'aib. How could I permit my daughter to do such a thing? What will people say if they see her? I told her I didn't care what they said, as far as we're concerned here, it's OK, no problem.

Without specifically stating this, Abu-Zeid and others point to the existence of a type of double standard in respect to honor, one for men and one for women. They argue that male honor is determined by things such as achievements, courage, generosity, class standing, social status and family origin.[15] A man is considered a man of honor if he keeps his promises and sticks to his word, if he revolts against injustices and declines to comply with any form of oppression, and if he shows sufficient eagerness and readiness in defending his own interests as well as those of his kin-group and his neighbors."[16] By contrast, female honor is determined by something totally different, namely, by women's sexual behavior, their "chastity" or "purity."[17] That distinction also arises from the responses of male and female interviewees who were asked to define what is a respectable man in comparison with respectable women. One of the young women, Ulfatb said: "In our society a respectable man is one who has money and supports his family well, someone with high status or from a well-known family. A respectable woman is one who does not go out with men, is not flighty, and preserves the good name of her family."

Not only is a woman's honor judged by a standard different from that applied to men, it also has a special term (in addition to the general expression for honor: *sharaf*), namely *i'rd*. According to the Al-Munjid dictionary (1986), one of the meanings of *i'rd* is "body," and in his book *Tribal Law*, Mazhar Aal-Far'un uses two alternative terms in referring to this kind of honor, sometimes *i'rd* and and sometimes *lahma* ("flesh"). He states: "When for example a man hears that a woman from his kinsfolk (*lahmatahu*) is accused of such a thing, then …"[18] The only term that describes the first type of honor is *sharaf*: "The Arabic word *sharaf* comes from the root verb which implies highness, both in physical position and in social standing."[19] Thus, the expression *i'rd* never refers to general human phenomena but is applied solely to female behavior. Lila Abu-Lughod notes that the subservience and submissiveness of women (and other weak agents in society) to males is what grants them the honor that men possess by dint of their *aqil* or reason.[20] That submissiveness entails social sensitivity and the fulfillment of laws of the existing social order, obedience to the code.

In addition to various features that distinguish the two types of honor mentioned above, Victoria Goddard points to another important characteristic distinguishing between male and female honor. Male honor is active while female honor (or more precisely, male honor bound up with female behavior), *i'rd*, is passive in nature.[21] We can understand this in light of the fact that it is always possible to add to *sharaf*, male honor, for example by acquiring wealth or defending the weak, just as it can be achieved, for example, by invading another tribe, i.e. gaining honor by humiliating another.[22] Thus, this kind of honor is not static; it can grow, develop and can of course also diminish. By contrast, *i'rd*, bound up with female behavior, is totally passive, ascribed, since it can only be lost. A woman and her relatives do not acquire or achieve honor because the woman's sexual behavior fulfills the expectations and conventional norms. Such honor can only be injured or besmirched — namely by non-adherence to those norms and by improper "unchaste" behavior.[23]

This concept embodies the entire world of views pertaining to family honor, whose basic principle is the fostering of female passivity, not just for the purpose of preserving virtues but as a virtue in itself. Yet that passivity does not nullify the fact that the honor of the patrilineal kinship group is connected to the body of the woman, or as al Sa'adawi puts it, "to her lower part of it."[24] This situation where all the agnatic male relatives of a woman can lose their honor as a result of her (mis)conduct underscores the chains of absurdity that hobble patriarchal society. The passive woman, thought to be inferior in status, holds within her body the public worth of all her male relatives, worth which she can directly damage and diminish, but which she cannot augment. Davis tries to an extent to broaden the ability of women to accumulate honor by taking good care of their husbands and children, and not just by preservation of their "chastity," trying to accord to them a more active character.[25] But it appears impossible to counterbalance these; no amount of maternal care for children can atone for a lack of chastity.

Family Honor and Economic Domination

The politics of *i'rd* is reflected not only in the enforcement inscribed in the codex of honor, but also in the fostering of female dependency on agnatic relatives. This dependency is facilitated by denying the right of the woman to inherit. According to Muslim religious laws, the woman is indeed entitled to half of the inheritance of the man, but in the family or her father's house, in most instances, she is denied even that portion too.[26] According to custom, a woman "renounces" her right to inheritance.[27] In exchange, her brothers oblige themselves not to abandon her in a strange *hamula*, i.e. to stand at her side and to pay regular visits to her in her husband's home, to give her presents on holidays and to offer her support if her husband should harm or beat her. They also oblige themselves to leave their door open to her should she be divorced by her husband or made a widow.[28] Certain scholars have praised this practice, viewing it as part of the beauty of blood relations, describing it in a manner bordering on romanticization. Hilma Granqvist, for example, observes that "The love between brother and sister finds expression in many ways and is most beautiful and attractive ... it is more beautiful than the love between wife and husband."[29]

This accolade of patriarchy is a distortion of reality. Not only is the woman deprived of virtually the only form of income permitted to her (which, in pre-modern society, could render her economically independent), but in return, her brothers "award" her the dubious burden of their honor, which she is bound to preserve in the vessel of her body and behavior, even when she is living in the house of her husband. In response to the question why she does not demand from her brothers the portion of inheritance due to her, even on the basis of religious law, one of the women I interviewed, Um M'hanna, stated: "That is *'aib*, how could I take from them? If I did that, none of them would take any future interest in me, they would not come to visit me and ask how I am. And if my husband should beat me, I would have no right to go to stay with them."

The woman's "renunciation" of her portion of the inheritance in return for apparent protection is a practice which, in my opinion, was established even before Islam. Its contractual nature is a kind of cover for women that have been dispossessed of the inheritance rights equal to those of men (which they had in the pre-patriarchal era). In return, the woman is entitled, according to tribal custom, to protection and support from her brothers even after she has married and relocated to her husband's house. 'Aref al-'Aref contends that a woman does not inherit according to custom, supporting this by the well-known pre-Islamic saying: "No one will inherit from us who does not carry a sword and defend the tribe." He notes that tribal law reserves the right of the woman to submit a complaint against her brothers if they fail to stick to their part of the deal, and they would be required to return to their sister her share of the inheritance, with one exception: land. Al-'Aref continues: "The inheriting males are obliged to care for the women whose inheritance has been robbed from them. The brother has a debt toward his sister in return for the inheritance robbed from her. It is his duty to bring her up, provide her with food and adorn her, and to defend her from mortal dangers. Should he neglect this duty, it is her right to bring him to court."[30]

It would thus appear that although the patriarchal system attempts to give a semblance of legality to the sisters' lack of inheritance rights, the recognition in tribal law of the right of the woman to bring to court a brother who fails to live up to his side of the "bargain" suggests that deep down within collective patriarchal consciousness, there is a recognition that the reason sisters do not inherit is not some natural law. Rather, it is bound up with an act of theft by their brothers, who took from them the equal and natural right to inherit. What happened here is that the patriarchal system has succeeded in turning thievery into a "natural right," and the women's natural right into a crime. In other words, it has turned the thief into the woman's guardian and labels the woman who resists the theft a rebel.

The denial to women of the right to inheritance appears to be the cornerstone of patriarchal politics. Women are taught that even though they can officially inherit, it is regarded as "something that isn't done," and can result in negative reaction from the brothers.[31] A woman who insists on her right to inherit is regarded as insolent and rebellious. In such a case it is likely that her disappointed brothers, whose dominion over her will be ended if she gains a share of the inheritance, will use arguments against her of 'aib — shame, banishment and ostracizing. Um Tariq told a story about such a defiant acquaintance: "Um 'Amir from our neighborhood filed a claim to receive what she had a right to, and her brothers gave her a dunam and a half. But do you think anyone came to speak to her after that? She is left abandoned in her husband's house and none of her brothers takes an interest in her or ever visits her." This banishment is not just a reaction to financial loss; it is punishment for the brothers' loss of control and domination, or an expression of their fear of losing that dominant control.

Following changes that have taken place in Palestinian society over the years, new paths were opened up for women leading to possible economic independence. Yet one of the ways fathers assure control over their daughters is the demand that they hand over their wages in "exchange" for being permitted to work. The penetration of capitalist relations into Palestinian society has left the single woman without good education, while living with her parents and experiencing disadvantages in the marriage market. In order to prevent an educated working woman from becoming independent, some fathers forestall that independence by taking the wages of their daughters in return for pocket money. This assures the continued domination by the males in the family over the women, but does not safeguard the family entirely; one act of misconduct by one single woman from the biological family can bring down an immediate curse on all her blood kinsmen. This is reflected in the story of Noha Ibrahim (fictitious name):

> I was working for a year and a half in a restaurant kitchen, and my father would demand at the beginning of each month that I give him my wages. He left me only a small amount of money, mainly for transportation and perhaps a bit of pocket money. Sometimes he went to my boss at the restaurant and asked him to give him my monthly wages in advance.... Now he just learned that I was hitchhiking with some stranger and he wanted to kill me. He told me I had to die because I'd caused a scandal for the family.

One thus can contend that behind what appears to be a basic "agreement" in which the woman "renounces" her right to a share of the inheritance for the benefit of her brothers "in exchange" for their continued protection, another agreement is concealed, pointing to a highly sophisticated patriarchal politics in the control and domination of women. In return for her relinquishment of her right to inherit, the woman continues to maintain in her body the honor of her patrilineal kinsmen, i.e. in return for the theft of her inheritance, they will continue to supervise her behavior even after she marries. This is, then, a zero-sum game in which the winner is chosen from the start.

Who Are the Potential Murderers — the Restorers or Avengers of Honor?

The male agnatic relatives of the woman are her brothers, father, uncles, cousins and her adult sons. The inviolable nexus between men's honor and their kinswomen's bodies is even more pronounced when compared with the relation between a wife and husband, as this is a relation that can be terminated and is thus weaker. If the woman violates the code of behavior, her husband (unless he is her cousin as well) is not only exempt from killing her

— he is not authorized in any way to do this. He is exempt because even if his pride as a husband is damaged, his *i'rd* and that of his family is not sullied if there is no blood relation between him and his wife. He is thus not authorized to punish her, because, according to laws of blood vengeance, if he murders his wife he will be obliged to pay blood ransom and his claim that his wife committed adultery will not be accepted by her family.[32] The betrayed husband has the right to return his wife (to divorce her and send her back to her parents) and to receive as compensation from her family the bride-price and all expenses for the wedding.[33] Only close blood relatives of the woman are authorized to take steps to redress the shame.

In Arab society, the case of a husband who murders his wife for reasons of jealousy or possessiveness is not subsumed under honor killings. Not only are there no close blood relations between the man and his wife which obligate him to cleanse the shame; in cases where a wife betrays her husband, the man is miraculously able to overcome his jealousy, restrain himself and make it possible for his wife's blood kinsmen to carry out the ritual of the purification of their honor. Kressel comments: "a man's jealousy does not justify the execution of his wife. In other words, the individual motivation of the betrayed party is secondary."[34]

In all instances where a husband murders his wife, he violates her patrilineal family, no matter what the reason for the murder. As mentioned, it is not his honor that is injured, even in a case where she has been unfaithful to him, since his wife is not his absolute property but only handed over to him for his use. That is evident from the fact that when he divorces his wife for her unfaithfulness, he is entitled to a return of the bride-wealth he paid to her family. This is not a payment for virginity or the loss of honor, as Kressel suggests, because when the wife is returned to her family she may already have given birth to several children.[35] It is thus clear that payment of the bride-wealth does not make the bride the property of her husband, since it does not sever the link between the honor of her agnates and her body. Rather, it is payment for the use of a "non-defective" commodity. It is permitted to the husband to beat her, of course, but he cannot under any circumstances take her life. Consequently, I suspect that instances of the murder of women by their husbands in Palestinian society were the result of "excessive" beating by their husbands. The "right" to beat one's wife is given to the husband, and if he "goes too far" and causes her death, then his act of killing is by conjugal entitlement — and nothing more.

The lack of a "right" on the husband's part to decide over the life and death of his spouse is also evident from cases in which the husband was opposed to his wife's killing even though she had been unfaithful to him. If her blood relatives decide to murder her, they will do that against his will, since it is *their* honor and not his that has been assaulted.[36] Kressel recounts a case where a husband even tried to defend his wife, and was himself injured in the attempt.[37]

The murder of a wife at the hand of her husband and the reactions to this killing are exemplified in the story of Ikhlas Zebeidat, 23, from Sakhnin, who married a man from Ibtin, Hussen 'Amriyeh. The husband and wife often squabbled and she was occasionally beaten by her husband and by members of his family. In September 1992, she was brought to the hospital after having been badly battered, and she subsequently died of her injuries. The autopsy showed traces of poison in her body. The husband and members of his family claimed the young woman had committed suicide. The police, who had detained her husband, his father and sister for some time, agreed to accept their testimony, despite signs of severe beatings on her body. The pathologist claimed that no connection had been proven between her death and the poison, a substance used for cleaning. Members of the dead woman's family objected and demanded ransom from the husband: it was clear to them that he had murdered his wife "illegally" and that her biological family was entitled to indemnification for her loss.

Why Are Women Murdered and Not Men?

In his book, *Jurisprudence among the Bedouin* (1933), 'Aref al-'Aref contends that anyone wishing to explore the truth of current customs, i.e unwritten law, in the Arab world must return to examine the customs of the Bedouin. As Bedouins have preserved their customs over the years, they can be used as a reliable reference point for grasping the roots of traditions and customs common today, even among non-Bedouin Arabs. He also states that based on his experience, there is virtually no essential difference between the laws and customs of Bedouin in different Arab countries. A comparison of literature documenting tribal law among different Arab peoples also points to an almost total similarity between diverse countries.[38]

The traditional legal system, which is called by a variety of names in Arabic, such as *al-qadaa, al-'ashaari* or *al-qadaa al-'urfi*, and which essentially constitutes a complete system of civil law, exists to this day in all the communities that make up Palestinian society, that is, among the rural population as well as the Bedouin, in the territories occupied in 1967 as well as within Israel. This system operates parallel to the civil and military legal systems of the State of Israel, although it becomes stronger or weaker at a given time or in a given place depending upon various political and social circumstances. Significantly, customary law goes beyond communal boundaries. Not only does it exist in all communities, but there is also no necessary connection between the community of the litigant parties and that of the judges. That is especially evident in Galilee, where three major religious

Palestinian communities live: Christians, Muslims and Druze.

The question of *i'rd*, or family honor, has an important place in the traditional legal system, and a special panel of judges called *al-Manshad* exists for the purpose of dealing with it. The various kinds of offenses against family honor and the punishments required for each of them are dealt with in great detail: there is kidnapping against the will of the woman, or with her consent, there is rape in broad daylight, in the woman's home, or at night, and there are also various sorts of indecent acts, slander, voluntary sexual relations, and so on.

However, it turns out that there is little in common between the fundamental principles of the traditional legal system and what occurs in reality, since as far as the traditional legal system is concerned, the guilty party is always the man and not the woman. Even if a woman has sexual relations with a man voluntarily, it is he who will be punished by the legal system and not she. The reason is that the system perceives the woman as lacking intelligence and weak and the man as perfectly intelligent and able to control himself and to prevent the occurrence of the offense.[39] In fact, the tribal legal system does not have anything at all to do with the women. It deals with interactions between men only: the injurer and the injured. That is to say, it is interested in the compensation that the man who has desecrated the honor of the woman's family is obliged to pay the men of that family, or in physical measures to be taken against the man. In this system, the woman is not an injured party at all, since according to the patriarchal way of thinking, the honor that has been desecrated is that of the men of her family and not her own.[40]

Nonetheless, 'Aref al-'Aref mentions the punishment apportioned to an adulterous woman — death or the cutting of the tendon in her right foot. Yet I suspect he is confusing two quite different domains: traditional law on the one hand, and customary law on the other. Tribal justice comprises a system of (oral) laws that constitute the frame of reference in tribal-customary courts. Customs, by contrast, are a category of accepted conventional acts that allow no possibility for a legal action before a court against the perpetrator of the act and are legitimized by public recognition. These might appear identical but are not. The woman whose blood may be spilled according to custom is not a party to traditional legal proceedings, and is not even a person under the law. The woman, who can be accused and punished according to the custom of honor, is not a litigant party or person in a custom-based legal action.[41] Consequently, the murder or lesser punishment of the woman does not interest the tribal legal system, which is public justice. Such punishment is an internal family matter, i.e. private. Sometimes this leads to confusion and misunderstanding. The question of women murdered (by blood kinsmen) for having dishonored the family or besmirched its reputation is never brought before the forum of customary justice. By contrast, that court can hear a complaint for compensation against the male involved in the affair brought by the family of the woman the blood kinsmen were "compelled" (by the honor code) to murder.[42]

An additional point that underscores the absence of women from the realm of traditional law is the fact that a woman does not need to be tried by the tribal court. The subjects of the lawsuit are her male relatives — her father and brothers, and not she herself. Even in the case of a woman who murders her child, her male blood kin must compensate her husband's family.[43] The woman is absent not only from the customary justice system. A number of studies by researchers on judicial processes relating to honor and its desecration, whether the charge is rape, abduction or some other crime, are silent about the fate of the woman. Sason Bar-Zvi, for example, presents the case of two lovers, a married woman and her paramour, who absconded. They hid in a cave for some time until their hiding place was discovered: "And when Ibrahim learned that their hiding place had been discovered, he got in a taxi ... intending to find refuge in another tribe ... the members of the Qawa'in discovered him ... and stabbed him to death."[44] What happened to the woman? Did she stay behind and escape? Was she also found and murdered? No answer can be found in this account — the woman simply doesn't exist!

The contradiction between customary justice and custom is also known through a phenomenon which is touched upon in Bar-Zvi's research: it is true that, according to tribal law, the father or blood relations of the family of the woman whose family has been dishonored have the right (if blood money was not paid) to avenge their dishonor by murdering the man who caused it, or any other man from among his kin, without male members of the murdered man's family having any right to demand that his blood be avenged. Yet it is clear that in reality the family of the murdered man will refuse to accept his death as proper punishment. Bar-Zvi contends that they will always find arguments and excuses for claiming the woman was responsible, and thus the circle of vengeance will go on and on. Aal-Far'un comments that family honor is one of the most brutal elements that can shatter the peace among Arab families, sparking bitter conflict.[45]

'Aref al-'Aref also stresses the close connection between blood revenge and family honor, including the personal responsibility of those it applies to. Not only does he comment that: "Murder is an abomination to the Arabs, except when it is committed in the name of revenge or the preservation of honor ... then they praise it."[46] He also illustrates an additional point of similarity between blood revenge and revenge for the sake of family honor: just as the laws of blood revenge apply to every man in the murderer's "hamsah," i.e. all males from his patrilineal family to his "fifth grandfather" (the sons of the individual, of his father, his grandfather and even the sons of his great-grandfather constitute a legitimate target for blood vengeance), if the family of the killer does not request a cease-fire (*'atwah*), so it is with the avenging of dishonor: the murder of any male from the *hamsah* of the person who dishonored the rival tribe, not necessarily the offender himself, is sufficient. It is the same group that is responsible for both the cleansing of family honor and blood vengeance.

The contradiction between traditional law and custom explains Bar-Zvi's above-mentioned illustration. In most cases where a family's honor has been desecrated, however, the offender's family will not allow the revenge-seekers to kill their men. Thus, despite the fact that traditional law states that it is permitted to spill the blood of the one who committed the desecration and that he, i.e. his family, is not entitled to blood revenge, if this law is followed, it can become the focus of reciprocal bloodletting on the part of groups, tribes or extended families. The traditional law that grants a woman's family the right to murder the man who desecrates her honor still exists side by side with the custom of the murder of young women, although it is seldom carried out. This suggests that the custom may have developed from this traditional law. Thus we see that the attempt to fulfill the dictates of traditional law and to carry out the official law by murdering the offending man gives rise to disparities between the application of the law of honor and that pertaining to blood revenge.

This unavoidable clash between the laws of avenging dishonor and the laws of blood vengeance, coupled with the infrequency of instances of men being murdered in the name of family honor (androcide to avenge family honor) and the fact that even women who were raped were subsequently murdered,[47] all suggest that women are murdered only because it is "cheaper" in social terms. That is, in tribal society, every injury to a man who violates the honor of a woman (and thereby desecrates her family's honor) will bring in its wake a vicious cycle of blood vengeance. Consequently, even though tribal law states that the male bears responsibility, it is clear that if the law were actually applied, the principles of blood vengeance would unleash unending tribal warfare. By contrast, the elimination of a woman by her own kin is an internal private matter.

This I believe is the main reason for the practice of the murder of women in tribal society which, otherwise, could self-annihilate through a vicious spiral of blood vengeance. It is possible to say that the apparatus of maintenance of the tribe or lineage found a way to avoid its weakening or destruction by constructing a scapegoat, a surrogate victim for execution of judgment. This introduces an additional aspect of the substitution of the man's for the woman's life: the sacrificial victim. The woman is sacrificed by the agnatic family, thus releasing itself from the obligation to murder the male who dishonored the family. This appears to be the basis underlying the ritual aspect in this act of cleansing and sacrifice, a feature familiar in the process of murder.

The Ritual Character of Murder

It is difficult to explain in precise terms the sentiments behind what anthropologists term a "social response to instances of deviation from sexual tradition,"[48] but it would appear that the ritual dimension of the act is meant to fulfill psychological needs and to convey a social message to the relevant community. Kressel notes:

> [P]rior to Western interference, "purging" the family honor was a public act. The elders of the Arab communities studied testify to the time … when the murderer would sprinkle his victim's blood on his clothes and parade through the streets displaying the bloody murder weapon … to increase his honor. He was considered a "purger," one who restored the honor, not a murderer.[49]

Kressel's description is correct, but his contention that this is an ancient heritage "prior to Western interference" is not quite correct. The ritualistic and public dimension exist today as well, even under Israeli rule.

On 6 July 1993, the newspaper *Maariv* carried a story about a young man of 19 who had entered the Israel Defense Forces (IDF) base at Anabta, a village near Tulkarem, carrying the head of his sister. It turned out that he had murdered his married sister Sanaa Bader Zubeidi, 22, because it was suspected she was having sexual relations with other men. After killing her, he decapitated the body and walked about the streets of the village for over an hour, with her head dripping blood. Only after that did he go to the army base. It is important to point out that not a single person in the village who witnessed this gory spectacle bothered to inform the police.

The journalist Khaled Abu T'umi conducted a detailed investigation of the circumstances surrounding the murder of Nura 'Asa'asha, a single woman aged 32 from Jiba' village, murdered in February 1989 after her family had discovered she was five months pregnant. After Nura confessed she had had sexual relations and was pregnant, her father gathered together the members of the family and told them it was necessary to cleanse the name and restore the honor of the family and the *hamula*. The father, who was from a Bedouin family which cooperated with the authorities, invited all the members of the *hamula* to the execution, especially the women, so they would see and be afraid:

> At 8 p.m. dozens of men and women gathered together in a circle in the room of Farid 'Asa'sah in the village of Jiba' near Jenin. They knew why they had come. The daughter of Farid, Nura 'Asa'ash … a single woman

aged 32, was brought into the center of the circle. Her pregnant stomach protruded from her dress like a badge of shame. Her father approached her and asked her to choose between the ax and the rope. She pointed to the rope. Her father then threw her to the floor, stepped on her head, tied the rope around her neck and began to strangle her. She did not utter a single word. As her father continued to press down on her head and strangle her, the members of the *hamula* began to clap and the men shouted: "harder, harder, oh hero (*ya batal*), you've proved you're not a scoundrel." And so this miserable chapter in the life of the beautiful young woman from Jiba' came to an end.

Among those present at the ceremony were Nura's mother and sisters. Not one of them cried. They prepared coffee for those in attendance, who praised the murderer, and then sat talking afterward for two hours. Only after midnight did the father and his brother walk over to the house of the village *mukhtar* (headman). They told him that "the father of the 'adulteress' has restored his honor." Once the *mukhtar* had gone to see the body, they went to the police in Jenin.[50]

The writer Fawaz Turki, a Palestinian from an urban family of Haifa shopkeepers that was expelled to Lebanon in 1948, narrates a similar murder ceremony. He tells the story of the murder of his sister Yasmin, who supported the family during the 1950s in Lebanon working as a waitress. When it became clear to her eldest brother Musa, who had become the head of the family after the death of his father, that Yasmin had lost her virginity, he pronounced the death sentence on her. The members of the family gathered together, and Musa prepared a mixture of poison which he then ordered Yasmin to drink. Yasmin obeyed without protest and died in agonizing pain "like a slaughtered bull" as the members of her family stood by and watched the spectacle. Not only did Fawaz Turki himself, who admired his sister, not think to assist her, he stated that he even felt no disgust or repulsion at the time witnessing this horrible scene. As he noted, he did not think at the time that the verdict of death pronounced on his sister was anything evil and tyrannical.[51]

Such atrocious incidents illustrate in vivid detail that before constraints were created, principally by the law, the act of "cleansing" was publicly and socially accepted. Today the process of "reporting" to the relevant community has in most cases become more refined and concealed. But it seems that along with the ceremonial-public aspect of the "cleansing" and the restoration of honor, there is also an element of expiatory sacrifice which influences those present at the ceremony, including the victim, to accept it as "right." All those present are rendered participants in the ritual act. The "gods" of primitive tribes apparently continue to accept human sacrifice many generations after disappearing from the conscious history of their worshippers.

However, it is also important to remember that the woman-victim who becomes a "willing" participant in the "ritual" deed is not the only model for behavior amongst Palestinian women. In my estimation — which is based upon my experience as an activist in the al-Fanar organization, which provides shelter to fleeing women — there are many women who have refused and continue to refuse to go "like lambs to the slaughter." Yet it seems that the enormous guilt ingrained in women sometimes causes only a hair's-breadth of difference between the decision to follow the path to death and the decision to choose life. It is also important to note that the victim does not always have the ability to flee, especially in situations where she is surrounded by vengeful family-members. In such cases, only outside intervention can save the woman.

Whatever the current importance of this ritual element in honor killings, it is rarer today than in the past. In most of Palestinian society nowadays, the principal effort is directed toward concealing the murder, by reporting the woman missing where no body is found, or declaring her a suicide or accident victim. Meanwhile, the "report" of the act to the community is becoming increasingly de-prioritized, and the details are hinted at rather than described directly.

Where Do Such "Crimes of Honor" Occur?

In order to have a more exact picture of the scope and extent of honor killings, more comprehensive and in-depth research is needed. A first investigation indicates that the murder of women for the sake of family honor exists in *all* Arab societies and communities. Consequently, to attribute this to Islamic religion or to some mixture between Islam and Arabness (i.e. that the phenomenon exists solely in communities that are Islamic and Arab), as Kressel contends, is a problematic assertion.[52] First of all, in Palestinian society and other Arab societies, the practice can also be found among Druze and Christian communities.[53] Second, there are reports both from the field and in the literature on the practice of honor killings in non-Arab Islamic societies, such as Pakistan, Turkey and Kurdistan.[54]

Ginat sought to explain the association of the practice with Islam by underscoring that in Islamic belief, extramarital sexual relations are regarded by the Koran as sinful.[55] Although this is true, it is not a sufficient explanation for the concept of family honor, and certainly not for the practice of murder for its sake. First of all, such forbidden relations are regarded as sinful in other religions. Second, not only do the Koranic verses dealing with punishment for such transgressors not mention the punishment of death, there is likewise no reference to who is responsible for punishing the offender (brothers, father, husband or some other authority). Moreover, one verse states that

punishment depends on the testimony of four persons, and another verse
metes out equal punishment to the male and female sinner, 100 lashes for
each.[56] As one can see, the equality of punishment meted out to the man and
woman as stated in the Koran is absolutely contrary to the code of family
honor.

The literature also contains references to this practice in Christian
communities of the European Mediterranean area.[57] Nonetheless, there is no
exclusive patrilineal "responsibility," that is, after the woman marries,
responsibility for defending her honor and "purity" is transferred to her
husband. A similar situation exists in non-Arab Muslim societies.[58]

State Politics and Honor

Palestinian society, both within the State of Israel and in the Occupied
Territories, has experienced huge and profound changes over the past four
decades. From being a people that was a majority in its own land before
1948, the Palestinian community was fractured into several groups: a
minority inside the State of Israel, with a "different" sort of citizenship from
that of the majority,[59] and refugees within the territory of historical Palestine,
in other Arab countries, and in a diaspora all over the world. Nevertheless,
within Palestinian society in Israel, social strata that existed in the past in
Palestinian society and disappeared after 1948 are beginning to re-emerge.
In the light of those myriad changes, a serious question poses itself: Why has
the practice of the murder of women for family honor, with its ritual
dimension, not vanished from Palestinian society? Does its continued
existence not confirm the assertion of Ezra Denin, an architect of the Israeli
intelligence community and a founding member of what later became the
Israeli Bureau for Arab Affairs, who stated: "We must get to know and learn
about the Arab mentality which, unlike weapons and other military
equipment, which are always being improved, is unchanging"?[60] The fact
that, as noted above, the practice of the murder of women for the sake of
family honor is not unique to Palestinian society in the State of Israel, but is
also found in most societies throughout the Arab world, would seem to
strengthen the presumption that its continuation is indeed the result of
internal factors and Arab mentality and culture.

I believe that assumption is fundamentally mistaken. One can note that
both in Arab countries and in the State of Israel, there are factors acting to
bolster the practice of honor killing and its associated patriarchal politics,
namely, state deference to the patriarchal leadership *for reasons that are clearly
and unmistakably in the interest of the state.* A glance at the law codices of
several Arab states can illuminate this: Jordanian law, for example, prescribes
the death penalty for murder; yet it exculpates from punishment a male who

murders his wife — or any woman from his *maharim*, i.e. a blood relation, if he discovers she is having sexual relations with a man who is not her husband.[61] Lebanese law also tends to show leniency towards men who murder for the sake of family honor. Mokbel states: "Lebanese law on punishment contains paragraphs which openly discriminate between the man and the woman in connection with what is termed crimes of honor."[62] The same holds true for Syrian law and laws in other Arab states.[63]

The regimes in most of those countries openly espouse such patriarchal views. Since most of these countries do not derive their power from free choice of their subjects but rather from submission and oppression, they also nurture these attitudes within the family. Moreover the government needs the stamp of legitimacy from the hand of religious leaders. Thus, state recognition of traditional values and special favors granted to the religious establishment function to ensure the loyalty of the believers and tie them to the regime; in addition, the state resorts to means of oppression when deemed necessary: one striking example of this was the campaign of terror and intimidation by the Saudi government in 1991, with the aid of the religious establishment there, against women demonstrating for their right to drive automobiles.[64] It is thus clear that the phenomenon of the murder of women for the sake of family honor in these countries is not just part of traditional heritage, but is at the very least a combination of tradition and open encouragement by the regime. The governmental reward granted to murderers of women ensures a united front between the government, the patriarchal and religious leaderships and anyone who fears social change.

Yet there is no reason that the same legal and political system that encourages and perpetuates an honor cultural belief system and honor killings in Arab states should exist in Israel. After all, Israel is a state that proudly proclaims it is a democracy, with a functioning civil society and freely elected government open to criticism. It boasts of laws that ensure the protection of equal rights for women (except with regards to matters of matrimony, of course), the equality of all citizens before the law and equitable just punishment. In such an ostensibly vibrant democracy, is it only the tenacious obstinacy of tradition that has led to the continuation of honor killings within Palestinian society in Israel?

Field research points to an accumulating number of cases of girls and women who fled from their homes for fear they might be murdered, only to be returned to their potential murderers by the police. For example, Kressel recounts the case of a 13-year-old girl, named Salwa, who fled from her paternal home because she feared for her life after she was seen shaking hands with a boy from another family. The girl was brought to the police and the police took her to the sheikh, "who promised the sheikh [another sheikh, father of the boy] and the police that no harm would come to her." He then took her back to her father. A short time later the body of the girl was found drowned in a well near her tribe's encampment.[65]

Another case is that of 'Aiysha, an unmarried girl of 20 who became pregnant. After she gave birth, she abandoned her infant in the field. The police conducted a search, thinking the mother of the abandoned child was Jewish, but in the end they came to 'Aiysha. Yet in spite of the fact that the police were apparently well aware, as is evident from the presentation of the case, that the girl's life would be in danger were she returned to her family, the police took her back to her family "in return for a promise from her father, uncle and his sons to the police that no harm would come to her. A few days later her body was discovered in a dry water hole."[66]

The engagement (with an official marriage licence) of a 24-year-old woman was annulled by the Shari'a court because her fiancé had heard rumors she was not a virgin, and her brothers demanded of her that she commit suicide. The woman went to the police to ask for protection, but they returned her to her home. Her life was rescued only after her mother had staged a fake "suicide" attempt for her daughter (first she poured boiling water on her and then bit off her left earlobe).[67]

The journalist Mati Regev tells the story of a girl from Tira who ran away from home. She went to the police and they brought her to the qadi. Members of her family visited the qadi and brought her medicine. A few hours later the girl was found dead, a suicide note in her pocket. The case was closed. Regev notes: "I am aware of a number of cases where the police delivered the girls (subsequently murdered) straight into the hands of their murderers."[68]

Ginat relates an incident from January 1983 where a woman married to her cousin was discovered with another man. She went to the police together with her lover to request protection. The police sent her to the local sheikh. A week later the woman was found dead. She had been stabbed twice. Ginat concludes: "The woman, and probably her lover as well, thought that by going to the police they would protect themselves from any dangerous sanction by her husband or agnates. This was to no avail."[69]

Sara Abu Ghanam, 16, who ran away from home and requested police protection was handed over by the police to the sheikhs and then murdered. Amal Musrati was handed over by the police to her family. Less than 24 hours later her dead body was found.[70] Rabab Salem (fictitious name), who was rescued from death, told me in an interview that in August 1977, when she was 17, the family decided to marry her to a close relative, against her will. She fled from her home and went to the police to request help and protection. The members of her family, together with the mukhtar of the village and other "notables" (highly respected men) discovered she was at the police and came to take her. She recounted: "When I saw them I knew that if I returned with them they would certainly kill me, just as they had murdered my cousin a year earlier when they discovered she was seeing a 'strange' man. I begged for my life before the chief of police, telling him that if he returned me to them, they would murder me. The police chief, in a gesture of dismissal, said: 'That's your problem, not mine,' and returned me back to them, but not before they had signed a declaration that no harm would come to me." That same day, the heads of the *hamula* met and decided to kill her, because her behavior had dishonored them. Rabab, who learned about this from her little brother, managed to escape before the hour set for her death.

These are just a few of the many cases that show that when a Palestinian woman attempts to escape being murdered for the sake of family honor, the police deliver her back into the hands of her potential murderers. In the majority of cases they make use of "notables" to mediate between her and her family, thus divesting themselves of responsibility for her life. In the case of Sara Abu Ghanam, Salah Nj'idat says: "*As customary in such cases,* the head of the Ramle police brought in the sheikhs and notables."[71]

In another instance the police had planned to involve the sheikhs from Kfar Kassem in the case of Ramziya (fictitious name), a girl who ran away because she feared her brother would kill her and went to the police to request protection. The journalist Mati Regev contacted the chief of Ramle police, Gamliali Harari, and asked: "And what if they don't keep their agreement and murder her?" He replied: "No one can guarantee that they'll keep the agreement. If you buy a car, can you be sure they won't cheat you? In any case, if the family members murder her, they'll have a serious problem with the police."[72]

At a symposium held in Beer-Sheva in December 1983, Negev District Police Chief, Michael Baz, stated that it was the policy of the police to put young runaway women under the care of *sheikhs*, whom they trust to deal with the matter.[73] Regev, who notes that this policy exists elsewhere in the country, opines that it is because of a lack of manpower in the police force.[74] This explanation does not seem adequate to me. It is much more reasonable to suppose that this policy does not originate with the police, but with the office of the Government Advisor on Arab Affairs, the bureau which sets out the policy guidelines for all government treatment of the Palestinian population inside the State of Israel. However, the great majority of these guidelines — even those from before the founding of the state — are still classified information and not accessible for research purposes.[75] The Advisor's office continues to operate mainly in the shadows, and only rarely is an inkling of its activities publicly revealed. For example, when a young woman was raped and became pregnant, she went to the Ministry of Welfare, which helped her to escape from the country. Her father petitioned the High Court of Justice, demanding that the ministry return his daughter, one of his claims being that the Ministry of Welfare had acted contrary to the opinion of the Advisor on

Arab Affairs (who apparently had advised that the raped woman marry the rapist — as recounted by Nisim Kazaz, Adviser on Arab Affairs at the time, at the above-mentioned symposium).[76] This case reveals that at the very least, the Advisor has a policy on matters involving women and family honor, and that the Arab patriarchy is well aware of this policy.

The Patriarchy and the Hamula

One way in which the *hamula* preserves its unity and power is by means of marriage of close relatives. Marriages among relatives within Palestinian society constitute 45 percent of all marriages. Some scholars have even noted a rise in the number of such marriages since the 1950s.[77] During that same period, the position of the *hamula*, which had begun to weaken before the establishment of the state, was reinforced. The *hamula* was strengthened by the state authorities through their preferential treatment of the traditional leadership.[78] According to Ian Lustick, the size of the *hamula* is a factor of considerable importance, since trying to control a society split up among many clans would make cooption of its leaders by the authorities impossible.[79] It thus seems that the government is interested in *hama'il* (plural of *hamula*) that are large and stable in order to reduce the costs of control. The way to preserve the *hamula*'s size and stability is by endogamous marriage among relatives. This can help explain why the authorities do not attempt to eliminate such marriages, even though many children born from them have defects or are retarded and later become a burden for the state.[80] Hence, the preservation of the patriarchal *hamula* structures and their strengthening became the cornerstone in Israeli policy toward the Palestinian population in Israel, as Henry Rosenfeld has noted:

> Politically, the government often continues to support patriarchal leadership, to generate and manipulate hamula factionalism, or to promote young men who are prepared to support "traditional" relations between it and the village.... The authorities exert pressure on the villagers to maintain the existing order, they support the traditional hamulas and grant favors to their representatives; manipulation from outside of patriarchal groups and factions assures their continuance on the inside.[81]

The motives driving the Israeli government to bolster the *hamula* by granting respect and economic and social preference and favors to the patriarchs, including those involved in party politics, are the same as those behind government support of Arab traditions that stabilize the dominant role of the Palestinian patriarchy. The support for tradition is nothing but a function of the need to buttress that same patriarchy in its encounter with the social changes threatening its stability and existence. Consequently, giving sheikhs and notables the possibility of playing the role of intermediary and mediators in Palestinian society, bypassing the official social agencies, strengthens their authority and public recognition. This is the only logical explanation for why the police persist in a policy that has proven ineffective in saving women from murder but nonetheless augments the respect paid to the guardians of tradition. If this is so, then the policy is a product of conscious social and political control whose price tag is minimal: no more than a few female corpses per year. The policy, therefore, encourages the continuation of the murder of Palestinian women.

The story of Sheikh Hussein Gadir from Bir al-Maksour, a former judge in a tribal court in the Galilee, can exemplify the extent to which branches of the government are prepared to favor the notables who are bent on preserving the values of the *hamula*. On 13 July 1991, the IDF Radio broadcast an interview with the sheikh in the regular feature program of Adi Talmor, "In the Present Situation." Introduced by the interviewer as the "Sheikh of Reconciliation from the North," Gadir stated: "It is necessary to preserve the honor of the family and if a young woman shames her family, they must do something to her and even kill her. This is accepted by all the respected families." The interviewer pressed the sheikh: "Even today in the modern, democratic State of Israel, where the law specifically prohibits murder?" The sheikh replied: "Yes, even today. Excuse the expression, but if a girl is a whore and walks the street and deals with one man and then another. If she marries and then goes out prowling, that is a matter of family honor. It will not forgive her to go on in that way. It's necessary to kill her." This interview took place just after the sheikh had left the presidential mansion in Jerusalem, where he had been given an award of special appreciation for his activities on behalf of the community. He belongs to the category of notables who are summoned to mediate in disputes or to return girls who have run away and requested police help back to their families.

In response to this broadcast, the Palestinian feminist organization al-Fanar sent a letter, dated 15 July 1991, to the Israeli attorney general demanding that the sheikh be charged with incitement to murder women. After months of correspondence the attorney general informed al-Fanar that "this is indeed a serious statement." After detailing at length the struggle by the justice authorities against the phenomenon, he recommended that the statement by the sheikh be seen, "despite the fact that it is without any legitimacy whatsoever, as the expression of a personal opinion." He reiterated the "important principle of freedom of expression in a democratic society which also extends to disturbing and deviant points of view," citing at length the judgments to support this argument. In the end, the attorney general informed al-Fanar that he had decided not to take any steps against the sheikh.[82]

By way of comparison, at that very same time, the Palestinian poet and Israeli citizen Shafik Habib was charged in court with incitement to terrorism based on a poem he had written in praise of the children of the *Intifada*. The poet was brought to court by the attorney general on the basis of paragraph 4a of the Decree on Terror Prevention (1949). That paragraph prohibits the publication of "words of praise, sympathy or encouragement for acts of violence which can lead to the death of a person or to personal injury." The subsequent request by al-Fanar to charge the sheikh on the basis of that same paragraph went unanswered.[83]

Joseph Ginat, who (as mentioned above) once served as the Advisor for Arab Affairs, comments in his book, *Blood Disputes among Bedouin and Rural Arabs in Israel:*

> Although the Israeli legal system makes no distinction between homicide for different reasons, the Israeli administration does. A murderer of a woman who engaged in illicit sexual relations … can be released by presidential pardon after no longer than 8–12 years in prison. Such release is not automatic and must be applied for, but it is the usual pattern in the majority of cases.[84]

It is important to recall that Ginat is referring here to murderers sentenced to life imprisonment — not persons convicted of manslaughter and sentenced to shorter periods of imprisonment, according to the discretion of the court. When a person is convicted of murder, the court must pronounce a sentence of life imprisonment, whereas in cases of manslaughter, various factors may be taken into consideration. Thus, if we take into account every man who was brought to trial for killing a female member of his family — whether convicted of murder or manslaughter — the average period of imprisonment would be even shorter.

In a conversation with me on 12 August 1994, Deputy State Prosecutor Yehudit Carp stated:

> The Pardon Committee was established many years ago. The police set the criteria according to which this committee should operate — who should not be pardoned and who should be considered for pardon. I have found that murderers were excluded, of course, but those who committed murder for the sake of family honor were included among those considered fit to be pardoned. I insisted that such cases be transferred to the category of murder. This I can tell you from my own experience — the last time they appointed a Pardon Committee.

That is to say, the police classify murders for reasons of family honor under a special category which, unlike with other murders, entitles the murderer to a pardon.

The State Prosecutor's Office also frequently arranges plea bargains with murderers for family honor. On 10 February 1993, for example, a father who had attempted to murder his daughter by forcing her to drink poison and stabbing her afterwards was sentenced, after a plea bargain, to only eight months. A brother from the village of Horfish, who attempted to murder his divorced sister in September 1991, was sentenced — after a plea bargain — to four years (rather than twelve). Yassir Hjirat, who murdered his sister by drowning on 11 November 1987, was sentenced to ten years. In the late 1970s a man who had murdered his sister in a village adjacent to Nazareth was sentenced to ten years, and released after seven.

The preponderance of cases in which the police release young Arab women to the custody of their murderers-to-be, via a cultivated stratum of "notables," points to policy rather than happenstance. The forgiving attitude of other Israeli authorities and their policy of fostering the *hamula* and its values produce a hothouse in which the poisonous plants of patriarchal oppressive tradition can thrive. There is a striking similarity between the encouragement of the practice of murder for family honor in the Arab states by means of the law and in other ways, and its encouragement in Israel via an apparatus originally intended for law enforcement.[85] Ginat attempts to justify this policy. He states: "The partial recognition by the state of traditional customs may indeed contribute to their continuity. But more probably the responsiveness it demonstrates limits the alienation of traditional communities within the modern state."[86] Ginat in effect sums up this policy and intention behind the encouragement and cultivation of patriarchal customs — such as the murder of women for the sake of family honor — on the part of the State of Israel. By "alienation of traditional communities" Ginat means the embitteredness and resistance of the Palestinian population to the policy of national discrimination and oppression, which must be limited — if possible, by channeling nationalist feelings in the direction of tradition. What he means by "traditional communities" is the patriarchal males — to whom the state almost says: we will compensate your lost national honor with 'necklaces': a few dozen women's corpses each year will symbolize the boundaries of the territory that we are leaving to you, the broad expanses of tradition.

Palestinian Views of the Practice

Until a few years ago, the practice of murder of women for the sake of family honor enjoyed almost total legitimacy within Palestinian society, a legitimacy abetted by the very silence of those who opposed it. The voices heard were mainly of those who supported the practice. In 1989, the Deputy Mufti Sheikh Muhammad al-Jamal was asked his opinion about a father who had murdered his daughter. He replied: "in the absence of Shari'a rule, it was permissible for him to do that … Had the man been brought before me, I would have found him innocent and even praised him."[87] In 1990, the head of the Supreme Monitoring Committee (which constitutes the informal leadership of the Palestinian population in the State of Israel), testified on behalf of a father who had murdered his daughter (who had been seven months pregnant). The father murdered her after her husband had suspected her of adultery and divorced her. The witness explained to the court that the father had acted in accordance with Shari'a law.[88]

However, on the whole, the practice was essentially taboo as a subject for discussion. Women's organizations, organizations on the left, and human rights groups — all were silent. Sometimes, when it was impossible to stay entrenched behind a wall of silence, there was simply denial: "It is something that once existed, but no longer does," or "there have been isolated cases," and so on. Journalist Mati Regev was given similar answers while preparing an article in January 1988 when he sought responses from Palestinian public figures and those active in women's groups (Samira Huri, from the organization Tandi.)

At the beginning of 1991, a group of Palestinian women, citizens of Israel, established the Palestinian Feminist Organization al-Fanar. In June of that year, Ibtisam Habashi was murdered by her father and brother after they claimed that she had dishonored the family. Al-Fanar's members decided not to remain silent but to organize a demonstration against Ibtisam's murder and against the practice in general. A public battle was launched. The taboo was finally broken. The public debate which it sparked and which has continued until today has divided participants into two camps, pro and con, thus revealing the existence of two polar cultures within Palestinian society. But despite the fact that this polarization has become more intense, there can be no doubt that the patriarchal culture of family honor remains at the moment hegemonic.[89] Spokesmen of that culture, such as the qadi of the Druze Shari'a court, Nur el-Din Halabi, were vocal after the murder of Ikhlas Kana'an: "Although it is forbidden to murder, a person who does not preserve the honor of his family is an infidel." Commenting on the murderer, he noted: "He is not considered a murderer; he is a man who decided to preserve his family's honor and does not deserve to be put in prison."

The subject's presence on the public agenda has aroused a new kind of reaction from people who cannot openly support the practice and who therefore turn their anger upon those bringing it to public attention. One such example is the stance of Muhammad Mi'ari, then a Knesset member and head of the political party Progressive List for Peace. In an interview given to the journalist Arye Dayan, Mi'ari commented on al-Fanar:

They decided to attack this issue in such a blatant and shrill manner.... If I could advise the members of this organization, I would tell them to be more restrained. We are living in a society that has certain patterns, and I would not advise that all the "dishes be broken" at once.

By contrast, as to the fundamentalists and their approach to the issue, Mi'ari stated: "They have their position and they are expressing it."[90] The statement also exemplifies a typical approach: women are shrill and men have a position.

The poet Samih al-Qassem, a public and political figure known throughout the Arab world, not only among Palestinians, editor of the weekly *Kol al-Arab* in Nazareth, published an editorial on 22 July 1994 in response to the demonstration against the murder of Ikhlas, in which he stated:

> We proclaim our clear and total opposition to the murder and to all forms of violence associated with the preservation of family honor.... Yet at the same time, we are opposed to rash action and a lack of discretion in dealing with this type of tragedy and reject the indictment of our society as a whole. This society does not specialize in the murder of women. It is a society that loves its women and daughters and protects them.

One public figure, Walid Sadik, gave a characteristic response when asked his position on the practice:

> I am opposed to murder, because no one has the right to kill another human being ... But it's hard to swim against a powerful current. Nor am I totally convinced it's necessary for me to condemn the practice and come out against it. Doing that could also have an influence on my political standing.[91]

Such expressions of an ambiguous attitude point to a deep sense of embarrassment and confusion. An explanation for this perplexity was given by one of the leaders of the organization Abnaa al-Balad (Sons of the Country):

> What do you expect from a traditional, tribal, *hamula*-oriented leadership? Do you expect them to denounce the thing and fight against it? That's impossible. Look, one of them was elected because he is active in protecting family honor, he's [also] collecting money for the murderer. How can you feminist leaders expect that these people will come out and fight against the phenomenon? You think it's all that easy for them to come out against the people who voted them in?[92]

Commenting on men who murder for family honor, former member of Knesset, Walid Sadik, observed: "Look, they're not criminals, they're victims of circumstances, of their education. How can you say they're criminals? They didn't steal, they didn't spy against the state."[93] A typical response from an Islamic religious leader: "If a person sins and should be executed according to Islam, the Shari'a justice system has sole authority to decide this. In the absence of an Islamic state, individuals are not authorized to take the law into their own hands."[94]

Acceptance of the patriarchal values associated with family honor does not, of course, bypass women. Intisar al-Wazir, known as Um Jihad, who served as minister of welfare in the autonomous government in Gaza and Jericho, was unwilling to speak out against honor killings before journalists from the Israeli daily *Ha'aretz*. She said: "We live in a Muslim society and there's a difference between the social integration of the woman [i.e. the public sphere] and her moral role. There is a social status to which a woman must reconcile herself until customs and mores have changed.[95] To the question, "What is the most important thing for a woman?", one typical response, especially from older female interviewees, was: "The most valuable and important thing to a woman is her honor and *sum'aitha* [her good name]" (Sohila). One woman, a divorcee of 37, even stated: "The murder of a woman who willingly gives herself to a man is *halal* [something positive and permitted]" (Najla). Aziz Haider contends that of a sample of 372 Palestinian university graduates (inside Israel) in 1980–1993, 70 percent were opposed to the idea of their sister's having a premarital relation, and 80 percent accepted the notion that the family should supervise the behavior of women.[96] A third-year law student asked to give his opinion on the matter replied:

> Look, academically speaking, I can tell you I'm against the phenomenon, against the killing of women for the sake of family honor. Many men will tell you they're against it. But it's necessary to understand custom, to understand education. Because believe me, at the moment of truth, I mean if something like that [dishonoring the family] happened, say, with my sister, I just don't know what I'd do. (Samir)

Walid Sadik said something similar to me: "It's impossible to completely free oneself from the sediments [left by] the past. I don't know how I'd react if I saw my daughter embracing some man who is not her husband. That's right, there's a gap here between my theory and my practice."[97]

The truth is that it is not the "sediments left by the past" that are hard to free oneself from, but the privileges that this past institutionalized for men. Some men see themselves as progressive by virtue of the fact that they are prepared to relinquish some of the privileges that most humiliate women — on condition that they are allowed to retain the rest. This is essentially the basis for the confusion and vacillation of public figures. Much of what most public figures say reflects how uncomfortable it is for them to even broach the topic, and their ambivalence when discussing it. The dilemma progressive Palestinian men face in Palestinian society was put quite well by Raja Ighbariya, an activist in al-Balad and a member of the Arab Monitoring Committee. When asked for his assessment of how people in Palestinian society related to the phenomenon, he was quite candid:

> Things are different nowadays. And the truth is, things have changed thanks to the actions of your group [al-Fanar].... After you criticized us, Abnaa al-Balad and the Communist Party came to the demonstration [against the murder of Ikhlas Kana'an] and published our opposition in the press.... Let me tell you, you're having quite an impact on a lot of leaders and politicians. Keep on pressing and criticizing us ... but don't curse us.[98]

In today's Palestinian society the predominant attitude towards honor killings is one of ambivalence. That attitude is dependent on the political realities and the pressures being exerted in the sociopolitical arena. There is also, in addition to al-Fanar, a coalition called "Badil," which is opposed to and active against the forces of tradition, made up of civil rights and women's organizations. It is also struggling against these "crimes of honor" and the honor cultural belief system that legitimizes them.

Epilogue

The concept "family honor" is a fortified wall behind which are entrenched all the forces seeking to restrict the freedom of women, to maintain their economic and social inferiority and perpetuate special male prerogatives, employing ideological and coercive means, all the way to murder. This is effected by the legitimating stamp of approval of tradition through education and the protection afforded tradition by the religious establishment, even defending elements of tradition in contradiction with Islamic religion, such as the special clemency showed by men who have violated the moral code.

Those who murder for the sake of family honor are the agnates (paternal kinsmen) of the woman, not her husband or in-laws, should she be married. Honor killings are premeditated, carried out in cold blood and carefully preplanned, sometimes with participation in the actual murder or its preparation by a number of family members (including women). Such killings are occasionally masked as accidents, at times as suicide, at times as cases of a woman gone missing. Yet there are instances where the murder is staged in order to eliminate the "stain" before it becomes known publicly. In such cases the murder is not perpetrated in order to restore honor but rather to conceal the disgrace and *protect honor*. Files on cases of murdered women are sometimes closed due to "a lack of public interest." Nj'idat cites the case of a girl who had relations with three boys and became pregnant. When family members learned of this, they decided to keep it a secret and to murder her. They threw her down a well and then reported to neighbors and the police that she had disappeared. The police closed the filed due to a "lack of public interest." Yet later on, the murderers filed charges in a tribal court against the family of the three boys, demanding they be compensated because they had been constrained to murder their daughter.[99]

This essay argues that women and not men are the victims of murders for the sake of "family honor" because they are "cheaper." The murder of adulterous men, and the cycle of blood revenge it would start, could result in an open, bleeding sore in the body of the tribe; therefore, murder of the "stranger" (i.e. the man from a different tribe or *hamula*) has been replaced by murder of the "offending" woman by her own kinsmen. One may even assume that the murder of women has its origin in lengthy experience with bloodshed as a result of the laws of blood revenge. It is mistaken to contend that such honor killings only occur in a Muslim society. The literature and reports from the field show that the phenomenon also exists among Christians and Jewish communities and that women and girls from all Palestinian communities — Muslim, Christian and Druze — are murdered for reasons of family honor.

In recent years, there have been significant changes in the *reasons* behind honor killings. The first murder that marked the beginning of that process was that of Ikhlas Kana'an from Ramah in the Galilee in the summer of 1994. Ikhlas's most serious "violation" of family honor was the very fact that she had encroached into the area of behavior reserved to men: public discussion, initiative and decision. Her request to the leaders to allocate land to the projects for which she had raised funds embarrassed her relatives, who apparently pressured the young Hussam, whose attitude toward his sister was highly emotional. By contrast, the united front demonstrated by religious leaders, who instructed people not to pray at the grave of Ikhlas, and even declared that her murderer was not a killer but a man who had cleansed and restored the family's honor, shows that the concept of family is in actuality a kind of patriarchal line of fortifications separating what is permitted to a man and forbidden to a woman, and exposes the ramparts behind which all those who support morality entrench themselves. Later attempts to offer an "explanation" by contending that Ikhlas's behavior was exaggerated and seemingly served as an example of sexual license expose the real essence of family honor: namely domination and control of female relatives in the patrilineal family. Ikhlas's behavior, manifest in personal initiative and independence within a defined area traditionally the preserve of males, was a new and different kind of threat to the patriarchal system, which explains why the representatives of the system used old concepts to explain a new situation. Thus, they had to wrap her behavior in the metaphor of the "mini-skirt" in order to lend legitimacy to the crime, i.e. there was a bid here to style Ikhlas's assertiveness as sexual permissiveness.

Ikhlas's murder thus heralded an important change in the reasons for honor killings. Women's style of dress in the patrilineal family, their way of behavior, obedience and submissiveness and way of life were always subject to that same codex of family honor. Yet until recently there had been no sororicide or filiacide for reasons not connected directly or indirectly (whether as suspicion, rumor or fact) to the core taboo of extramarital sexual relations. From this new juncture on, it is not just prohibited to embark upon sexual relations that constitute an extremely serious stain on a women's chastity, as Ginat has argued,[100] but also to refuse to obey traditional mores. One murderer, 17 years younger than his victim, told his investigators in court that before he had murdered his sister she had said that no one could tell her how she had to behave, and that is why he had murdered her.[101]

This murder and later incidents all exemplify the fact that the entire matter of honor is actually a rationale for maintaining male control over women: for example, a woman from Nazareth was murdered by her brother because she refused to stop smoking; another woman, Amira Mujrabi from Rarmali, was murdered in January 1997 by her cousin because she refused to stop working outside the home; another woman was murdered because she decided, against the wishes of her brother, to return to her husband; and a girl from Yerkha village, Masarra Ma'di, was murdered by her brother in February 1996 because she dared to file a complaint against her father accusing him of having abused her and her sisters. I believe there is evidence to suggest we are witnessing a new pattern in the murder of women for the sake of family honor — one in which men who enjoy significant privileges under patriarchal rule attempt, through violent means, to bring stability to a world that is continually changing before their eyes, seeking more and more fervently to defend their traditional status vis-à-vis women. In this pattern, sexual relations and the ideology of control are so intermingled as to become confused with one another, thus exposing the connection between them.

In this way, in addition to the fact that the circumstances surrounding the murder of Ikhlas reveal the true physiognomy of what is called family honor, her murder marked the beginning of a deepening spiral of brutality in the patriarchal system, its very existence now endangered by the waves of social change buffeting it. It is likely there will be many more victims as a result of the final shudders and convulsions of that system, which, like most anachronistic structures, refuses to exit the social stage. The large proportion of cases in which it was revealed that there had been an effort to make the murder look like suicide or accident reinforces the assumption that in certain cases this was done successfully.

Regarding the argument that honor killings are part of some essentialist

"Arab mentality" and constitute a meta-historical phenomenon separate from social changes in a particular time and place, this essay aims to show that the existence of the phenomenon in Arab societies and states is buttressed inter alia by the legal system, in particular the paragraphs in criminal law that exempt murderers from punishment. Those legal systems are one of the important reasons for perpetuation of the practice, because they serve both the governments and the guardians of tradition, forging an alliance between them. One should not accept the societies and regimes in Arab countries as "natural" and homogeneous phenomena; rather, one must analyze the interests of the rulers and other groups and their influence on these societies. Neglect of the latter has caused scholars to overlook the rulers' support, in the interests of the regimes, for the practice of gynocide, and instead to attribute this practice to tradition.

When it comes to what is happening in Palestinian society within the State of Israel, it appears that the encounter between patriarchal politics and state politics ultimately leads to the perpetuation of the practice. The ideology underlying state policy can at times pretend to be "recognition of the different culture of the Other," or "multicultural," but this is merely a guise for a policy that sanctifies and actively nurtures the values of obedience and resignation in Palestinian society. Thus the preservation of women's inferior status is the currency with which the authorities pay off "notables," sheikhs and the wise men of tradition and religion as well as those party leaders who were elected with the support of the traditional leadership. Therefore, even people with a supposedly modern political outlook see this respect for tradition on the part of government agencies not as a strategy that exploits internal apparatuses of Palestinian society in order to enhance Israeli control of this society, but as a sort of "diplomatic recognition" of a border between the domains of state and traditional authority.

Those who determine the direction of Israeli policy towards Palestinian Arab society in Israel, i.e., the Advisors for Arab Affairs, are a central part of the Israeli defense establishment. In their estimation, the nurture of tradition and the division of the different religious communities which make up the Palestinian people, are necessary to prevent Palestinian nationalist organizing.[102] Ultimately, a separate distinctive "Arab" strategy was developed in Israel regarding social questions which bears a strong similarity to strategies customary in a number of Arab countries. The product of that strategy was the preservation of the old social structures in Arab-Palestinian society, manifest in the perpetuation of honor killings, and perhaps even in their fostering.

By contrast, the state pursued precisely the opposite policy towards the Jewish immigrants from Arab countries who arrived in Israel during the great immigration wave of the 1950s: here they sought to eliminate the old social structures, such as the extended family, and systematically destroyed the authority of the family heads. This was a conscious policy of assimilation that aimed to integrate Oriental Jews from the Arab world into the melting pot of the Israeli nation in its formative stages. Yet there was never any desire to integrate the Palestinians. Rather the aim was to isolate them and maintain a battery of means for their control. Asked to comment on the murder of Palestinian women for the sake of family honor, civil rights activist Shulamit Aloni stated:

> We live under a kind of apartheid. The system does not wish to apply the same values among Israeli Arabs, adapting them to a modern society where murder is murder and a woman is also a human being. The State of Israel does not deal with Arabs as equal citizens. It doesn't care about backwardness. One thing they did distribute though: birth control pills, so that Arab women would not have a lot of babies.[103]

The transition from the ideology of developed civilization and a "light unto the nations" to an ideology of "multiculturalism" or "cultural relativism" is meaningless in the context of actual colonial rule. The stratagem is simply to mobilize liberal ideology, either from the nineteenth century or in a current form, for the sake of preserving traditions that ensure the continued economic and political control of Palestinian society in Israel.

NOTES

* This essay is a slightly revised and shortened version of "Ha-politikah shel ha-kavod: Ha-patriarkhiyah, ha-medinah ve-retzah nashim be-shem kvod ha-mishpahah," published in Dafna N. Izraeli et al., *Min migdar politikah* (Sex, Gender, Politics: Women in Israel) (Tel Aviv, 1999), pp. 267–305. It is based on my M.A. thesis, "Murder of Women for Family Honour in Palestinian Society and the Factors Promoting Its Continuation in the State of Israel" (University of Greenwich, 1995). I wish to express my heartfelt gratitude to my thesis advisor Professor Nira Yuval-Davis for her dedicated guidance and support.

1   *Jerusalem Post* and *Ha'aretz*, 31 August 1994.
2   See Edward Said, *Orientalism* (New York, 1978); Gil Eyal, "Bein mizrah ve-maarav: Ha-si'ah al ha-kfar ha-aravi be-Yisrael" (Between East and West: The Discourse on the "Arab Village" in Israel), *Teoriyah u-Vikoret*, No. 3 (1993), pp. 39–55; Dani Rabinowitz, *Antropologiyah u-falestinim* (Anthropology and the Palestinians) (Raanana, 1998).
3   Gideon Kressel, "Harigat ha-ahot/harigat ha-bat: Retzah le-shem kvod ha-mishpahah" (Killing of the Sister/Killing of the Daughter: Murder for the Sake of Family Honor), *Ha-Mizrah he-Hadash*, Vol. 30, Nos. 1–4 (1981), pp. 69–98; Joseph Ginat, *Women in Muslim Rural Society* (New Brunswick, NJ, 1982).
4   The use of the term "patriarchal" here is based on the definition by Halim Barakat, *The Current Arab Society* (in Arabic) (Beirut, 1984) who defines the Arab family as a hierarchical social unit based on gender and age. Males are at the higher rungs of the ladder, with older males at the top. Older women have a higher status than younger women.
5   Lila Abu-Lughod, *Veiled Sentiments* (Berkeley, 1998).
6   Tawfiq Canna'n, "Unwritten Laws Affecting the Arab Women of Palestine," *Journal of the Palestine Oriental Society*, Vol. 11, Nos. 3–4 (1931), pp. 172–203; Nawal al-Sa'adawi, *Women*

and Sex (in Arabic) (Beirut, 1971).

7   Nadia Youssef, "The Status and Ferttility Patterns of Muslim Women," in Lois Beck and Nikki Keddie (eds.), *Women in the Muslim World* (Cambridge, MA, 1978), pp. 69–99; Sanna al-Khayyat, *Honour and Shame: Women in Modern Iraq* (London, 1992); Hilma Granqvist, *Marriage Conditions in a Palestine Village* (Helsingfors, 1935); Ginat, *Women in Muslim Rural Society*; Germaine Tillion, *The Republic of Cousins* (London, 1983); Nikki R. Keddie, "Introduction: Deciphering Middle Eastern Women's History," in idem and Beth Baron (eds.), *Eastern History: Shifting Boundaries in Sex and Gender* (New Haven and London, 1991), pp. 1–21; Ilsa Glazer and Wahiba Abou Ras, "On Aggression, Human Rights, and the Case of Murder for Family Honour in Israel," *Sex Roles*, Vol. 30, Nos. 3/4 (1994), pp. 269–87.

8   This interview and others which will be cited below are part of a series of interviews with men and women conducted in 1994–95 as field research for my M.A. thesis.

9   Tamar Rapoport, E. Lomski-Feder and M. Masalha, "Female Subordination in the Arab-Israeli Community: The Adolescent Perspective of Social Veil," *Sex Roles*, Vol. 20, Nos. 5–6 (1989), pp. 225–69.

10   A. H. Abu-Zeid, "Honour and Shame among the Bedouin of Egypt," in J.G. Peristiany (ed.), *Honour and Shame: The Values of Mediterranean Society* (London, 1965); Jane Schneider, "Of Vigilance and Virgins: Honor, Shame and Access to Resources in Mediterranean Societies," *Ethology*, Vol. 10, No. 1 (1971), pp. 1–24; Nadia Youssef, "Culture Ideals, Feminine Behaviour and Family Control," *Comparative Studies in Culture and Society*, Vol. 15, No. 3 (1971), pp. 326–47.

11   Al-Khayyat, *Honour and Shame*; Glazer and Abou Ras, "On Aggression."

12   Abu-Zeid, "Honour and Shame."

13   Al-Khayyat, *Honour and Shame*, p. 22.

14   Ikhlas was born in the village of Ramah in the Galilee in 1956 and was 37 years old when she was killed by her youngest brother Hussam on 8 July 1994. Ikhlas attended High School in the nearby town of Akko and studied chemistry at the Hebrew University. After graduating, she went to the United States where her older brother and other relatives lived, continued her studies for a master's degree and decided to settle there. She worked for ten years in a local hospital, and four years in a school for disabled children. Shortly before her murder she had begun a new job with the United Nations (as narrated by her sister Zeinat, *Al-Itihad*, 22 July 1994). In addition to her work, Ikhlas was also very active in the Druze community there, dealing mainly with fund-raising for projects of orphans' homes and cultural centers within the Druze community in Israel. Members of her family came to visit her in the US. Hussam, the brother who killed her, stayed with her from the age of 14, returning in 1991 to serve in the IDF, obligatory military service required of all Druze men in Israel, the only such military obligation for the Palestinian communities in Israel. Ikhlas arrived in Israel on a visit two weeks before her murder, mainly, it seems, to help implement social and cultural projects in the Palestinian community. To that end, she met with Druze representatives in the Palestinian community, members of the Knesset, heads of municipalities and other leading figures. Her sister Zeinat recounted that these public officials had been very enthusiastic about the idea, and even competed among one another for possible projects in their village. On the day she was murdered, Ikhlas was interviewed on Israeli TV. She spoke of her plans and the meetings she had had for that purpose with leaders of the community. After the program was over, she returned to her home in Ramah. Shortly before the program was broadcast at 5 o'clock that same afternoon, her brother murdered her. He shot her 20 times in the upper part of the body with a rifle he had brought with him from the army. The then deputy mayor, Hatem Fares, told the paper *Ha'aretz* for its 22 July 1994 edition: "Together with other notables, we negotiated until 2 a.m. for them to take care of her funeral. The imam clearly stated that because of her improper behavior, he was not prepared to accept responsibility and deal with the matter, and told us to turn to the Shari'a court. In accordance with Druze religious belief, all those who stray from the straight path are not prayed for by the sheikhs. There is no expression of forgiveness and they do not say 'Allah yirahmo' (God have mercy on him)." The Shari'a court also ruled that none of the sheikhs should be involved in the funeral. Her body was buried at 4 a.m. in a hasty

and degrading manner, without any religious ceremony. As mentioned, her brother, the murderer, told police investigators that he had killed his sister because of her improper behavior, since she had worn a mini-skirt and thus dishonored the family. The deputy mayor explained his action and motives for the killing: "In matters of honor, morality and modesty, there are clear red lines: women do not wear mini-skirts, do not dress immodestly, exposing either the front or back of their body, do not wear jewelry or earrings, do not consort with boys and preserve their chastity. Ikhlas violated all these rules" (ibid.) The rumors circulating in the village after the murder suggested that Hussam's cousins had instigated him to kill his sister. (See also discussion in "Epilogue" below.)

15   Al-Khayyat, *Honour and Shame*; see also Abu-Zeid, "Honour and Shame"; Samir A'bdo, *Arab Women between Backwardness and Liberation* (in Arabic) (Beirut, 1980); Jalal Amin, "The Concept of Honor," *Hajar — Women's Book*, Vol. 1 (Cairo, 1993), pp. 166–7 (in Arabic).

16   Abu-Zeid, "Honour and Shame," p. 245.

17   Ibid.; see also Sasson Bar-Zvi, *Masoret ha-shiput shel bedu'ei ha-negev: Iyunim mevusasim al maga'im im ziknei ha-bedu'im* (Jurisdiction among the Negev Bedouin: Studies Based on Contacts with Bedouin Elders) (Tel Aviv, 1991); Victoria Goddard, "Honour and Shame: The Control of Women's Sexuality and Group Identity in Naples," in Pat Caplan (ed.), *The Cultural Construction of Sexuality* (New York, 1987), pp. 166–92.

18   Mazhar Aal-Far'un, *Tribal Law* (in Arabic) (Baghdad, 1941), p. 95. In Hebrew as well the word *she'er* refers both to meat as food, and in the expression *she'er basar* to a blood relation. The closeness in two Semitic languages betwen food and blood points to an ancient common tongue from which Hebrew and Arabic derive and an ancient period in which each group of blood relatives was a participant in the meal, thus the semantic nexus.

19   Abu-Zeid, "Honour and Shame," p. 245.

20   Abu-Lughod, *Veiled Sentiments*.

21   Goddard, "Honour and Shame."

22   Abu-Zeid, "Honour and Shame."

23   Joseph Ginat, *Blood Disputes among Bedouin and Rural Arabs in Israel* (Pittsburgh, 1987).

24   Nawal al-Sa'adawi, *The Face behind the Veil* (in Arabic) (Beirut, 1978).

25   Cited in Goddard, "Honor and Shame," p. 168.

26   See 'Aref al-'Aref, *Jurisprudence among the Bedouin* (in Arabic) (Jerusalem, 1933); Aal-Far'un, *Tribal Law*; Rima Hammami, "Women in Palestinian Society," in *Palestinian Society in Gaza, West Bank and Arab Jerusalem*, a FAFO survey of living conditions (Oslo, 1993).

27   Halim Barakat, *The Current Arab Society* (in Arabic) (Beirut, 1984).

28   Henry Rosenfeld, *Hem hayu falahim: Iyunim ba-hitpathut ha-hevratit shel ha-kfar ha-aravi be-Yisrael* (They Were Peasants: Studies in the Social Development of the Arab Village in Israel) (Jerusalem, 1964).

29   Granqvist, *Marriage Conditions*, pp. 253–4. See also Michael E. Meeker, "Meaning and Society in the Near East: Examples from the Black Sea Turks and the Levantine Arabs," *International Journal of Middle Eastern Studies*, Vol. 7, Nos. 1–2 (1976), pp. 383–422.

30   Al-'Aref, *Jurisprudence among the Bedouin*, p. 125.

31   Annelies Moors, "Women and Property: A Historical-Anthropological Study of Women's Access to Property in Jabal Nablus, Palestine" (Ph.D. diss., University of Amsterdam, 1992); Rosenfeld, *Hem hayu falahim*.

32   Abu-Zeid, "Honour and Shame"; Tillion, *The Republic of Cousins*; Bar-Zvi, *Masoret ha-shiput*.

33   Grandqvist, *Marriage Conditions*; Abu-Zeid, "Honour and Shame"; Aal-Far'un, *Tribal Law*; Al-Aref, *Jurisprudence among the Bedouin*; Tillion, *The Republic of Cousins*.

34   Kressel, "Harigat ha-ahot," p. 73.

35   Gideon Kressel, "Ha-mohar: Bhinah hozeret" (A Re-examination of the Mohar), *Ha-Mizrah he-Hadash*, Vol. 26, Nos. 1–2 (1976), pp. 203–31; Al-Aref, *Jurisprudence among the Bedouin*; Aal-Far'un, *Tribal Law*.

36   Manar Hasan, "The Murder of Women for Family Honor"; *Princesses Dead or Doomed to Die*, Sentinelles Report (Geneva, 1982).

37   Kressel, "Harigat ha-ahot."

38   See also Aal-Far'un, *Tribal Law*; Bar-Zvi, *Masoret ha-shiput*; Salah Nj'idat, "Pishei min ba-hok
     ha-bedu'i" (Sex Crimes in Bedouin Law) (M.A. thesis, Hebrew University, Jerusalem, 1992);
     Abu-Zeid, "Honour and Shame."
39   Al-'Aref, *Jurisprudence among the Bedouin*; Aal-Far'un, *Tribal Law*; Bar-Zvi, *Masoret ha-shiput*.
40   Ibid.
41   See Bar-Zvi, *Masoret ha-shiput*; Nj'idat, "Pishei min."
42   Aal-Far'un, *Tribal Law*; Nj'idat, "Pishei min"; Bar-Zvi, *Masoret ha-shiput*.
43   Bar-Zvi, *Masoret ha-shiput*; Aal-Far'un, *Tribal Law.*
44   Bar-Zvi *Masoret ha-shiput*, p. 54. See also Nj'idat, "Pishei min."
45   Bar-Zvi *Masoret ha-shiput*; Aal-Far'un, *Tribal Law.*
46   Al-'Aref, *Jurisprudence among the Bedouin*, p. 77.
47   See Kressel, "Harigat ha-ahot"; Aal-Far'un, *Tribal Law*; Abu-Zeid, "Honour and Shame";
     Hasan, "Murder of Women for Family Honour."
48   Kressel, "Harigat ha-ahot," p. 73.
49   Ibid.
50   Abou Touma, *Yerushalayim*, 10 March 1989.
51   Fawaz Turki, *The Making of a Palestinian-American Exile's Return* (New York, 1993).
52   Kressel, "Harigat ha-ahot"; see also Richard T. Antoun, "On the Modesty of Women in Arab
     Muslim Villages: A Study in the Accommodation of Tradition," *American Anthropologist*,
     Vol. 70, No. 4 (1968), pp. 617–97; Ginat, *Women in Muslim Rural Society*.
53   Hasan, "The Murder of Women for Family Honor".
54   Quoted in Kressel, "Killing of the Sister"; Shujauddin Qureshi, "Another Taliban Regime?"
     Women's International Net, 17A (January 1999), welcome.to/winmagazine.
55   Ginat, *Women in Muslim Rural Society*.
56   The Koran, Sura 'el-Nisaa', verse 15; Sura 'el-Nur, verse 2.
57   John K. Campbell, *Honour, Family and Patronage: A Study of Institution and Moral Values in a
     Greek Mountain Community* (Oxford, 1964); Schneider, "Of Vigilance and Virgins"; Tillion,
     The Republic of Cousins; Gideon M. Kressel, "On Sororocide/Filiacide for Family Honour,"
     Current Anthropology, Vol. 22, No. 2 (1981), pp. 152–3; Keddie, "Deciphering Middle
     Eastern Women's History."
58   Kressel, "Harigat ha-ahot."
59   Yoav Peled, "Zarim be-utopiyah: Ma'amadam ha-ezrahi shel ha-palestinim be-Yisrael"
     (Strangers in Utopia: The Civic Status of Israel's Palestinian Citizens), *Teoriyah u-Vikoret*,
     No. 3 (1993), pp. 21–35.
60   Ezra Danin, *Te'udot ve-dmuyot* (Certificates and Images) (Tel Aviv, 1944).
61   Ginat, *Blood Disputes*; Mona Rishmawi, "The Legal Status of Palestinian Women in the
     Occupied Territories," in Nahi Toubia (ed.), *Women of the Arab World: The Coming Challenge*
     (London, 1989), pp. 79–92.
62   So'ad Mokbel, "Women in Lebanese Law," *Mawakif*, Vol. 73–74 (1994), pp. 248–58 (in
     Arabic).
63   Lama Abu-Odeh, "Crimes of Honour and the Construction of Gender in Arab Society," in
     Mai Yamani and Andrew Allen (eds.), *Feminism and Islam: Legal and Literary Perspectives*
     (New York, 1996), pp. 141–94.
64   See *Soltat al'aba'im: Women in the Saudi Island: The Committee for Women in the Arabia Island*
     (Cologne, 1991).
65   Kressel, "harigat ha-ahot," p. 85.
66   Ibid., p. 87.
67   Ibid.
68   *Monitin*, No. 112 (January 1988), p. 24.
69   Ginat, *Blood Disputes*, p. 124.
70   For details of the two cases, see Nj'idat, "Pishei min"; and Hasan, "Murder of Women for
     Family Honour."
71   Nj'idat, "Pishei min," p. 97 (author's emphasis).
72   *Kol ha-Ir*, 8 November 1991.
73   Cited in Ginat, *Blood Disputes*.

74 *Monitin*, No. 112 (January 1988).
75 Uzi Benziman and Atallah Mansour, *Dayarei mishneh: Aravyei Yisrael, maamadam veha-mediniyut klapeihem* (Subtenants: Israeli Arabs, Their Status and the Policy towards Them) (Jerusalem, 1992).
76 *Monitin*, No. 112 (January 1988).
77 Rosenfeld, *Hem hayu falahim*; Aharon Layish, *Marriage, Divorce and Succession in the Druze Family* (Netherlands, 1982).
78 See Majid al-Hadj, *Social Change and the Family Process* (Boulder and London, 1978); Abner Cohen, *Arab Border Villages in Israel: A Study of Continuity and Change in Social Organization* (Manchester, 1965); Henry Rosenfeld, "Hamula," *Journal of Peasant Studies*, Vol. 1, No. 2 (January 1974), pp. 243–4.
79 Ian Lustick, *Arabs in the Jewish State: Israel's Control of a National Minority* (Austin, TX, 1980), p. 319, n. 5.
80 Manar Hasan, "Marriage between Relatives in Palestinian Society in Israel: Tradition or Product of Government Policy?" (typescript, 1993).
81 Cited in Lustick, *Arabs in the Jewish State*, p. 204.
82 Letter to al-Fanar from Attorney General, file no. 107/91/12, on file in the Al-Fanar organization.
83 Letter from al-Fanar to Attorney General, 10 May 1992, on file in the Al-Fanar organization.
84 Ginat, *Blood Disputes*, p. 240.
85 See Sentinelles Report, *Princess Dead or Doomed to Die*.
86 Ginat, *Blood Disputes*, p. 27.
87 *Yerushalayim*, 10 March 1989.
88 As we have noted, the claim that an honor killing is based on Shari'a law is incorrect. What is interesting though is that there was no response whatsoever to this from the side of the Shari'a judges.
89 Glazer and Abou Ras, "On Aggression."
90 *Ha'aretz*, 1 September 1991.
91 Walid Sadik, former Knesset member, Meretz Party, interview, 11 November 1994.
92 Raja Ajbariya, interview, 6 December 1994.
93 Walid Sadik, interview, 11 November 1994.
94 Sheikh Abdulla Nimr Darwish, head of the Islamic Movement, *Al Sunara*, 22 July 1994.
95 *Ha'aretz*, 26 August 1994.
96 *Al-Sennara*, 2 December 1994.
97 Walid Sadik, interview, 11 November 1994.
98 Raja Ajbariya, interview, 6 December 1994.
99 Nj'idat, "Pishei min."
100 Ginat, *Blood Disputes*.
101 *Kolbo*, 29 July 1994.
102 See Benziman and Mansour, *Dayarei mishneh*.
103 *Monitin*, No. 112 (January 1988).

Familism, Postmodernity and the State: The Case of Israel

Sylvie Fogiel-Bijaoui

In Israel, as in other post-industrial societies, social institutions, including the family, are undergoing a process of individualization. The family is becoming a private concern, and state involvement in matters of marriage, divorce and fertility is being reduced to mediating between the individual and the society and to setting a legal seal to the individual's preferences and decisions. The perception is that adults, both men and women, are autonomous individuals, entitled to shape their own biography in the private and public spheres. As a result, the rate of marriage is declining, the divorce rate rising, total fertility rates are decreasing while the percentage of out-of-wedlock births is growing.

These developments have enabled various and sundry family structures to come into being, including "two-career families," "second families" (following divorce or separation), "single-parent families," and "single-sex families." Members of these families live together under the same roof or separately; they are married or cohabit without marriage; they are married in accord with religious law and/or signed a civil contract. The number of children in these families is generally small, and parent–child relations tend to be democratic. The literature calls these families "the new families" or "postmodern families."[1]

In Israel today, the same post-industrial processes are taking place. Yet along with them, one sees a remarkable persistence of familism. Familism continues to characterize Israeli society, and for Israelis "the family" continues to play a crucial role, at both the individual and collective levels.[2] As a cultural code, familism takes for granted an unequal gender division of labor. The woman is constructed as a mother and wife, whose primary obligations are to bear children and take care of her home and family. Her paid work is accepted, if at all, as a secondary contribution to the family livelihood. Familism also entails the construction of marriage as the only framework for the birth of legitimate children and the construction of divorce as an aberration of the norm. As a cultural code, it thus dictates to the individual his/her proper way of life: the duty of heterosexual marriage, rejection of divorce, bringing (many) legitimate children into the world, prohibition of out-of-wedlock births, and, as stated above, an unequal and gendered division of labor. This code is exemplified both by the modern nuclear family which characterizes industrial society (with the father, who supports the family, the mother, who is a housewife, and the children, all in a single household) and by the traditional family (a multigenerational structure, consisting of the father, his children and their wives, and unwed daughters living together under the same roof and managing a joint household).

The aim of this study is to explain the paradoxical continuation of the centrality of familism in Israeli society, despite the processes of individualization the society is undergoing and despite its affinity with Western culture. To this end, the first section of this study, "Familism in Israel: The Limits of Individualization," presents data that point to the continued existence of familism in Israeli society in comparison with other post-industrial societies. The second section, "Familism as a National Asset," argues that familism is a marker of Israeli society because it rests on the institutionalization of religious laws pertaining to marital status.[3] In fact, every ethno-religious group conceives of these religious laws as a "national asset," which serves as a boundary between the groups and as a basis for their "normative collective memory" and their "normative collective identity."[4] The third section, "Familism and Class among Israeli Citizens," contends that class stratifications and geographical differentiations, which not infrequently overlap with ethno-religious dimensions, are also structural mechanisms that strengthen and perpetuate familism among both Israeli Jews and Israeli Palestinians.[5] In other words, I claim that the different forms of familism in Israel and the continued cultural dominance of familism in Israeli society are the products of the conjunction of the country's institutionalized religious laws and its stratified post-industrial reality. In the conclusion, I deal with the future of "the family" in Israel.[6]

Familism in Israel: Individualization and Its Limits

By economic and technological criteria, Israel belongs to the industrial nations. In fact, since 1994 Israel has been a member of the exclusive club of the industrialized nations with the highest incomes.[7] One of the features of these countries since the 1960s has been the consistent and significant rise in the level of education among women and the massive participation of women, especially of middle-class, married women with small children, in the labor force. Post-industrial society required a huge, varied, available and cheap labor force, and women definitely formed the major reservoir of such labor. More and more women became "working mothers," and this dramatic process became the lever for family change in post-industrial societies.[8]

A similar process took place in Israel, especially after the 1967 Six Day War. Over the years women came to make up an increasingly marked proportion of the recipients of academic degrees. For example, in the 1997–98 academic year, women constituted 57 percent of those who received academic degrees, as opposed to 48 percent in 1987–88.[9] At the same time, the rate of women (aged 15 and older) in the labor force, which had not exceeded 30 percent till the 1970s, reached 47.3 percent in 1998, when it amounted to 45 percent of the entire Israeli labor force (men and women). Also in 1998, 55 percent of all the married women in Israel — that is, more than 70 percent of all the married mothers of children under fifteen years old — were in the labor force.[10]

As a result of the massive entry of married women/mothers into the labor force, the normative model of the family in Israel — of the father-provider, mother-housewife, living under the same roof with their biological/adopted children — steadily declined.[11] The two-provider family became the prevailing model of the family in Israel.[12] These structural changes were accompanied by processes of liberalization, both on the institutional and cultural levels. Israel became a more pluralistic society and created social mechanisms and institutional arrangements which freed various groups in the society from the supervision and control of the political parties and state machinery. The individual, his/her rights and wishes, became more central in the public discourse, and greater emphasis was placed on the individual's ability to determine his/her own destiny. These developments were reflected in legislation, in court rulings, and in what has been termed the Supreme Court's "constitutional revolution."[13]

It is thus no wonder that between 1985 and the end of the 1990s, marital rates fell from 6.9 to 6.7 (1998), divorce rates rose from 1.2 to 1.7 (1999), and total fertility rates declined from 3.12 to 2.98, while the percentage of live births by never-married women rose from 1.3 to 2.5 (1998).[14] During these same years, the percentage of single-parent families also rose from 5 percent of all households with children under 17 in the mid-1980s to 10 percent in 1998.[15] Nonetheless, and despite the processes of individualization that have been described, a glance at Table 1 confirms the claim that Israeli society is the most familistic of the post-industrial societies: Israelis "marry a lot," "divorce little," "give birth to many (legitimate) children" and to relatively few children out of wedlock. Even in Japan, which, much like Israel, is considered a post-industrial society with a clear familistic tradition, total fertility rates are 50 percent lower than in Israel.

In addition, even a cursory look at Table 2, which provides data on three indicators of familism among the ethno-religious groups in Israel, shows that different forms of familism exist among these groups. Among the Jews, there has been a moderate process of individualization of the institution of the family, and the dimensions of familism have declined somewhat in the last 15 years. The situation is quite different among the Palestinian Arab citizens of

TABLE 1
DEMOGRAPHIC INDICATORS —
COMPARISON BETWEEN ISRAEL AND OTHER POST-INDUSTRIAL
SOCIETIES, 1996

Demographic Indicators	Marriage Rates (%)	Divorce Rates (%)	Total Fertility Rates (%)	Live Births to Never-Married Women (%)
Country	(*)	(**)	(***)	(****)
Israel	6.6	1.6	2.9	2.3 (Jews only)
European Union[1]	5.1	1.8	1.4	24
United States	8.8	4.4	2.04	32
Canada	5.2	2.6	1.62	31
Japan	6.4	1.6	1.44	1 (1994)

Notes:
*   Number of marriage certificates issued per 1,000 persons by a recognized official licensing authority.
**   Number of legal divorce certificates issued per 1,000 persons.
***   Number of children a woman is expected to bear in her lifetime.
****   Births to never-married women per 100 live births.
[1]   The 15 countries of the European Union are: Austria, Belgium, Britain, Denmark, Finland, France, Germany, Greece, Holland, Ireland, Italy, Luxemburg, Portugal, Spain, Sweden.

Source: Central Bureau of Statistics, Shnaton statisti le-Yisrael (Annual Statistical Abstract of Israel) (hereafter CBS), No. 51 (2000), Tables 3.1, 3.12, 3.16; Eurostat Yearbook, 1998–1999, pp. 84, 86, 88.

Israel, whether Muslims, Christians or Druze. Despite slight fluctuations in the various dimensions, Arab society in Israel retains very high levels of familism in all its dimensions.

The percentage of births to never-married women is not included in Table 2. It appears only in Table 1, and only for the Jewish population. This is not accidental: Among the Muslim, Christian and Druze citizens of Israel, giving birth outside wedlock is viewed as a violation of family honor, which may be punished by the murder of the "deviant woman" by her father, brother or, in recent years, husband.[16] As a result, births to never-married women are not reported.

It is also evident from Table 2 that familism has different forms and different dimensions among the different groups of Palestinian-Arab citizens of Israel: the Muslims have particularly high marriage and birth rates, the Christians (most of them Catholic) have very low divorce rates, and the Druze

TABLE 2
FAMILISM IN ISRAEL'S ETHNO-RELIGIOUS GROUPS,
DEMOGRAPHIC INDICATORS, 1985–99

	Population	1985*	1999
Marriage Rates	Total	6.9	6.7 (1998)
	Jews	6.7	6.1
	Muslims	8.6	7.9
	Christians	6.2	5.7 (1998)
	Druze	9.5	9.3
Divorce Rates	Total	1.2	1.7
	Jews	1.3	1.9
	Muslims	0.8	1.1
	Christians	0.2	0.2
	Druze	0.7	0.8
Fertility	Total	3.12	2.98 (1998)
	Jews	2.85	2.67 (1998)
	Muslims	5.54	4.76 (1998)
	Christians	2.41	2.62 (1998)
	Druze	5.40	3.10 (1998)

Note: * 1985 was the year in which the first National Unity Government instituted the neoliberal economic policy that still characterizes the Israeli economy.

Source: CBS, No. 37 (1986), Tables C.1, C.3; CBS, No. 51 (2000), Tables 3.1, 3.12.

have high rates of marriage and low rates of divorce, accompanied, however, by a consistent decline in fertility since the 1970s. They are the only ethno-religious group in Israel to have seen such a decline. In addition, the average age at first marriage among Arab women has remained more or less stable since the 1970s, while among the Jews there has been a gradual, moderate rise. In 1998, the average age at first marriage among Christian women was 23.7; among Muslim women, 21.6; among Druze women, 21.2; and among Jewish women, 25.5. Among men, the average age at first marriage in that year was 29.3 for Christians; 26.3 for Muslims; 25.9 for Druze; and 28.5 for Jews. Moreover, the average difference between the mean age of the bride and groom among Israeli Palestinians has remained more or less stable, while the average difference among the Jews has somewhat decreased over the years.[17]

How can one explain the strength of familism in Israel in comparison to other post-industrial societies? How can one account for the different dimensions of familism among the different ethno-religious communities?

Familism as a National Asset

In order to explain the familism that characterizes Israeli society, we must consider first and foremost the institutional arrangements that govern the society, that is, Israel's family laws. The laws that regulate marriage and divorce in Israel, namely the Rabbinical Court Law-1953 (Marriage and Divorce) and the Druze Religious Courts Law-1962, take the place of civil law and bestow exclusive authority over personal status (marriage and divorce) to the religious courts of Israel's four ethno-religious communities. In other words, familism is institutionalized and perpetuated by the country's laws.[18] As Carmel Shalev writes: "The most salient feature of the marriage and divorce laws in the Israeli legal system is the almost total application of religious law to matters of personal status. This means that, with certain exceptions, Israeli law does not contain civil mechanisms for marriage and divorce."[19] In this section, I analyze the implications that these religious laws have for men and women in Israel, and then explain why most Israeli Jews and Israeli Palestinians consider these laws "national assets" even though they violate basic human rights.

Religious Laws and Familism[20]
In the world view underlying all the recognized religions in Israel, the man, the husband, is regarded as the pillar of the family and is given authority over his wife and children. The man's power is based on an unequal gender division of labor in the family: the wife belongs to her husband and must obey him. In exchange, the husband is responsible for the physical and economic security of the home, including his wife. The main aim of marriage is to produce legitimate children. Hence, while men are allowed a certain amount of sexual freedom, women are permitted to have sexual relations only with their husbands. In this way, religious laws legitimize a double standard in family life, characterized by strictness towards women and leniency towards men. In addition, there are many restrictions on the right to marry and divorce.

Among Jews, the following categories of persons are not allowed to marry:

1. Illegitimate children (*mamzerim*): These are children born of a relationship between a married woman and a man not her husband. (Children born of a union with an unmarried woman are defined as legitimate.) *Mamzerim* may not marry a "kosher daughter of Israel," but only another *mamzer* or a convert. The status of illegitimacy (*mamzerut*) lasts for ten generations, being passed on from one generation to the next till the tenth.
2. Cohens: As descendants of the priests of the ancient Temple, Cohens are forbidden to marry divorcees.

3. Adulteresses: These are women who had a relationship with a man other than their husbands while they were married. Such women are sexually forbidden both to their husbands and to the men with whom they had intercourse.

4. *Agunot:* These are women whose husbands have disappeared, whether through unproven death or otherwise, or who refuse to grant them a writ of divorce. They are viewed as still married and are not permitted to remarry for fear of adultery and *mamzerut* (the children they bear will be considered illegitimate). Men, however, whose wives have disappeared or refuse to grant them a writ of divorce may obtain permission to marry from the rabbinate, though the process is long and cumbersome.

Religious law thus strengthens marriage and hinders divorce, at least for women whose husbands do not agree to it.

The situation is similar in the other religions, and in some cases even more problematic. Catholics cannot divorce at all. In Islam and in the Druze religion, a woman cannot divorce her husband, though in certain cases she may ask the Qadi (the religious authority) to permit her to do so. In Islam, which is polygamous, a man can easily divorce his wife: in most cases, it is enough for him to tell her "You are divorced" before witnesses, with no need for judicial proceedings, since the Sharia Court (Muslim Court) will authorize the divorce retroactively. In many cases, women are divorced without appropriate compensation and lose their children, who remain in the custody of their husband's family. In the Druze religion, although it is monogamous, the situation is similar: a wife cannot divorce her husband, though a man can divorce his wife with relative ease. Moreover, Druze women may not remarry after being divorced (or after being widowed). In addition, among Muslims in Israel, there are polygamous marriages (made in religious ceremonies) that are not reported to the Ministry of Interior. Among Muslim, Druze and Christian Arabs, girls are sometimes married as children. In many cases, such marriages are arranged by the girl's relatives, without the girl's participation in the decision and without her consent or agreement. Most of these practices, it should be noted, occur in circumvention of Israeli civil laws prohibiting polygamy, child marriage and one-sided non-judicial divorce.

Israeli law also discriminates between Jews, Druze and Christians, on the one hand, and Muslims, on the other. In the event of divorce, Jews, Druze and to a fair extent also Christians may turn to a civil court with regard to alimony, child support and the division of assets. That is, they can choose between the religious and civil courts. Women generally hasten to turn to the civil courts, which mostly pay more attention to their civil and human rights. Men generally prefer the religious courts, which, in accord with religious law, usually give them preferential treatment. For the Muslims in Israel, however, the only legal authority, even with respect to the practical matters related to the termination of the marriage, is the Sharia Court. Thus Muslim women citizens of Israel do not have the freedom of choice that is available to the country's other women, whether Jews, Druze or Christians.[21]

Women as a Threat to the Social Order
The religious laws of all the religions institutionalize, to one degree or another, a single central value, *modesty* (*tzni'ut*), which consigns women to a lower status by virtue of their being women. Modesty is a value stemming from the construction of women as a danger to men and to the social order because of their sexuality. Modesty thus requires that women suppress all expression of their sexuality and conceal it in the public sphere. Modesty is also a value that applies to men. However, it does not have the same far-reaching implications in the public and private sphere for men as for women.

Modesty as a value is differently interpreted in the various religions, and sometimes in the different streams within each religion. This value is nourished by customs and traditions, most of which are ancient and which derive from different sources. However, for all the variations, there are basic similarities in the way modesty is socially constructed: modesty excludes women from the public sphere and institutionalizes the wife's subordination to her husband's authority within her home, where she is obliged to channel her sexuality to the highest aim of helping her husband fulfill the commandment "be fruitful and multiply."

- Among Jews, Muslims and Druze, though not among Christians, modesty entails the separation between men and women not only in the public sphere, but also in the private sphere. In the latter, there are various degrees of separation between "strange" (meaning unrelated) men and women and even between husband and wife. For example, Jewish religious law (*Halakhah*) constructs the menstruating woman as "unclean" and forbids sexual contact and even touch between her and her husband (*niddah*, according to Leviticus). These restrictions come on top of the fact that her perceived "uncleanliness" bars her from participation in the public sphere, in synagogue, cemetery and so forth.
- In all the religions, the ultimate meaning of marriage is the bringing of legitimate children into the world so as to ensure the biological and cultural continuity of the collective. In this context, virginity constitutes the highest value. In the best case, loss of virginity means losing the chance of marrying or even of being considered a possible match (among a substantial portion of Muslims and Druze and a not insignificant portion of Jews marriages are arranged). In the worst case, loss of virginity can lead to the murder of the "deviant woman" by the men in her family, usually her

father and brothers, with the cooperation of her mother. We will return to this subject below.

- Modesty also means that girls and women must cover and conceal their body and head, to one degree or another, by a veil, wig and/or long dress, so as not to arouse the "evil instinct" in men. Although there is little consensus about the age at which the body must be covered, the means by which it must be covered or how thoroughly it must be covered, this moral code is found among Jews, Muslims and Druze (as well as among Christians, to a more limited extent). Covering the body and head is important to the woman as well, since the cover serves as a kind of passport that gives her a certain, though sometimes most limited, "freedom of movement." When her body is covered, a woman may leave her home and move about in the public sphere, to one degree or other.

- Modesty also means that women's sexuality has no valid existence in and of itself, but only in connection with childbearing. As a result, decisions about contraception, abortion and related matters are not left to the individual — to the woman — but are precisely coded by religious norms and laws. Among Catholics, contraceptives and abortions, that is, the voluntary prevention and cessation of pregnancy, are totally forbidden. Muslims and Druze take a similar approach, though they sometimes apply more liberal interpretations or permit "exceptions," mainly when the pregnancy endangers the mother. Contraceptives are also forbidden among Jews, though different streams of Judaism, even some of the Orthodox streams, allow women to use them under certain circumstances. Jewish women are permitted abortions when the fetus endangers their life.

- Violation of the norms of modesty leads to different responses in accord with the context, the persons and the type of violation. The strongest and most extreme reactions are found among some Muslim, Druze and Christian groups and come in response to the "violation of family honor." Such a violation can occur as a result of the woman's dress, contact of any sort with "an outsider," loss of virginity, etc.. In such instances, the men of the family are expected to restore the family honor, to show the society that they can enforce proper social order in their household and to punish — that is, to kill — the "deviant" woman or girl. Every year between 20 and 30 women — Muslim, Druze and Christian citizens of Israel — are murdered for "violating family honor." Police files (and media reports, when the information reaches the media) refer to these women as "missing," "accident victims," or "suicides." The police and courts in Israel treat such murders with understanding and clemency. Their "liberalism" is prompted by their reluctance to upset the delicate balance between the Arab citizens of Israel and the state's governing bodies, since many, though not all, Palestinian Arab citizens of Israel accept and even support "family honor" killings.[22]

Naturally, the question arises of how such laws and customs exist in a state that is committed to democracy and human rights. These laws infringe the human and individual rights of both men and women, though not to the same extent. As Shalev reminds us:

> The right to marry and establish a family is recognized as one of the basic human rights in international law, in several agreed upon treaties. Complementing this recognition is the obligation of the state to protect the family as "the basic unit of society." Every adult — regardless of race, citizenship, or religion — has the right to equality in all that relates to marriage, married life and divorce.[23]

Part of the answer is undoubtedly anchored in the delicate balance in Israel between religious laws and the various means of circumventing them. Alongside the religious courts, which have exclusive jurisdiction over marriage and divorce as such, Israel has a system of family courts that rule in accord with civil law and have jurisdiction in matters relating to property, alimony and custody and visiting rights. With the exception of Muslims, Israeli citizens can choose between the two instances. Moreover, as stated above, marriage abroad (for example, "Cyprus marriages") are recognized. In addition, many laws lend legitimacy to cohabiting couples, both heterosexual and homosexual, and cohabitation is well anchored in Israel's legal and social systems. This situation makes possible a kind of *modus vivendi* which enables Israelis to live in this legal-institutional framework. Nonetheless, it is still necessary to explain the hegemony of religious laws — the hegemony that serves as the major mechanism for the institutionalization of familism.

Familism as a Jewish National Asset

Many researchers have analyzed the relation between the Jewish religion and Jewish nationhood in the State of Israel. According to Kimmerling, one of the most taken-for-granted assumptions among Israeli Jews is the non-separation of religion and nationhood in the construction of Jewish Israeli identity. The collective Jewish Israeli identity, values, symbols and memory are anchored in the Jewish religion.[24] As Hervieu-Léger notes, religion plays a major role in the formation of "normative collective memory" and its transmission and perpetuation over generations: "Religion is an ideological, practical, and symbolic system through which consciousness, both individual and collective, of belonging to a particular chain of belief is constituted, maintained, developed, and controlled."[25] Moreover, according to Shifman, more than anything else family laws symbolize for many Israeli Jews the symbiosis of religion and nation. For these Jews, whether religious or not, marriage carried out in accord with Jewish law is an essential component of the integrity of the Jewish people and of its historical continuity in Israel and the diaspora. It is also an essential component of the connection between Israel and the diaspora.[26] This is one of the most taken-for-granted and difficult-to-challenge assumptions among Israeli Jews.

Moreover, as Durkheim argues, religion plays a major role in all that relates to the social integration and cohesion of the community.[27] In the eyes of many Jews in Israel, the religious laws play an integrative and unifying role in at least three areas:

1. Religious laws are needed to prevent mixed marriages between Jews and non-Jews both in and outside of Israel. In other words, the family laws in Israel delineate the boundaries of the Jewish collective and serve as a dividing line between the Jewish and Arab citizens. For all practical purposes, this demarcation is the desired situation, not only in the eyes of religious Jews but also in those of most Jews who are not religious.[28] In other words, religious laws are instrumentalized on behalf of a national project, which can be defined as preserving the boundaries of the national collective.
2. Out of similar motives, much of the Jewish Israeli public accepts (Orthodox) religious laws as a means of facilitating the identification of the religious people with the state. Their readiness to do so is accompanied by ambivalence towards the Conservative and Reform streams of Judaism and their family laws (marriage and divorce),which are not recognized in Israel. Although a not inconsequential proportion of Israeli Jews declare that they support Jewish pluralism, many of them, including not only those who define themselves as religious but also those who define themselves as secular, feel that non-Orthodox marriages will lead to a split in the nation (not to a split in the religion!), and oppose these marriages.
3. The religious and family laws, at the core of which is the commandment to "be fruitful and multiply and fill the land," make a substantial normative contribution to the "demographic competition" which exists both overtly and covertly between the Jewish and Palestinian Arab citizens of Israel. "The demographic problem," that is, the need to ensure a Jewish majority for the future of Zionism, is raised in many and varied discussions: in discussions about the Palestinian–Jewish conflict, in discussions on the civil status of the Arab citizens of Israel; in discussions on abortion, and others.[29] As a normative discourse, religious law fosters attitudes, values and behaviors that construct childbirth as a national commandment for perpetuation and numerical enlargement of the nation. It forms a major component of what Anson and Meiri term the "strategy of group survival."[30] It is thus clear that religious laws, and the institutionalization of familism in marriage, divorce and childbirth, constitute a central component in the crystallization of the Jewish collective at both the symbolic and the demographic levels.

Aside from its religious aspects, familism is a "national asset" in another way as well. In the perpetual state of war in Israel, familism reinforces and justifies as self-evident a clear and rigid unequal gender division between the "fighting man" in the public-national sphere and the "protected woman and her children" in the private-personal sphere. This gendered division acts as an organizing principle that is interwoven, both overtly and covertly, in all areas of life: in the language, in images and myths, in norms and customs and in the legal system. As a result, the (Jewish) "fighting" man is situated at the center of society, while the (Jewish) woman, who participates only partially in the defense of the nation, is located at the margins of society and at the margins of "the family," in her view as well as that of the society.[31]

Familism among Jews, though "dressed in religious garb," constitutes a central component of the social and cultural weave, in that it is one of the pillars of the national identity. A similar situation exists in the other national community that lives in the State of Israel: the Palestinian Arab community.

Familism as a Palestinian National Asset
Among the Palestinian citizens of Israel, religion and religion-based family laws also constitute a basis for "normative collective memory," as well as a basis for "normative collective identity" in face of the Jewish majority. For Arabs, as for Jews, religious laws provide a "boundary marker" both between Arabs and Jews and among themselves: as Muslims, Christians and Druze. Moreover, religious laws, particularly among Muslims and Druze, are viewed as reinforcing Arabs' historical identity as a fortress against Westernization — increasingly perceived as a danger in today's age of globalization. In addition, religion and religious laws serve as a bridge to the world outside: to the Christian and Muslim worlds, with which the Israeli Palestinian-Arab communities have ramified connections on both the personal and collective levels.

As among Jews, demography is regarded as a major issue and is seen as a "strategy of survival" of a minority against a majority, a strategy that Jews define as a "demographic threat." In other words, demography is also a major component of the national strategy of the Palestinian-Arab collective,[32] and, as among the Jews, the religious discourse contributes to this strategy. It is thus no wonder that Shifman found that "among non-Jewish ethnic groups, there is hardly any opposition to that legal-religious domination. On the contrary, this situation is interpreted as an important part of the legal-religious autonomy which these religions enjoy."[33]

The importance of religious laws and family laws as a basis for national (not only religious) identity for both the Jewish and Palestinian citizens of Israel is precisely the reason that religious family laws are institutionalized in Israel, despite Israel's commitment to democracy. The religious family laws are seen as promoting the "common good," even at the price of infringing upon basic human rights, especially women's basic human rights. This approach explains the findings in Table 1, which compares the dimensions of familism in Israel with those in other post-industrial societies.

I will now discuss the various dimensions of familism among the different ethno-religious groups that comprise Israeli society .

Familism and Class among Israeli Citizens

For this discussion, we must take into account the positioning of the different ethno-religious groups in the Israeli economy and their exposure to the patterns, values and norms that have been created by capitalism in Israel.[34] The positioning of each group in the Israeli economy in the age of globalization refers, above all, to the access that the group and its members have to the structures of educational and occupational opportunities created by post-industrial capitalism. This access is what enables the mass participation of women in the labor market, which, as recalled, has been the major lever in changing the institution of the family. In addition, access to educational and occupational opportunities exposes women to the ethos of individualism, which is based on competition and achievement and which emphasizes the individual's abilities, wishes and responsibility for his/her fate. Clearly, not every person who is exposed to and lives in an individualistic environment will support this ethos in the family. The opposite is quite often the case. On the other hand, the absence of an environment that enables people to live on their own, economically and normatively, will make it difficult for persons to think in individualistic terms and even more difficult for them to realize their individualism in practice.

In Israeli society, exposure to individualism as a norm and access to educational and occupational opportunities correspond almost entirely with the division of the population into ethno-religious groups. Here too there is a clear division both *between* Jewish and Arab citizens of Israel and *among* the Jews and Arabs. Israeli society is characterized by ethno-religious and class stratification in addition to gender stratification. As a result, familism takes on different forms in the various groups, in accordance with each group's encounter with post-industrial capitalism and globalization.

Among those groups which, as a result of the country's ethno-religious and class stratification, have not been exposed or have been only minimally exposed to the processes of globalization, the level of familism is high: married women do not join the work force *en masse* and family patterns have changed only slightly. In contrast, among those groups who have been maximally exposed to post-industrial capitalism or who have led the post-industrial processes, the dimensions of familism are much lower: many women/mothers have joined the labor force and have become working women/mothers — the very experience defined as the lever for family change in post-industrial societies.

Familism among Palestinian Arab Citizens of Israel

About 22 percent of Arab women, in contrast to 51.1 percent of Jewish women, are in the labor force.[35] This means that about 78 percent of Arab women in Israel do not work outside their homes. Moreover, most of those who do work are employed in simple, ill-paid and low-status jobs, mostly without social benefits, in agriculture, industry (textiles, food), personal services and low-level clerical work. However, about 20 percent of working Israeli Arab women hold semi-professional jobs, in education, social work and nursing, and about 4 percent are in the liberal professions.[36]

This situation stems from the geographic and occupational stratification of Arabs and Jews in Israel: about 85 percent of the Arabs in Israel live in separate communities and about 15 percent live in mixed cities but in separate neighborhoods.[37] The "Arab sector" lacks a developed economic infrastructure, and its business activity is most limited. Unemployment, especially for skilled and educated workers, is chronic in their areas of residence. Moreover, with the exception of some spheres, the "Jewish sector" and the public sector are reluctant to include Arab citizens. The exceptions include government services, local authorities, institutions of higher learning, the electronic and printed media, finance and law, and the arts, in which Israel's Palestinian-Arab citizens are somewhat more integrated. On the whole, however, most Arab citizens of Israel have hardly any access to the post-industrial society — and if they do have access, it is generally in low-status and low-paid occupations. It is no wonder that under these conditions the structural economic changes that would permit the massive entrance of Arab women into the paid labor force have not taken place and that there has been no significant change in the social construction of Arab women in the private and the public sphere.

Given this state of affairs, the power of the *hamula*, the extended family, is still significant, even though it has somewhat declined. Granted, the economic dependency of the individual on the *hamula* has declined, mainly because of the entrance of the young men into the paid labor force, and the *hamula* tends to interfere less in the lives of its members than it previously did and tends less than before to impose rigid norms. Nonetheless, the *hamula* still plays a major role in promoting, rather than obstructing, its members' adjustment to the processes of social change that the Palestinian-Arab population in Israel is undergoing. It serves as a basis of identity and belonging, as an economic security net, and as a source of functional support in the light of the limited state services in the Arab sector, as well as a base for political organization and activity at the local and national levels. For women, however, the centrality of the *hamula* in the life of the community generally means control and domination by the men and women of the *hamula,* that is, the enforcement of familistic patterns of behavior.[38] Given all these factors, one can understand the continued existence of the most traditional family patterns among the Arabs in Israel, though there are also other family patterns.

Familism among Christian Arab Citizens of Israel

In general, this is a familistic population (see Table 2 above); however, since a not insignificant portion of the population is urban, it has been somewhat exposed to the educational and occupational opportunities of Israel's post-industrial society. It is thus not surprising that of all the female Palestinian citizens of Israel, Christian women make up a relatively large group in the labor force. About 33 percent of Christian women of working age are in the paid labor force.[39] Similarly, for women to go out to work is increasingly perceived as a norm.[40] It is thus not surprising that among the Christians in Israel, modern and postmodern family patterns are found alongside traditional ones.

Familism among Muslim Arab Citizens of Israel

In general, this is the population with the most familistic family patterns (see Table 2). It has high rates of marriage along with the highest birth rates (more or less stable since the 1980s) of all the ethno-religious groups in Israel, whether Jewish or Palestinian.[41] It is true that the divorce rate has risen somewhat in recent years (Table 2); but one must ask what this means in a society in which only 13 percent of the women work for wages[42] and in which it is unacceptable for a woman to live alone. On the whole, despite slight fluctuations here and there, it seems that the power of familism is stable and strong among the Muslim citizens of Israel, even if it sometimes takes on new expressions. I contend that the main cause of this state of affairs is the lack of civil equality, which entails an inequality in access to educational and occupational opportunities. With structured economic inequality and underdevelopment, only a small number of Muslim women, in both villages and cities, can join the paid labor force, even if they studied for many years. In consequence, the necessary condition for changing the family structure — access to paid employment — exists only for a small proportion of this population. Most Muslim Arab citizens of Israel thus preserve many traditional family patterns, with all that this implies for the role of women and mothers in the family and society. The preservation of familism seems to be occurring along with the strengthening of religious and fundamentalist trends in the population, or as an expression of these trends.

Familism among the Druze Citizens of Israel
The most salient phenomenon among the Druze citizens of Israel is the steady
and substantial fall in their birth rates (Table 2), even though these rates are
still high in comparison to those of the Christians and Jews in Israel. Druze
birth rates have not yet stabilized and continue in a steady annual decline: the
fertility rate among Druze women was 7.21 in the mid-1950s, 4.19 in the mid-
1980s, and 3.10 in 1998.[43] It may be that the status of the Druze as a "preferred
minority" which does compulsory military service in the Israel Defense Forces
has given them somewhat more access to the various resources of Israeli
society. Indeed, in recent years the rate of Druze women in the paid labor force
has steadily increased and reached 29 percent in 1996.[44] However, in-depth
and comprehensive research is needed to enable us to better understand this
process.

Familism among the Jewish Citizens of Israel
A different reality, in terms of both structures and values, exists among Israeli
Jews. In general, Jewish society has entered the post-industrial world, though
there are substantial differences between different groups of Jews, between the
"center" and the "periphery." Jewish families in Israel have been formed by the
conjunction of Israel's institutionalized family laws and the class stratification
that is created and reinforced by post-industrialism. Three types of family have
been formed through this meeting.

Ultra-Orthodox (Haredi) *Families*
These families are not a single bloc. *Haredim* vary in their geographic and
ethnic origins, and they are very much stratified by class. Nonetheless, *haredi*
families are similar in some basic features. The marital age is low: girls
generally marry at 18. The purpose of marriage, in accord with religious law
(*Halakhah*) is to perpetuate the Jewish people and to enable the man to fulfill
the commandment to "be fruitful and multiply." Most marriages are made
through arranged matches, though today there are more personal ways to
meet a future spouse. At home, there is a clear, hierarchical gendered role
division: between husband and wife, parents and children, boys and girls. The
number of births is very high, sometimes over ten. From a young age, the girl
covers her body with a long dress and long stockings (the length differs in
different streams). When the young bride marries, she covers her head with a
wig, kerchief or hat (here too there is little agreement, and the issue is highly
disputed among the *haredim*).

   However, many changes are also occurring in the Ultra-Orthodox world.
As a result of the Compulsory Education Law (1949), all the girls go to school,
most of them till the age of 18, though in a school system that does not
provide high school matriculation. More and more women, including mothers

of young children, join the labor force so as to realize the ideal of Ultra-
Orthodox society, which, since the 1950s in Israel, has become a "society of
scholars." Going out to work has become part of the "household" chores
performed by women and mothers so as to free their husbands to devote
themselves entirely to the study of Torah, without having to work for pay.[45]
As a result, more and more Ultra-Orthodox women work in places that
respect the rules of modesty: in education and small businesses, in clerical
jobs, in Ultra-Orthodox institutions; in the arts and crafts: graphics, drawing
and music; and recently in computers, literature, journalism and radio. There
are even Ultra-Orthodox women who work as "rabbinic pleaders" (to'anot
rabbaniot) — women who represent women in the rabbinical courts.[46] These
processes — which partly explain the high poverty rate among the haredim —
are beginning to affect the normative role division in Ultra-Orthodox
families, as the man takes upon himself some of the household chores, since
his wife is sometimes the main or the sole provider.[47] As Friedman
summarizes: "The Ultra-Orthodox woman is today a dynamic factor who is
certainly changing the patterns of Ultra-Orthodox life."[48] In other words, the
more Ultra-Orthodox women assume the role of "working mothers," the
more changes one can expect in Ultra-Orthodox communities and their
families.

Neomodern Families
The typical, normative family in Israel is the nuclear family headed by a
heterosexual couple who have an average of three children. The couple
marries according to Jewish Law, and both spouses do paid work: the man as
the "main provider," the woman as the "second wage earner" — a distinction
that perpetuates the dependency of wives on their husbands.

In 1998, the rate of women in the labor force was about 51 percent; in
1999, it rose to 52.5 percent. However, in the 25–34-year-old cohort, 76.1
percent of the women were in the paid labor force; and in the 35–44-year-old
cohort, 78.5 percent were. Women's participation in the labor force varies
somewhat depending on whether the father was born in Israel, Asia-Africa
(i.e. of eastern origin, or *Mizrahi*), or Europe-America (i.e. of western origin,
or Ashkenazi). However, in both cohorts and across ethnic origin, over 70
percent of the women were in the labor force.[49] The gap between women of
"eastern" and "western" origin does not lie, therefore, in the very fact of
working for wages, but rather in the type of work they can obtain. In general,
the "westerners," the Ashkenazim, work in more prestigious and better-paid
"feminine jobs," the "easterners," the *Mizrahim,* in lower-paid and lower-status
"feminine jobs."[50] This is a class difference that reflects the still-existing
inequality of educational and occupational opportunities between Israeli Jews
of eastern and western origin.

In addition to both spouses having paid employment, there are other postmodern parameters in the "normative Israeli family": increased involvement of fathers in taking care of and bringing up their children ("the new fathers"), democratization of intrafamily relationships; and more participatory and more egalitarian decision-making processes, especially with regard to children and their needs. In fact, these are all modifications that alter central aspects of "the family" in Israel without changing its essence, i.e. the superiority of the man and dependency of the woman. In other words, these are all changes that enable preserving "the normative Israeli family" in the postmodern age.

Postmodern Families
As defined at the beginning, postmodern families are families in which the individual, his/her wants, his/her needs are the center and purpose of the institution. These families include two-career families, single-parent families, homosexual and lesbian families, second families, families established through marriages (whether between Jews or between persons of different religions) that circumvent the religious establishment or through common-law marriages, cohabiting couples, and couples where the spouses live separately. The members of these families are characterized by the fact that they are not religious in the sense accepted in Israel, but are either religious in accord with their own definition or completely atheist. These families generally live in urban centers, since, sociologically, cities not only enable access to the developed capitalist economy and to varied services but also make it possible to live far from the social control of the family and community and in an atmosphere in which individualism is both legitimate and approved. The vast majority of postmodern families live in Tel Aviv and other cities in the center of Israel, as well as in the cities of Haifa, Beer-Sheva, Eilat and Jerusalem.[51] Postmodern families are also found in rural areas, such as in kibbutzim.

From the above analysis, we can deduce that there are not very many postmodern families in Israel. The members of these families are mostly Ashkenazim. But there are also a fair number of *Mizrahim*, as well as a small number of Palestinian Arabs, who by their education and income belong to the middle class or above.

Welfare Policy and the Establishment of the Normative Family

As many studies have shown, welfare policy can support or discourage the creation of different family forms by fostering or thwarting the economic autonomy of men and women. Where wage policy, social services and welfare allowances do no permit women to live on their own means, the welfare policy perpetuates women's dependency on men. Thus it can be said that welfare policy contributes substantially to the "stability of the family" by preventing women from being economically autonomous.[52]

One of the salient features of Israel's wage policies, social services and welfare payments is that they are based on the "obvious" distinction between "the man, the provider" and "the woman, the second wage earner."[53] One of the outcomes of this distinction is the economic deprivation of single-parent families, especially those headed by women. As recalled, single-parent families constitute 10 percent of the households in Israel with a child up to 17 years old: 11 percent among Jews, 5 percent among the Palestinian citizens.[54] Approximately 90 percent of single-parent families in Israel are headed by women.[55] About 30 percent of single-parent households are poor, in contrast to 16.7 percent of the households in the population as a whole.[56] As Gal explains:

> This should not be surprising. It is not only that these families do not have a second provider; often the need to take care of the children prevents the head of the family from finding full-time employment with reasonable wages. That is, the single parent may not earn a living at all or only a partial living, and the family is dependent on social welfare payments. As a result, many children in single-parent families are classified as "poor children."[57]

These data clearly show the negative effects of wage and welfare policies on women. Moreover, the very fact that poverty and single parenthood are associated in public discourse creates an ideological mechanism that supports "normative families," since the association implies that women will find it difficult to live and raise children at a reasonable standard of living outside of marriage.

Today, when the issue of wife beating is on the national agenda, these points must be kept in mind. My claim is that Israel's legal system, social norms, unequal wages (in 1998 women's average gross hourly wage was 83 percent of that of men for similar or identical work)[58] and welfare policy make the vast majority of women in Israel dependent on their husbands. Against this background, we can understand why only a small portion of women who are beaten by their husbands, whose total number in Israel stands at around 200,000,[59] report the abuse to the authorities. We can also understand why, after their stay in shelters, about two-thirds of abused women return to their homes. Their home becomes a death trap for about 20 women every year. This was already pointed out 30 years ago by radical feminists who raised the issue in Israel and abroad.[60] No fundamental change in this situation is to be expected without changes in the factors that create and perpetuate this dependency in all of its psychological, legal, social and economic aspects.[61]

Summary and Conclusions

Despite the "mutations" (in Wilfrid Dumon's term)[62] of the institution of the family in postmodern societies, familism clearly remains a marker of Israeli society. The main reason for this is that familism in Israel rests on the institutionalization of religious family laws for the country's various ethno-religious groups. As this study has argued, for all the ethno-religious groups in Israel, religious law serves as a "national asset": as a boundary marker between groups and as a foundation for the "normative collective memory" and "normative collective identity" of each individual group. In addition, religious laws and the familism they foster are a major mechanism in the process of biological and cultural reproduction of the different ethno-religious groups and thereby also contribute to the covert and overt "demographic competition" that exists between Israeli Jews and Israeli Palestinians.

Capitalist development works in the opposite direction. It fosters individualism in both discourse and practice and thereby promotes and accelerates the individualization of Israeli institutions, including the institution of the family. Capitalist development is also the main lever for the integration of women/mothers into the paid labor force, while the massive entrance of women/mothers into the labor force is a major factor in the changes the family has undergone in post-industrial societies.

The conclusion to be drawn from these two trends is: the different dimensions of familism in the Israeli population are the product of the encounter between Israel's post-industrial ethno-religious stratification and its institutionalized religious laws.

The educated, urban stratum of the middle and upper-middle classes (also found to a certain extent in kibbutzim) is the smallest stratum and the stratum most exposed to post-industrial processes and, in part, is the vanguard of these processes. This stratum has the lowest levels of familism and the bulk of the postmodern families (with the exception of a certain portion of poor single-parent families). In these families, women/mothers are in the labor force. The vast majority, though not all, of these families are Jewish. A small number are Palestinian Arab citizens of Israel.

In keeping with the class-religious-national and gender stratification that characterizes Israel, the social strata with the highest level of familism are those with low access to educational and occupational opportunities. In these strata, the proportion of women/mothers in the labor force is relatively low. These strata are generally located on the "periphery" of Jewish society (that is, in development towns, poor neighborhoods and Ultra-Orthodox neighborhoods), and they include a substantial portion of the Arab population as well.

Between these two poles are neomodern families which combine religious elements with "postmodern" features. In these families, the couple is married in an Orthodox religious ceremony, but is also exposed to postmodern processes. Both husband and wife work for wages, the husband as the "main provider," the wife as the "second wage earner." Sometimes the husband "helps" the wife at home. The Jewish families in this category have an average of three children, the Arab families an average of four. In general, the family atmosphere is nonauthoritarian. The neomodern family is the most prevalent family model in Jewish society and is beginning to become stronger in Palestinian Arab society in Israel.

No significant change is expected in the near future in the institution of the family in Israel or in the familistic character of Israeli society. One of the main reasons for this is that no improvements which would promote the (economic) autonomy of "working women" are expected in welfare policy or in the status of women in the labor market. On the contrary: as these lines are being written (December 2001), with the Al-Aqsa *Intifada* in process, the economy in deep recession and unemployment high, women are being pushed out of the labor force. But the main reason that no significant changes are expected in the institution of the family in Israel is the institutionalization of religious laws and the norms that this institutionalization creates. Today more than ever, when we hear the trumpets of war, religion and religious law serve as major devices in the crystallization of the collective identity and sense of belonging of all the ethno-religious groups in Israel. The "civil revolution" about which Prime Minister Ehud Barak spoke in the summer of 2000 seems further away than ever today.

NOTES

1   See, for example, Judith Stacey, *Brave New Families* (New York, 1990); Barrie Thorne and Marilyn Yalom (eds.), *Rethinking the Family: Some Feminist Questions* (Boston, 1992); Ulrich Beck and Elizabeth Beck-Gernsheim, *The Normal Chaos of Love* (Cambridge, 1995); Wilfried Dumon "Ha-mishpahah u-matzavah be-Eiropah ha-maaravit" (The Western European Families: An Overview), *Bitahon Sotziali*, No. 44 (1995), pp. 5–23; Janet S. Chafetz and Jane Hagan, "The Gender Division of Labour and Family Change in Industrial Societies: A Theoretical Accounting," *Journal of Comparative Family Studies*, Vol. 27, No. 2 (1996), pp. 187–210; Jan Trost, "Family Structure and Relationships: The Dyadic Approach," *Journal of Comparative Family Studies*, Vol. 7, No. 2 (1996), pp. 395–408; Eva Illouz, *Consuming the Romantic Utopia: Love and the Contradictions of Capitalism* (Berkeley, 1997); François de Singly, *Libres Ensembles: L'individualisme dans la vie commune* (Paris, 2000).
2   Yohanan Peres and Ruth Katz, "Mishpahah u-mishpahtiyut be-Yisrael" (Stability and Centrality: The Nuclear Family in Modern Israel), *Megamot*, Vol. 26, No. 1 (1980), pp. 37–56; Leah Shamgar-Handleman and Rivka Bar-Yossef (eds.), *Mishpahot be-Yisrael* (Families in Israel) (Jerusalem, 1991); Dafna N. Izraeli, "Ha-migdur ba-olam ha-avodah" (Gendering the Labor Market in Israel), in Dafna N. Izraeli et al. (eds.), *Min, migdar, politikah* (Sex, Gender, Politics) (Tel Aviv, 1999), pp. 167–217; Sylvie Fogiel-Bijaoui, "Mishpahot be-Yisrael: Bein mishpahtiyut le-post-moderniyut" (Families in Israel: Postmodernism, Feminism and the State), in ibid., pp. 107–67; Liat Kulik, "Intrafamiliar Congruence in Gender-Role Ideology: Husband-Wife Versus Parents-Offspring," *Journal of Comparative Family Studies*, Vol. 31, No. 1 (2000), pp. 91–106.

3 Israel had about six million inhabitants in 1999: approximately 80 percent Jewish, 15 percent Muslim Arabs, 2 percent Christian Arabs, 1.5 percent Druze Arabs, and only 1.5 percent or so without any religious classification. Central Bureau of Statistics, *Shnaton statisti le-Yisrael* (Annual Statistical Abstract of Israel) (hereafter CBS), No. 51 (Jerusalem, 2000), Table 2.1.

4 The term "ethno-national groups" refers to the Jewish community (with no distinction between the religious and national dimensions of Judaism), and to the three religious groups that comprise the Arab-Palestinian community in Israel.

5 Majid Al-Hadj, *Hinukh bekerev ha-aravim be-Yisrael: Shlitah ve-shinui hevrati* (Education among Arabs in Israel: Control and Social Change) (Jerusalem, 1996); Sami Smooha, "Tmurot ba-hevrah ha-yisre'elit le'ahar yuval shanim" (Changes in Israeli Society after Fifty Years), *Alpayim*, No. 17 (1999), pp. 239–398; The Adva Center, *Tmunat matzav hevrati 2000* (Israeli Society in 2000: An Overview) (Tel Aviv, 2000); Uri Ram, "Bein ha-neshek veha-meshek: Yisrael ba-idan ha-olamekomi" (Between Nation and Corporations: Liberal Post-Zionism in the Global Age), *Sotziologiyah Yisre'elit*, Vol. 2, No. 1 (1999), pp. 99–145; Oren Yiftachel, "Ethnocracy: The Politics of Judaizing Israel/Palestine," *Constellations*, Vol. 6, No. 3 (1999), pp. 364–90; Ahmed Saadi, "Incorporation without Integration: Palestinian Citizens in Israel's Labour Market," *Sociology*, Vol. 29, No. 3 (1995), pp. 429–51.

6 In this study, the family is defined as the legitimate framework adults create to raise their children. This legitimacy is necessary because the family is still the major framework for the biological and cultural reproduction of society — notwithstanding the achievements of medical technology.

7 *World Bank Report* (Washington, 1996), pp. 238–9.

8 Dumon, "Ha-mishpahah u-matzavah"; Stacey, *Brave New Families*; Thorne and Yalom (eds.), *Rethinking the Family*; Beck and Beck-Gernsheim, *Normal Chaos of Love*; Chafetz and Hagan, "The Gender Division of Labour"; Trost, "Family Structure and Relationships"; Illouz, *Consuming the Romantic Utopia*; de Singly, *Libres Ensembles*.

9 CBS, No. 51 (2000), p. 5.

10 Anat Maor (ed.), *Nashim, ha-ko'ah ha-oleh: Niputz "tikrat ha-zkhukhit"* (Women, the Rising Power: The Breaking of the "Glass Ceiling") (Tel Aviv, 1997); Izraeli, "Ha-migdur ba-olam ha-avodah"; CBS, No. 51 (2000), Tables 12.4, 12.5.

11 Shamgar-Handleman and Bar-Yossef (eds.), *Mishpahot be-Yisrael*, pp. 1–7.

12 Izraeli, "Ha-migdur ba-olam ha-avodah."

13 Jonathan Shapira, *Ha-demokratiyah ha-yisre'elit* (Israeli Democracy) (Ramat Gan, 1977); The Association for Citizens' Rights in Israel, *Zkhuyot ha-adam be-Yisrael: Tmunat matzav 1996* (Human Rights in Israel: An Overview) (Jerusalem, 1996); Aharon Barak, "Tafkido shel beit ha-mishpat ha-elyon be-hevrah demokratit" (The Role of the Supreme Court in a Democratic Society), in R. Cohen Almagor (ed.), *Sugiyot yesod ba-demokratiyah ha-yisre'elit* (Basic Issues in Israeli Democracy) (Tel Aviv, 1999), pp. 129–41; Frances Radai, "Kol ha-ishah be-demokratiyah ha-yisre'elit" (Woman's Voice in Israeli Democracy), in ibid., pp. 143–66; Alon Harel, "Aliyatah ve-nefilatah shel ha-mahapekhah ha-mishpatit ha-homoseksualit' (The Rise and Fall of the Homosexual Revolution in Israeli Law), *Ha-Mishpat*, No. 12 (July 2001), pp. 10–20.

14 CBS, No. 37 (1986), Table C/1, C/3; CBS, No. 51 (2000), Tables 3.1, 3.12, 3.16.

15 Idit Geist, *Yisrael-2000 do"h hevrati: Indikatorim hevratiim* (Israel 2000 Social Report), Report No. 3 (Jerusalem, 2000).

16 See in this volume Manar Hasan, "The Politics of Honor: Patriarchy, the State and the Murder of Women in the Name of Family Honor," pp. 1–37 above; see also Izraeli, "Migdur ba-olam ha-avodah."

17 CBS, No. 51 (2000), Table 3.5. These ages are lower than the normative ages in the post-industrial countries, including the ages in the 15 countries of the European Union. See *Statistiques Demographiques, Thème 3: Population et conditions sociales* (Commission Européenne, 1999), p. 134.

18 Radai, "Kol ha-ishah"; Carmel Shalev, "Hofesh ha-tikshoret le-nisuim vele-hayim meshutafim" (The Freedom to Choose? Marriage in Israel), in Frances Radai, Carmel Shalev and Michal Liban-Koobi (eds.), *Maamad ha-ishah ba-hevrah uva-mishpat* (The Status of Women in Israeli Law and Society) (Jerusalem and Tel Aviv, 1995), pp. 459–502.

19 Ibid., p. 460. As Shalev points out, the State of Israel recognizes civil marriages only if they are made outside of Israel. It also recognizes marriages carried out by an emissary when the couple does not leave the country, as in so-called "Mexican" and "Paraguayan" marriages. A "Mexican marriage," for example, is conducted by a person in Mexico who has been given power of attorney before a public notary in Israel to marry the couple in their absence. The marriage certificate is then sent to Israel. Marriages conducted by non-Orthodox rabbis (Reform, Conservative, etc.) and "mixed marriages" (between persons of different religions) are not recognized in Israel. For their marriages to be recognized, mixed couples and those who do not marry within the accepted legal and religious frameworks must hold a civil marriage abroad (e.g., in Cyprus, the Russian Federation) and then register as married in the Population Register. Guest workers in Israel can marry in their country's consulate.

20 This section is based on comprehensive bibliographic material. The Hebrew sources are: Tamar El-Or, *Maskilot u-vurot: Me-olaman shel nashim harediyot* (Educated and Ignorant: From the World of Ultra-Orthodox Women) (Tel Aviv, 1993); Dalila Amir, "'Ahrayot', 'mehuyavot', ve-'nevonot'": Kinun nashiyut yisre'elit ba-vaadot le-hafsakat heryon" ("Responsibility", "Commitment", "Intelligence": Abortion and the Constitution of the "Israeli Woman"), *Teoriyah u-Vikoret*, No. 7 (1995), pp. 247–54; Aaron Layish, "Maamad ha-ishah ha-muslemit be-veit ha-din ha-shara'i be-Yisrael" (The Status of the Muslim Woman in the Muslim Court in Israel), in Radai, Shalev, and Liban-Kooby (eds.), *Maamad ha-ishah*; Pinchas Shifman, *Mi mefahed mi-nisu'im ezrahiim?* (Civil Marriage in Israel: The Case for Reform), Jerusalem Institute for Israel Studies, Research Series No. 62 (Jerusalem, 1995), and "Mishmoret u-mezonot yeladim" (Custody and Child Support), in Radai, Shalev, and Liban-Kooby (eds.), *Maamad ha-ishah*, pp. 534–45; Carmel Shalev, "Hofesh ha-tikshoret," and "Dinei poriyut ve-zkhut ha-prat lihiyot horeh" (Fertility Law and the Right of Parenthood), in Radai, Shalev and Liban-Koobi (eds.), *Maamad ha-ishah*, pp. 508–33; Ronen Shamir, Michal Shitrai and Nelly Elias, "Shlihut, feminizm u-profesionalizm: To'anot rabaniyot ba-kehilah ha-datit-ortodoksit" (Faith, Feminism and Professionalism: Rabbinic Pleaders in the Orthodox Religious Community), *Megamot*, Vol. 38, No. 3 (1997), pp. 313–48; Fogiel-Bijaoui, "Mishpahot be-Yisrael"; Hasan, "The Politics of Honor"; Radai, "Kol ha-ishah"; Rachel Elior, "'Nokhehot nifkadot', 'teva domem' ve-'almah yafah she-ein lah einayim': le-she'elat nokhehutan ve-he'adran shel nashim be-lashon ha-kodesh, ba-dat ha-yehudit uva-metzi'ut ha-yisre'elit" ("Present Absent, "Still Life" and "a Sightless Beautiful Maid": On the Question of the Presence and Absence of Women in the Jewish Religion and Israeli Reality), in Yael Azmon (ed.), *Ha-tishma koli? Yitzugim shel nashim ba-tarbut ha-yisre'elit* (Will You Listen to My Voice? Representations of Women in Israeli Culture) (Jerusalem, 2001), pp. 41–82; Harel, "Aliyatah u-nefilitah shel ha-mahapekhah ha-mishpatit"; Nitza Yanai and Tamar Rapaport, "Nidah ve-le'umiyut: Guf ha-ishah ke-tekst" (Ritual Impurity and Religious Discourse on Women and Nationalism)," in Azmon (ed.), *Ha-tishma koli?* pp. 213–24; Hannah Naveh, "Ha-havayah ha-yisre'elit veha-havayah shel ha-yisre'elit — girsah beit ha-kvarot ha-tzva'i o: eifoh Shulah Mellet?" (The Israeli Experience and the Experience of the Israeli Woman in the Military Cemetery, or: Where is Shula Mellet?) in ibid., pp. 305–25. The English and French sources are: Nawal El-Saadawi, *La Face cachée d'Eve* (Paris, 1982); Michel Foucault, *Histoire de la sexualité*, Vol. 1, (Paris, 1976), Vols. 2 and 3 (Paris, 1984); Manar Hassan, "Growing up Female and Palestinian in Israel," in Barbara Swirski and Marilyn P. Safir (eds.), *Calling the Equality Bluff: Women in Israel* (New York and London, 1991), pp. 66–74; Fatina Shaloufeh-Khazan, "Change and Mate Selection among Palestinian Women in Israel," in ibid., pp. 82–9; Fatima Mernissi, *Women's Rebellion and Islamic Memory* (London, 1996); Sylvie Fogiel-Bijaoui, "Women in Israel: The Social Construction of Citizenship as a Non-Issue," *Israel Social Science Research*, Vol. 12, No. 1 (1997), pp. 1–30; N.G.O. Report, *The Working Group on the Status of Palestinian Women Citizens of Israel* Submitted to C.E.D.A.W., United Nations (1997); Alean Al-Krenawi and John R. Graham, "Divorce among Muslim Arab Women in Israel," *Journal of Divorce and Remarriage*, Vol. 29, No. 3/4 (1998), pp. 103–19.; Nadera Shaloub-Kervokian, "Law, Politics and Violence against Women: A Case Study of Palestinians in Israel," *Law*, Vol. 21, No. 2 (1999), pp. 189–211; Valentine M. Moghadam, "Gender, National Identity and Citizenship: Reflections on the Middle-East and North Africa," *Hagar, International Social Science Review*, Vol. 1. No. 1

(2000), pp. 41–69; Haideh Moghissi, *Feminism and Islamic Fundamentalism: The Limits of Postmodern Analysis* (London and New York, 1999); Mira Tzoreff, "Fadwa Tuqan's Autobiography: Restructuring a Personal History into the Palestinian Discourse," in Boaz Shoshan (ed.), *Discourse on Gender/Gendered Discourse in the Middle East* (Westport, CT, 2000).

21 Layish, "Maamad ha-ishah ha-muslemit"; Shifman, *Mi mefahed mi-nisu'im ezrahiim?*; N.G.O. Report, *Status of Palestinian Women*; Hassan, "The Politics of Honor."

22 Hasan, "The Politics of Honor," and "Growing up Female and Palestinian in Israel."

23 Shalev, "Hofesh ha-tikshoret," p. 462.

24 Baruch Kimmerling, "Dat, le'umiyut ve-demokratiyah be-Yisrael" (Religion, Nationalism and Democracy in Israel), *Zmanim*, No. 50 (1994), pp. 116–31. See also Yoav Peled, "Ethnic Democracy and the Legal Construction of Citizenship: Arab Citizens of the Jewish State," *American Political Science Review*, Vol. 86, No. 2 (1993), pp. 432–43; Sami Smooha, "Ha-mishtar shel medinat Yisrael: demokratiyah ezrahit, i-demokratiyah o demokratiyah etnit?" (The Regime of the State of Israel: Civil Democracy, Lack of Democracy or Ethnic Democracy?), *Sotziologiyah Yisre'elit*, Vol. 2, No. 2 (2000), pp. 565–630; Eliezer Ben-Raphael, *Qu'est-ce qu'être juif? 50 sages répondent à Ben-Gourion* (Paris, 2001). It should be emphasized that in the Israeli (Jewish) collective memory the Shoah is mainly constructed in terms of nationhood as conveyed in the Hebrew expression "Shoah ve-tkumah" (Shoah and National Resurrection); cf. Yosef Gorny, *Bein Auschwitz le-Yerushalayim* (Between Auschwitz and Jerusalem) (Tel Aviv, 1998).

25 For discussion of the significance of the Sociology of Religion, see Danièle Hervieu-Léger, *Religion as a Chain of Memory*, trans. Simone Lee (New Brunswick, NJ, 2000), p. 82; and Roberto Cipriani, *Sociology of Religion: An Historical Introduction* (New York, 2000).

26 Shifman, *Mi mefahed mi-nisu'im ezrahiim?* especially pp. 1–32. See also Ben-Raphael, *Qu'est-ce qu'être Juif?*, pp. 23–95.

27 Emile Durkheim, *The Elementary Forms of the Religious Life: The Totemic System in Australia* (New York, 1995).

28 Shifman, *Mi mefahed mi-nisu'im ezrahiim?*, pp. 1–32.

29 Carmel Shalev, "Nesi'at ubarim (pundaka'ut): Ha-miskhar be-sherutei holadah" (Carrying Fetuses: The Commerce in Childbirth Services), *Bitahon Sotziali*, No. 46 (1996), pp. 87–100; Nitza Berkowitz, "Eshet hayil mi yimtza? Nashim ve-ezrahut be-Yisrael" (Women of Valor: Women and Citizenship in Israel), *Sotziologiyah Yisre'elit*, Vol. 2, No. 1 (1999), pp. 277–318.

30 Jonathan Anson and Avinoam Meiri, "Datiyut, le'umanut u-firyon be-Yisrael (Religiosity, Nationalism and Biological Reproduction), *Bitahon Sotziali*, Vol. 46 (1996), pp. 43–63. See also Nira Yuval-Davis, "The Bearers of the Collective: Women and Religious Legislation in Israel," *Feminist Review*, Vol. 11, No. 4 (1980), pp. 1–27, and idem, *Gender And Nation* (London, 1997).

31 Rivka Bar-Yossef and Dorit Padan-Eisenstark, "Role System under Stress: Sex Roles in War," *Social Problems*, Vol. 20, No. 1 (1977), pp. 135–45; Dafna N. Izraeli, "Gendering Military Service in the Israel Defense Forces," *Israel Social Science Research*, Vol. 12, No. 1 (1997), pp. 129–66; Hannah Herzog, "Homefront and Battlefront and the Status of Jewish and Palestinian Women in Israel," *Israel Studies*, Vol. 3, No. 1 (1998), pp. 61–84; Berkowitz, "Eshet hayil"; Naveh, "Ha-havayah ha-yisre'elit."

32 Al-Hadj, *Hinukh bekerev ha-aravim.*

33 Shifman, *Mi mefahed mi-nisu'im ezrahiim?*, p. 5.

34 See Saadi, "Incorporation without Integration"; Al-Hadj, *Hinukh bekerev ha-aravim*; Ram, "Bein ha-neshek veha-meshek"; Smooha, "Tmurot ba-hevrah ha-yisre'elit"; Yiftachel, "Ethnocracy"; Adva Center, *Tmunat matzav hevratit 2000.*

35 Geist, *Yisrael 2000*, p. 59.

36 N.G.O. Report, *Status of Palestinian Women*, p. 33.

37 Al-Hadj, *Hinukh bekerev ha-aravim.*

38 Majid Al-Hadj, "Social Research on Family Life Styles among Arabs in Israel," *Journal of Comparative Family Studies*, Vol. 20, No. 2 (1989), pp.175–95, and "Kinship and Modernization in Developing Societies: The Emergence of Instrumentalized Kinship," *Journal of Comparative Family Studies*, Vol. 26, No. 3 (1995), pp. 311–28; N.G.O. Report,

Status of Palestinian Women.

39 CBS, *Women in Statistics* (Jerusalem and Tel Aviv, 1998), p. 8.

40 N.G.O. Report, *Status of Palestinian Women.*

41 Aaron Sabatello, et al., "Hitpatehut ha-piryon bekerev nashim muslemiyot be-Yisrael ba-asor ha-aharon — mehkar orekh" (Fertility Rates among Muslim Women in Israel in the Last Decade), *Bitahon Sotziali,* No. 48 (1996), pp. 64–86.

42 CBS, *Women in Statistics,* p.8.

43 CBS, No. 51 (2000), Table 3.12.

44 CBS, *Women in Statistics,* p. 8.

45 Elior, "Nokhehot nifkadot"; El-Or, *Maskilot u-vurot*; Menahem Friedman, "Ha-ishah ha-haredit" (The Ultra-Orthodox Woman), in Yael Azmon (ed.), *Eshnav le-hayeihen shel nashim be-hevrot yehudiyot* (A View into the Lives of Women in Jewish Societies) (Jerusalem, 1995), pp. 273–90.

46 Shamir, Shatrai and Elias, "Shlihut, feminizm."

47 Friedman, "Ha-ishah ha-haredit.". See also El-Or, *Maskilot u-vurot*; Amnon Levy, *Ha-haredim* (The Ultra-Orthodox) (Jerusalem, 1989).

48 Friedman, "Ha-ishah ha-haredit," p. 289.

49 CBS, No. 51 (2000), Table 12.3

50 Deborah Bernstein, "Economic Growth and Female Labour: the Case of Israel," *The Sociological Review,* Vol. 31, No. 2 (1983), pp. 264–92; Fogiel-Bijaoui, "Women in Israel."

51 On Tel Aviv as the "City of Freedom," see Bat-Ami Bar-On, "Sexuality, the Family and Nationalism," in Hilde Lindemann Nelson, (ed.), *Feminism and Families* (New York and London, 1997), pp. 221–34.

52 See Shulamit A. Orloff, "Gender and the Social Rights of Citizenship: The Comparative Analysis of Gender Relations and Welfare States," *American Sociological Review,* Vol. 58, No. 2 (1993), pp. 303–28; Linda Haas, "Family Policy in Sweden," *Journal of Family and Economic Issues,* Vol. 17, No. 1 (1996), pp. 47–93; Julia O'Connor, "From Women in the Welfare State to Gendering Welfare State Regimes," *Current Sociology,* Vol. 44, No. 2 (1996); Gosta Esping-Andersen, *Social Foundations of Postindustrial Economics* (Oxford, 1999).

53 Johnny Gal, *Yeladim aniim be-Yisrael* (Poor Children in Israel) (Jerusalem, 1997); Dafna Izraeli, "Ha-migdur be-olam ha-avodah," pp. 167–217; Mimi Eisenstadt and Johnny Gal, *Migdar be-medinat ha-revahah be-Yisrael: Hitpathuyot ve-sugiyot* (Gendering the Welfare State in Israel: Issues and Developments) (Welfare Research Institute, Hebrew University, Jerusalem, 2001); Sylvie Fogiel-Bijaoui, "Women in Israel"; Barbara Swirski, "A Short Exercise on Sameness and Difference in the Israeli Welfare State," paper presented at the founding meeting of the Israeli Association for Feminist and Gender Studies, Bar-Ilan University, 1998.

54 Geist, *Yisrael 2000,* p. 26.

55 Data for 1998, CBS, No. 51 (2000), p. 3. The fact that legitimacy is given to a situation in which a woman and her children live on their own (without the control of her family or her husband's family) is what makes women-headed single families "postmodern families" even if they are poor.

56 Geist, *Israel 2000,* p. 96.

57 Gal, *Yeladim aniim be-Yisrael,* p. 8.

58 CBS, No. 51 (2000), p. 8.

59 Shoshana London-Sapir, *Progress in the Status of Women in Israel since the 1995 Beijing Conference: A Feminist Perspective,* submitted to the Beijing + 5 Conference, New York, 2000.

60 Barbara Swirski, "Shlitah ve-alimut: Hakaat nashim be-Yisrael" (Violence and Control: Wife Beating in Israel," in Uri Ram (ed.), *Ha-hevrah ha-yisre'elit: Hebetim bikortiim* (Israeli Society: Critical Aspects) (Tel Aviv, 1993), pp. 201–21.

61 Swirski, "Shlitah ve-alimut"; Leora Bilsky, "Nashim mukot: Me-haganah atzmit le-haganat ha-atzmi'ut" (Beaten Wives: From Self-Defense to Defense of Selfhood), *Plilim,* Vol. 6, No. 5 (1997), pp. 65–78; Erella Shadmi, "Policy Handling in Wife Beating in Israel: Radical Feminist Critique and Public Policy," *Israel Social Science Research,* Vol. 12, No. 2 (1997), pp. 55–74; London-Sapir, *Progress in the Status of Women in Israel.*

62 Dumon, "Ha-mishpahah u-matzavah."

Women and the Changing Israeli Kibbutz:
A Preliminary Three-Stage Theory*

Amia Lieblich

I have been involved in studying the kibbutz in Israel since 1978. In addition to studying two kibbutzim in depth, Beit Hashita (in 1978) and Gilgal (in 1994–98), using the oral history approach,[1] I have followed the published literature on the kibbutz, talked to many kibbutz members and scholars all over Israel, and participated in numerous conferences, lectures and discussion groups on the topic. Much has been written and discussed about the "problem of the *haverah*" (female member), and being a researcher of gender I have always been intrigued by this. As a result of this prolonged scholarship, I propose in the present article a three-stage theory about the place of women in the kibbutz, specifically in initiating and leading changes in the kibbutz's lifestyle and values. At this stage, the theory is not fully supported by empirical evidence. Much of it is based on unrecorded conversations with my kibbutznik friends. When recorded empirical support is available, however, I will try to provide it. Nonetheless, this theory manages to provide a coherent framework for describing and understanding the historical and sociological gender-related processes that took place in the kibbutz in its (almost) hundred years of existence. I hope that other kibbutz scholars will add to this attempt from their own studies, experiences and reflections.

A word of caution should be placed here: By its nature, a theory is highly general and cannot describe in great accuracy individual cases or subgroups. Moreover, when gender differences are at focus, much caution is required in order not to enter the pitfall of essentialism, to create a false dichotomy, namely the impression that all women (or men) are this or the opposite by their sheer nature. I firmly believe that all of us have male *and* female components in our identity, and talking about "man" and "woman" as opposing poles is misleading. However, gender is a useful concept for organizing our experience and knowledge, and will be utilized for that purpose in the article.

Gender has been a major dimension for the description, research, discussion and criticism of kibbutz life. The mere prevalence of such a differentiation in the context of what aimed to be an egalitarian utopia may be taken as evidence of the sum and substance (or the depth of our introjection!) of the gender distinction. My theory originated from the impression and documented evidence that in the past women were less satisfied than men in the kibbutz.[2] In many of the cases of leaving the kibbutz, this step was initiated by women, who hoped to have a better life elsewhere. Men, in the past, were much more content with their lives in the kibbutz because it provided them with challenging, productive work, often including military or political careers. Thus, as kibbutz members, men could experience "success" and high prestige within the kibbutz as well as in the general Israeli society. Today, I have observed a reversal of the trend: with the decline of the status of the kibbutz and its growing economic problems, men feel frustrated. Many of them believe that they could accomplish more for themselves and their families outside of the kibbutz. Women, however, often press for staying in the kibbutz, since they have achieved their goals in the family domain, are less professionally ambitious and feel comforted by the intimacy of the group around them and their children. Thinking from a psychological perspective about my interviews on the early history of the kibbutz, I realized that in the past there was too little family intimacy and privacy for women. Generally speaking, this atmosphere was more suitable for men, because of their general need for "boundaries" and resentment of intimacy,[3] and their larger involvement in the work and public leadership spheres.

Put in very simple terms: was the past kibbutz better or more suitable for men, while the present kibbutz may be better for women? Sociologically, this idea in itself would imply a decline of the status of the kibbutz (like the fate of medical professions once women dominate them), something that is clearly happening. If this is so, the kibbutz may be currently better for women *in spite of* the fact that in the majority of the kibbutzim, like in traditional families, most of the child-care and household work is the responsibility of women. With these initial ideas in mind, I examined my research data and the previous research I had conducted, and as a result formulated a three-stage theory of women's place in the changing kibbutz.

Theory Outline

The place of women in the history of the kibbutz, and specifically their contribution to leadership and the initiation of changes, can be summarized as a three-stage process:

Stage 1 (roughly 1910–50): In the very early history of the kibbutz, female members, who even then had (objectively speaking) a lower status in the kibbutz as compared with men, joined the communal ideological platform with enthusiasm. They were a minority, however, and their voices or specific needs did not carry much weight in the community, its organization or decisions. Those who survived the hardships and did not leave were "kibbutz-religious" as much as men. They rarely complained of their dire straits, and performed the "mitzvah" of total communal child-care and education (*ha-hinukh ha-meshutaf*), in spite of their emotional difficulties. Some of them even felt no such difficulties at the time (a sign of repression?).

Stage 2 (roughly 1950–80): With the gradual normalization and stabilization of the kibbutz lifestyle, with greater affluence and a larger number of female members and growing families, women started to resent the communal sleeping arrangements (or permitted themselves to speak openly against it). Women led the reform in this domain, becoming much more active and political for that purpose. This may be termed the "feminine revolution," when men were the less involved followers and women the leaders of this drastic reform, which resulted in minimizing the communal child-care and educational system and bringing the children back home to their parents. Consequently, women were empowered in the sense that they became heads of their large families and households. They had more influence in the community and probably more satisfaction — yet also more housework. Having achieved this major change, however, they gave up their political power and did not dare demand additional changes, as if they might be responsible for "breaking the kibbutz."

Stage 3 (roughly 1980–present): Male members' dissatisfaction emerged in this stage, due to the political and value changes in Israeli society and the extreme economic crisis of the kibbutz. Problems emerged around equality of effort and contribution, or the "economic worth" of one man's work as compared to another's. This realization and the changes it produced may be termed the "masculine revolution." It brought about a rethinking of the basic kibbutz values in a much more profound manner than the "feminine revolution" of stage 2, which could still be accepted within the framework of the basic kibbutz values of equality and communality. The third stage is marked by the process of privatization, the movement towards differential salaries and first steps towards dividing the collective property, namely, private ownership of kibbutz assets. It is seen by many as the end of the kibbutz,[4] the abandonment of basic kibbutz norms and values. Women are relatively passive in this process and sometimes seem to protect the old kibbutz lifestyle.

While the "feminine revolution" stemmed from motherhood, from women's motivation to care for their families and children, the "masculine revolution" stems from economic concerns, and perhaps also from men's ambition and personal need for success. The question is where does it leave women? I suggest, as my Gilgal research indicates, that women would prefer to return to the second stage, when their priorities were actualized. In the third stage, when, on the one hand, an individual's value is measured by the worth of his/her work and, on the other hand, the major burden of housework is still shouldered by women, they are again — as in the first stage — experiencing an inferiority position compared with men.

In the following pages, I will elaborate on my explanations of the three stages and will provide some preliminary evidence for the three-stage scheme.

Stage 1: Apparent Equality and Underlying Discontent

Historical evidence documents that in the early days of the kibbutz women were a minority of only about 20 percent.[5] Among the entire group of immigrants of the Third Aliyah (1919–23), 70 percent were male. Women were not just a minority in numbers, they were generally accepted to the early "kvutzot" (singular form: *kvutzah,* the earlier name for the kibbutz) as house-mothers, and had no direct earnings. Some women, who wanted to participate with the male workers in "the conquest of labor," rebelled and started to work with the dairy herd or in other branches of agriculture. But when the first children were born, they were given the prime responsibility for child-care.

In 1916 Joseph Bussel laid down the ideological basis for what was later named "the communal child-care system": "Child-care is not only the responsibility of the mother, but of all the women."[6] This was the outcome of a dual principle: the mother's right to work, and the *kvutzah*'s duty to care for its children. In the earliest stages, no formal role of child-care worker was defined or assigned. One of the mothers would look after all the infants, enabling the others to go to work in agriculture. This spontaneous arrangement had been institutionalized by the time Bussel made his famous declaration: child-care — the role of "metapelet" (plural: *metaplot*) — became a job for female members, and the "educational group," i.e. the peer group of children who live, study and work together from birth to the age of 18, was defined. The communal child education helped to knot the community closer together.

Three facts should be emphasized here: men never became "metaplot." Women took on this position willingly, since they would not trust a man to be the primary caretaker of their own infants. With time, however, many female members resented the fact that a major part of their adult work-life had to be dedicated to work in child-care and education, occupations in which a high level of attrition is a well-documented phenomenon.[7]

The early kibbutz had its special attitudes and practices regarding the family as well. In Eliezer Ben Rafael's words, the early kibbutz can be characterized by "its virulent anti-familism."[8] When a couple was formed, it was usually in secret, and no privacy was allowed for intimacy.[9] A couple or a family was perceived as threatening the fabric of the community, the collective. Yet children were greatly desired in the kibbutz and made the nuclear family an accepted, or at least tolerated, fact. Henry Near claims that "despite the tensions which it caused in certain periods, the acceptance of the nuclear family was a means of stabilizing and expanding the kibbutz."[10]

While officially the kibbutz attempted to combine the principle of equality between the sexes with the preservation of the family unit, there was always a predominance of women in the "services," while men were free to work in the high-status "productive" branches. Thus, women's work was of lesser community value. The more children were born, the greater the proportion of women that had to work in child-care and other child-related services, including, of course, education on different levels. A pattern was clearly established: men engaged in traditional male occupations — agriculture, industry and other productive work — and women in "services" — child-care, education, kitchen and laundry. Moreover, from its earliest days, the kibbutz's democratic institutions were almost entirely dominated by men. "Women spoke far less in the general meetings, were rarely elected to the central decision-making bodies of the kibbutz, and virtually never held such administrative posts as farm manager or secretary."[11] Women were active only in committees within their own occupational domains, namely education, health, clothing and the distribution of consumer goods. They did participate to some extent in the defense or military activities organized during these times, especially the guard duty within the kibbutz.

In spite of this situation, Near concludes that until the rise of feminism in the West in the 1960s nobody challenged the view that "the problem of the women was very largely solved in the Kibbutz society."[12] As will be shown below, this claim is clearly supported by my interviews with the female founders' generation of Beit Hashita. Yet, a more careful listening and analysis reveals the cracks in the apparent egalitarian idyll.

Empirical Evidence for Stage 1
I looked closely at the detailed life-stories of ten women of the first generation whom I interviewed in Beit Hashita. At the time of the research, they were in their sixties. In the sections used for the following analysis, they talked about their lives in the early years of the kibbutz, 30–45 years prior to our meeting. Ten main themes were brought up in these stories regarding life in Beit Hashita in the years prior to 1950:

1. the hard work and living conditions;
2. idealism: the importance and awareness of life according to kibbutz values, even when in conflict with family needs;
3. Zionism: the importance and awareness of the kibbutz's contribution to Israel;
4. the strong collective discipline that controlled personal life and choices;
5. the strong friendship among members, the importance and love of the group's social life;
6. conflicts between loyalty to kibbutz values and individual preferences,

especially in the areas of intimate relationships and motherhood, as well as work, study programs and personal possessions;

7.   longing for family left behind in Europe;
8.   criticism: awareness of the inequality of women and new immigrants;
9.   criticism of women for their passivity and lack of initiative in public life;
10. in retrospect: regrets for the rigidity of child-education practices.

This list shows that first-generation female members of the kibbutz talked about values and public life as well as about their families and their private lives. In fact, these two domains, the public and the private, filled about equal space in their discourse. The above topics demonstrate — as previously claimed in other writings[13] — that the expected personal revolution in women's identity, as compared to men's, was twofold: to change the old "Jewish identity" into that of a manual laborer, and the traditional feminine identity into a new, previously unknown identity, that of a kibbutz-wife-and-mother. This can obviously be better understood in retrospect. While all topics above are constructed from the present viewpoint of the narrators, later construction (or reconstruction) is most apparent in the last three themes, which add critical perspectives to the memories. I had the impression that criticism of the kibbutz regarding its treatment of "inferior" groups, especially women, stemmed from memories of the early period, while criticism of women themselves, and regrets about the mistakes of the communal education practices, were a result of a later understanding. The list of topics suggests that while women identified with the aims of the commune, they also experienced some discrimination, doubt and self-criticism. They expressed intense conflicts in the relational sphere, regarding their male partners and children.

When a similar narrative analysis is applied to men's life stories, the comparison reveals that men predominantly described public life, namely the evolution of the kibbutz and/or its special branches (e.g. the food-canning industry), political, ideological and security dilemmas, organizational development, etc. When conflicts were depicted, they were mainly between individual wishes and the collective system. The men's discourse allowed much less space for emotional aspects, family stories, concerns about their children, and criticism of the kibbutz. The major mood was of satisfaction and pride, rather than regrets.

Because of limitations of space, quotes cannot be provided to illuminate all the themes listed above. I have selected some quotes, however, to demonstrate how women of the first generation expressed dissatisfaction with or regrets about their status in the kibbutz, on the one hand, and described conflicts concerning the communal sleeping system for their children, on the other hand. These ideas and feelings contain the seeds for the feminine revolution of the next historical stage.

Na'ama was one of the most critical women I met at the time, yet also most moral and idealistic in her values. About her work as a "metapelet" and experiences as a young mother she told me the following:

> Our methods of child-care were simply ascetic — bathing children in cold water the year round, for instance, because we thought it was healthy.... At night, they slept on wooden boards, which was considered healthy for their posture. I'm not normally a strict person, far from it, so the whole time I was raising children this way, it was out of a sense of duty. For me it was a long, ongoing nightmare. (p. 35)[14]

Later in our conversation she told me a story about her experience of mothering within the strict rules of the kibbutz at that time — a story that reduced her to tears. Every evening, when Na'ama (whose husband was on a mission in Europe) went to eat in the dining hall, she had to leave her young daughter alone in the room before putting her to sleep in her dormitory for the night:

> Makom had a rule that children were not allowed into the dining hall .... There was no way to eat in the room then, there wasn't even an electric kettle to boil water in. Who imagined that some day we would be cooking whole meals in the room? So my daughter used to stay alone in the room ... and she never protested or said a word. I cannot forgive myself. Only years later did I find out how frightened this little girl was, how she lay in my bed, trembling.... Why did we not understand it then?... Our rules and regulations were very strict then, even cruel, one might say. (pp. 37–8)

From a different perspective Chana, a very active member in the kibbutz, expressed her conflicts and solutions as follows:

> I still truly believe that I did the right thing with my life, although we might have developed into a happier family had we lived in town. Who knows? My difficulties with my children stem from the fact that I have always been very active publicly, expressed my opinions, and openly fought for my values. I have assumed, perhaps incorrectly, that family relationships would take care of themselves.... Zvi has always been busy with his own public duties and was away from home very frequently, leaving me in charge of our four children.... So frequently in the afternoon or evening, I used to put my young children in their baby carriage, and walk around the kibbutz with them to my various meetings and errands. I didn't see this as a crime towards my children. (p. 91)

The very fact that she insisted that she had not seen her behavior as "a crime" may, of course, hint at the opposite. In a later section of our conversation, talking about her difficulty in pleasing everyone and being both a perfect mother and kibbutz member with public responsibility, Chana said: "Probably I have disappointed many." Thus, she voiced the sad conclusion that a woman in the classic kibbutz could not be a good member, wife and mother simultaneously.

A minority of women had no regrets about child-rearing practices. Ester, for example, supported the practice of communal lodging wholeheartedly: "I'm one of the ardent supporters of the children's dormitory arrangement. I'm certain that it does not harm our children, and at the same time, it frees both parents in the later evening hours for social activities and studies, which are such central aspects of our kibbutz life" (p. 86). On the other hand, she was highly critical of women, who did not take the opportunity to become real partners in building the new kibbutz society: "They are not too active anyway these days" (ibid.).

To sum up, women of the first generation, at least those of Beit Hashita which had always been a highly ideological community, shared the ideological conviction of the male members and combined full membership in the kibbutz activities and practices with their role as mothers. At the same time, much more then the men of that generation, they experienced conflicts and dilemmas, focused mainly on child-care as regulated by the kibbutz, which often disagreed with their personal preferences and intuitions. These concerns, however, were rarely expressed directly and forcefully at the time, when collective practices were still highly believed and enforced. Some stories were shared about the daring mother who had refused to put her infant in the dormitory — stories that usually ended up in enforcement of the rules, or in the family's being made to leave the kibbutz. Women who were strongly against the kibbutz child-care practices evidently left the kibbutz, so that their voices are absent in the present account.

Stage 2: The Mid-Century "Feminine" Revolution

The ambivalence of women as described above, germinated the second stage, or the first major transition in the kibbutz lifestyle, in which female members took leadership in bringing their children back into the home, thus changing the kibbutz from a collective of individuals to a community of families. Regarding the two major issues of their discontent: their lower status and their separation from their children, women chose to fight against the second. As a gender group, they did this with energy, unity and political know-how unequalled by any other struggle in the kibbutz history.

Ben Rafael agrees that women were the dominant faction to promote the place of the family within the kibbutz. He attempts to analyze the origins of this process by presenting three alternative arguments. The first theory was proposed by Yonina Talmon-Garber as early as 1972. She conceptualized the process of empowerment of the kibbutz family as related to modernization and to a decline in the revolutionary nature of the kibbutz due to the routinization of its existence. More famous was the sociobiological theory presented by Lionel Tiger and Joseph Shepher, who saw the process as a return to female natural, biological inclinations. According to this school, "biogrammar" determines that women will be motivated to stay close to their children, thus undermining the attempted revolution of the first generation of the kibbutz members.[15] A third original theory was proposed in a 1984 article by Ben Rafael and Weitman. Their explanation combines the two areas of female dissatisfaction in the kibbutz — their lower status and their unwillingness to delegate child-care to the collective. The authors suggested that women turned to the family domain out of their frustration with the discrimination against them in the early kibbutz. Women, segregated in the inferior "service" branches and cast aside from political and economic power positions, found refuge in their families. Furthermore, by tending towards larger families, with more responsibility for the essential life-maintaining functions within the family home, women guaranteed their status and power within the kibbutz community.[16]

The transition to familial lodging of the children happened gradually in all the kibbutzim in Israel. Not only was it a tremendous change in people's lives, but it required rebuilding the family apartments to accommodate the children, an immense expense for all kibbutzim. This entire process, as already stated, was dominated by women.

Empirical Evidence for Stage 2
At the time of my study in Beit Hashita in 1978, the kibbutz still retained the communal sleeping system, although many other kibbutzim had already abandoned it. This fact obviously affected the accounts of the interviewees about the topic.

Women of the second generation, born in the kibbutz, were at the time already mothers of children of various ages. Like the men, some of them remembered growing up in the communal dormitories during their own childhood. One generalization clearly emerged from my study: men of the second generation usually expressed completely positive memories of their childhood in the communal sleeping system, while the majority of women described the same system as mostly negative or even traumatic. Men talked about the camp-like atmosphere, with constant fun and freedom from adult supervision. Women talked about the lack of privacy, constant noise, and messy boys who disturbed them. They told me about running home at night, where parents often forced them to go back to sleep in their dormitories. "I desperately longed for silence and solitude, for a corner of my own," said Maya

(p. 96), now herself a mother of three. This is just a moderate version of much more severe memories collected by Nurit Leshem in her book *The Song of the Lawn*. Born herself in a kibbutz, she stated: "we grew up without the basic security needed for survival." She quotes another woman who recalled "no hugging, or kissing, or physical warmth."[17]

Although less extreme, my second-generation female informants openly revealed their criticism of the communal sleeping arrangements for their children and expressed concern over the quality of the child-care, whether during day or night. This is, for example, the account of Michal, a mother of three, who speaks about the situation in a somewhat objective style, as a teacher with a professional view of the system:

> These moments of leaving your young child after putting him [*sic*] to bed at night are very significant and difficult moments. I believe they are difficult for the mother, even more so than for the child. The child often reacts to the mother's unspoken feelings. If a child senses his mother's worry, nervousness, or lack of confidence, he will tense up and cling to her and prolong the moments of departure.... Some parents can't do it, because of their doubts.... I remember a time when I, too, wanted my children to sleep in my room. I was intolerant of people and resented those hours of sitting with four strangers, reading a story to my child and not having any sense of privacy or intimacy with him. (pp. 291–2)

About her own daughter she merely said: "It's frequently very difficult for me to leave her [in the dormitory], and I do so completely out of logical considerations and against my strongest feelings. A mother must be strong in order not to tie her children to herself" (p. 292).

Very few of the interviewees of Beit Hashita, women or men, dared to criticize the communal sleeping arrangements directly, although their dissatisfaction was fairly apparent. Marginal people, newcomers and those who had left sounded the dissenting voice. Joan, a new immigrant from the USA, recalled her difficulty in adapting to motherhood within the kibbutz system:

> I had another crisis when my first daughter was born and we arrived together at the infants' home. I couldn't figure out what my responsibility was and what was the *metapelet*'s ... I felt utterly dumb.... My daughter was a very difficult baby. She screamed a lot and I lived under the impression that the whole kibbutz was watching to see how I coped. The competition between the mothers in the infants' home was overwhelming. They were constantly comparing: whose baby was the most calm, whose gained more weight, ate better, sat up first, was the most friendly. It made me terribly tense. (pp. 213–14)

People left the kibbutz for such reasons, as divulged by Dan, a kibbutz-born man, whose family had left Beit Hashita in the 1970s because of his wife's displeasure with the communal education: "Her problems focused around our son's education. She had many conflicts with the *metapelet* and with the other mothers of our son's group of infants … following which I announced that we would leave the kibbutz" (p. 270). Obviously, this narrative presents the criticism and conflict as part of the *woman's* experiences and not of the narrator himself. Nevertheless, he acted upon it.

Another woman also attributed her decision to leave the kibbutz mainly to the communal educational system.

> I experienced this system both as a child and later as a *metapelet* … As a child I felt terribly pressured by my peer group and the constant togetherness. I felt deprived. For me the children's society was like a closed institution … no personal attention, no warmth … I think that a child needs a family, parents and siblings, warm and personal attention, the feeling of natural belonging, his or her private corner — all these things, and not the forced framework of our children's homes. (p. 278)

No similar themes were expressed by the men I interviewed in Beit Hashita concerning their own experiences or attitudes.

While in Beit Hashita this feminine revolution occurred a few years after the termination of my study, Gilgal underwent this transition a decade before my arrival on the scene. It was narrated to me as part of Gilgal's history in my research interviews during 1994–98. There is clear agreement among Gilgal's members that the transition to family lodging was initiated and led by the female members, young mothers or mothers-to-be. This change was constructed in the members' memory, however, as a collective, well-organized process engaging the entire community. It was not an outcome of a process whereby individual families deviated from the rule and created another "lifestyle" which was later institutionalized by the community, as happened in other kibbutzim, and in Gilgal itself with regard to other "changes" that will be discussed in the third stage. Rather, Gilgal's female members led a political process, the kibbutz as a whole made a decision and then prepared the transition in a well-orchestrated manner.

To illustrate this process, I shall quote a long passage from my interview with Vered, which took place during the first year of my study, in 1994. Vered is one of the early child educators in Gilgal. It should be noted how Vered describes her own inner conflict, and the difference between her and her husband in this respect. Furthermore, although ideologically against this step, Vered played a leading role in implementing it in the best organizational manner:[18]

There is a lot to be learned from the process whereby we switched from the communal sleeping system to the familial arrangement. This happened more than ten years ago. First we had a discussion of the matter in the General Assembly, and many informal discussions in various circles. There was already one mother who vehemently objected to having her child sleep in the children's home, but she, too, conformed to the rule. This shows you how strong the kibbutz system was at the time. Even had she threatened to leave the kibbutz, this would not have led to a compromise of any sort. A strong kibbutz can impose its rules on the members. She was in great pain about this, I know for sure, but she waited for the collective decision, which happened very late for her — when her son was already five years old. I know because I was his kindergarten teacher (*ganenet*) at the time.

True, the process started from the pressure of some parents, especially mothers. There were many discussions and home-groups, I can't remember them all. I remember only the last two assembly meetings, at the end of which the proposition was adopted by a large majority. The eldest child in Gilgal was nine years old then. I had an adopted girl who was about this age, and my own son was one-and-a-half years old. Even the single people voted on the matter, feeling that it was natural to include them in this decision. I and Jonathan [her husband] objected to the transition. Jonathan was much more extreme in his objection than I was, however. You have to understand: the communal education was my dream. I had dreamt of collective life, a commune. But the moment my own son came home, all my objections evaporated. I must have been waging an inner struggle between my feelings and my principles, and my feelings won the moment my child came home. Jonathan's reaction to this change was entirely different.

The entire process was very well planned. We formed a committee for the implementation of the transitions, and I was one of its leaders. Following the decision we said: Not yet! You are not to take your child home as of tomorrow. Not even those parents who were very adamant. We considered every detail seriously. We prepared the transition for six months or more, and it did not happen till everything was ready. First of all, we needed to prepare the housing. The houses had been partitioned into three small apartments. During these months, a big construction process was undertaken in the kibbutz, and every unit of three apartments was turned into a two-apartment unit, so that a children's room was added to each of the family homes. We then bought the necessary equipment to furnish the rooms. Then we set a date on which the transition would take place. A party was planned after which every child would go home to his or her parents.

I remember we traveled to several older kibbutzim which had already established the familial sleeping arrangements. We studied not only the physical conditions, but also the rules relevant to family lodging. We created our own set of rules, so that on the day the transition took place, every parent knew exactly his or her role. For example — what was the latest that children could play outside, at what time they had to arrive for their morning activities in the children's homes, and what would happen to the "hour of love"[19] for which the kibbutz was so famous.

I remember the day when the truck arrived from the factory with all the children's furniture, and the children witnessed the unloading, which was a very happy event. Then on the day of the transition itself, all the children came to the dining room in their pajamas, we had a big party, and then they accompanied their parents home. Everything was completely organized. (pp. 62–3)

Vered further explained how the community purchased beepers for the parents to enable them to continue taking part in the various evening activities of the kibbutz, without worrying about the child left alone in the apartment. Thus, an attempt was made to preserve the nature of the collective life in spite of the extra burden of parenting that was added to the families. In practice, however, mothers — more than fathers — gave up many of their communal activities for the sake of staying home with their children.

When she summarized this part in our conversation Vered said:

The communal sleeping institution was one of the major symbols of kibbutz life. In abandoning it, our kibbutz was neither among the first kibbutzim nor among the last. Jonathan grew up in a communal sleeping situation, and for him it was synonymous with kibbutz life. I grew up in the city, and longed for the kind of experiences that Jonathan shared with me. Had I wanted to raise my kids in a family environment, I wouldn't have joined a kibbutz. Therefore, my vision of the kibbutz was somehow damaged in this transition. And in fact, once this transition occurred, many more followed: pretty soon the privatization process took place in different areas, and today we are on the verge of differential salaries! In a little while it will take a special effort to discover what is still a kibbutz here. For me, the abandonment of the communal sleeping arrangement was the beginning of the dismantling of the kibbutz way; the dismantling of a dream, of a vision, of an ideal — I don't know which. But as I told you, in my individual experience, my emotions won; the change must have agreed with my inner wishes, and I was happy to have my children at home with us. (p. 64)

To sum up, during the second stage as defined above women brought about a profound change in the kibbutz lifestyle and experienced leadership and public involvement as never before. In creating a strong family base within the kibbutz, they acted out of personal-psychological motives and did not directly contribute to their occupational status. In fact, this move cannot be viewed (from a present-day perspective) as a "feminist revolution." It originated from, and actually reproduced, the traditional gender position allocated to women in patriarchy. This self-produced "feminine" revolution resulted in some adverse outcomes for women in that it limited further their ability to participate in the collective activities and public functions of the kibbutz. But, as claimed by Ben Rafael and Weitman, it may have contributed to their status in a different, indirect, manner: By becoming the "matriarchs" of their large and highly desirable families, female members of the kibbutz gained implicit power and influence in the collective through their husbands and children.

Stage 3: The Present "Masculine Revolution"

As usual, it is most difficult to characterize the present moment without the distance that provides a better perspective. The last decade has brought about far-reaching changes in kibbutz practices and values. Some scholars have termed this "awakening from utopia" or "a state of turmoil," and others a "partial revolution" and "crisis and transformation" or "normalization."[20] Like the wider Israeli society, the kibbutz has become much more materialistic and much less collectively oriented. The political, ideological and economic weakness of the old kibbutz movements has produced a situation in which every kibbutz decides for itself on what is vaguely termed "the changes." Some go to the extreme of abolishing all cooperative aspects from their lives, while others adhere to various combinations of old and new rules and practices. Much of the closeness and togetherness characteristic of the old kibbutz has disappeared. Many of the kibbutz services have been privatized and can be purchased for money by the individual members. A number of kibbutzim have established a system of differential payments to members, thus breaking their basic egalitarian tradition. Few of them have gone all the way towards real salaries and distributing the collective assets among individual members. (The legal question of whether these villages may still be called "kibbutzim" or should be called something else instead, such as "community settlements," remains to be answered.)

What has been the role of women in these recent processes of transition? I would like to begin this exploration from an original idea proposed in Gavron's recent study, *Awakening from Utopia*. According to this perspective, the present crisis is not only an outcome of the economic collapse of the kibbutzim (which started in the mid-1980s), nor of their declining status within Israeli society, but a manifestation of the failure of the kibbutz education. Women members, as mothers, child-care workers, teachers and nurses, who bore the brunt of kibbutz education, failed to instill communal and egalitarian values in their children. Consciously and unconsciously, women transmitted to the next generation the legacy of resistance to the collective. Contrary to the old kibbutz values, they encouraged children to value individual attainment.[21]

It is impossible to support or refute this far-reaching claim on the basis of empirical evidence. Generally speaking, the transmission of cultural values and practices in all societies involves both men and women alike. In any case, such a theory attributes implicit power to female members as motivating or influencing the masculine revolution. Is this power evident in the external reality as well?

To investigate the place of women vis-à-vis the current changes, a special forum dedicated to the issue of gender equality and women's opportunities in the kibbutz was convened in 1994.[22] Its main conclusion was that women still feel inferior to men within the kibbutz community, both in the work sphere and in the political sphere. In response to the question about the future, namely, the effects of the present transformation of the kibbutz on women's opportunities and status within it, many of the participants of the forum saw it as a mixed blessing. On the one hand, many of the collective services that alleviated the traditional housewife's chores (e.g. caring for children at night, cooking, laundry) have been gradually returned to the responsibility of the family, thus burdening women and restricting their freedom. On the other hand, the kibbutz is now more liberal concerning professional choices. The services that remained as a collective responsibility (e.g. daycare of infants and children, kitchen services) are often allocated to hired workers, while female members are — theoretically — free to develop careers of their choice, even outside the kibbutz, like many of the male members do.

According to sociologist Michal Palgi, a veteran female kibbutz scholar, "even today, women in the kibbutz ... make up a powerless, marginal minority group, removed from the public scene and without control over economic resources."[23] This corresponds well with my impression from the study of Gilgal, which provides evidence for my claim that the present revolution is run by men. While men certainly have the interests of their entire family in mind (e.g. in increasing the income of the family, or its freedom from collective discipline), this new set of changes may serve them better than it serves women.

Empirical Evidence for Stage 3
A qualitative study by Aviva Zamir indicates that while in recent years men take on more of the family housework in the kibbutz, and female members tend to be a little more active in its public life, women still feel restricted in

their professional opportunities.[24] Interviews with a sample of 55 female members from four kibbutzim were also conducted in another recent study by Dana Blank. The majority of the women interviewed reported that they were publicly active in implementing the recent changes in their kibbutzim, and believed that the kibbutz must change in order to survive. They were convinced that it would be better for everyone to be less dependent on the collective and to take charge over their own lives.[25] A more comprehensive survey conducted by Ben Rafael in the late 1990s compared the change aspirations of 295 male and 329 female kibbutz members and found only few significant differences between them.[26] These studies, however, tell us little about the role of women in bringing about the changes in their communities. It is my impression from the limited example of the history of Gilgal, that women have had very little influence or involvement in the present "changes." They certainly did not assume any leadership positions in this social-political-economic process. Judging from the stories of Gilgal's members, the opposite is true: while men, especially members of the kibbutz elite, pushed energetically towards far-reaching changes, women have had an inhibitory role, in slowing the changes and trying to preserve the community as a whole.

My interview with Ayelet (aged 35, a mother of three) took place at the beginning of 1997. At that time Gilgal had already established privatization and commercialization of most of the services and started a preliminary system of differential payments. While her general comments seem to be supportive of the changes, Ayelet's mood and examples indicate the opposite.

> The changes that were implemented in our kibbutz are positive in my view, but we pay a high price for them. I have no problem with the ideology behind these changes ... but I have to admit that much of our comfort of kibbutz life has vanished with their introduction. All those central functions — eating in the dining hall, having your clothes cleaned and cared for by the common laundry — enabled us to have more "quality time" with our families. If you wanted to bake a cake, you could do it, but you didn't have to bake or cook or do the laundry. Now I have to devote a lot of time to housework. I have always wanted my house to be clean and tidy, but now all this work takes so many hours! (p. 335)

When I asked Ayelet why she had not objected to these changes, she shrugged my question off, like many other female members, as if they were helpless in the face of a tide. Ayelet said that "I am pretty cut off from the decision making process," and repeated:

We lost some of the comfort, our quality of life has gone down. Maybe others don't mind as much as me. I, however, didn't mind the differential salaries, because I am a professional accountant and my income is fine …. Yet I think that it could be enough to compensate people by the hours they put into work, and not by its worth in the market. I am more conservative than men in this respect. (p. 336)

She speaks about the need to protect people from inequality and also from being hurt or insulted by their evaluation as low-income individuals, and concludes:

I have here a group of very close friends, and I feel close to them, even more so lately. I don't want money to come between us…. To sum up, I have a good life here, especially because the kibbutz life is so good for my children, and their educational framework is perfect as far as I see. This is extremely important for me." (pp. 336–7)

What Ayelet is saying, therefore, is that being a mother, and having achieved the "correction" of the kibbutz's communal sleeping system for children, she is satisfied with her life. She has good friends and a comfortable life, and would like to preserve the situation as it is, rather than proceed with changes that may damage the interpersonal fabric of the community. Given that a relatively satisfactory standard of living is maintained, friendship stands above material gains in Ayelet's priorities.

This message sounded even more clearly in the interview with Vered, conducted at the same time. She, too, seemed to be sad about the changes:

Today I don't push for anything in the kibbutz, I don't think about the changes whatsoever. I prefer not to touch these things at all, for I can't influence the process in any way. Whatever happens, happens because this is what men want…. People voted for these things, yes, I know. Maybe they would like Gilgal not to be a kibbutz anymore … I give in to the process out of no choice. Things don't happen in the proper way, it's not like the decision we once carried out to shift to the family lodging for children…. (p. 352)

She went into a description of the changes that had recently occurred in the area of communal dining and laundry, and lamented: "All these new practices return women home, to the housework they so much wanted to get rid of!" When talking about the salaries, she said:

I repress this issue of the salaries. When a vote is taken, I vote against. But I don't go to the assembly meetings … I am worried that we will have classes in Gilgal, the poor and the rich. It is a situation of disintegration, that's what it is. It all stems from the weakness of the

> kibbutz.... What do people want? Don't they see how much each of us receives from the kibbutz? (p. 353)

It is true that Vered felt herself to be a much weaker individual now, because she was recently widowed and needed the support of the community. However, she did not hide her severe criticism regarding the changes and the decline of ideology in the present kibbutz, and, knowing her before her personal tragedy, I imagine she would have expressed the same views in any case. Like Ayelet, when trying to express what she is trying to protect in her passive objection to the changes, she says: "There is something about this place which is hard to describe, it is some kind of togetherness. There is this feeling of cohesion among us, even if we do less things together than we used to.... I know I am secure as long as I live in this community" (p. 354).

During the final period of my study in Gilgal, in the summer of 1998, Gilgal had elected a female secretary.[27] The differential salaries had already been implemented and, out of financial considerations, decisions were pending to close the infant daycare center (and bus the infants to a neighboring village for the day) and the dining hall, even for the paid lunch it had been providing since the previous changes. While men seemed to be satisfied with the changes and to be looking forward to even more, women — including the secretary — frequently expressed feelings of dismay and regret.

The quotes above (and there were many more expressing the same idea) have already demonstrated that women felt that the changes put the burden of housework back on their shoulders. Another aspect of women's place in the current transition of the kibbutz relates to the occupational domain. The new climate of the kibbutzim allows for hired hands to take the traditional jobs of women in child-care and early education — jobs that many women resented. At the same time, collective kitchen and public laundry jobs do not exist anymore. This should have allowed female members to develop more interesting careers, but can they?

In my first conversation with Pnina, right after she had been appointed to the position of kibbutz secretary, she said about the differential salary:

> I support this change. It is important to reward those who work harder, and you can already see the results of this principle. People work harder, they look for better-paying jobs, for additional work, since they know that their pay will be better. This is a good beginning.... However, the main problem is the work of women. Women are very passive. It is true that in Gilgal itself there are not too many jobs for women, and working outside is not easy. If you don't have a meaningful job, you start to feel worthless. They should try harder.... (p. 447)

Furthermore, it is true that Gilgal is a rather isolated settlement in the Jordan

Valley, and it is not easy to work outside the kibbutz. The roads are not safe in the region, and hours of commuting are added to the woman's absence from the kibbutz. Men manage to do it, however, relying on their wives to be in Gilgal in time to take care of the children in the afternoon. In other kibbutzim as well, women find it hard to use their new occupational freedom and develop meaningful careers, since this requires unusual initiative within the kibbutz or leaving the kibbutz daily to work in the city.[28]

In a later interview with Pnina, she discussed with me the possibility of closing down the dining hall and the infant-care services.

> The dining hall is in constant deficit. Only a small number of people eat there. Our financial advisors say we have to close it completely during the week, and offer meals only Friday night. The situation of the children's home is similar.... Believe me, I am trying to fight for these institutions. After all, they are the main symbols of the kibbutz. I make financial calculations all day long.... I believe I will fight harder for saving the infants' homes than for the dining hall, though. (p. 455)

In a more general manner, she stated towards the end of our conversation:

> Look, we have here a very complicated situation. All the functionaries of Gilgal [all men! A.L.] are striving to establish here real salaries for the members ... I don't know. If I were asked today whether I would like to live today in the kibbutz of 20 years ago, I would certainly like that! I would be as hard working without a salary, with no differential reward. But not everyone is like me. (p. 456)

Yael, a 35-year-old single mother whom I interviewed around the same period, was more blatant than Pnina:

> For several years now we have been undergoing a gradual process of dismantling the kibbutz. It's like stages: the laundry, the food, the salaries, one after the other. What remained was the communal child-care and the dining-room facility for lunch. But nobody has determined — not decided, not even discussed — where we are heading. What sort of a place shall we become? What is the red line we shouldn't cross? ... And look what happens to the status of women! The decisions are made by men, but the burden falls on women. Everything, everything is falling on women. (p. 450)

When I asked Yael why women did not participate in the decision-making process, why they did not vote against changes they disliked, she said: "All we do is sit and complain. No woman has a leadership position here, except Pnina, which is a very recent change." And she ended by echoing Pnina's words exactly: "Now I hear people saying that they wish we could go back in time to have the kibbutz of 20 years ago. We want that old kibbutz! We lost many good things in the transition. Only after the changes were made did we realize how much we lost, the mistakes we made" (p. 451).

Concluding Remarks

In making comparisons between male and female members of the kibbutz, I am aware of my unwarranted generalizations. Young single women who do not raise children may have different attitudes and expectations vis-à-vis the kibbutz as compared with the ones outlined here, which are based on interviews with mothers of different ages and generations.[29] Moreover, not all kibbutzim are alike, naturally. Each kibbutz has its own history of changing and not changing in certain respects, and their individual members may have different attitudes and experiences.

The scheme presented in this article may aid in finding some coherence within this complex of realities and experiences. In this 100-year journey of kibbutz life, women started out with great enthusiasm and willingness to create a new society, yet were given, from the very beginning, only secondary citizenship by the dominant males. Being care-oriented people, they then became deeply interested in changes that would make at least their family life more satisfactory, changes that would allow them to be closer to their children and more responsible and active in their care and upbringing. Thus, the first drastic transition, which was highly family oriented, was initiated and led by the female members, particularly the mothers, of the kibbutz. Women gained some power and status through this development, but only apparently, as explained above. They paid a price, however, in resuming child-care functions and accepting the work this involved, previously the responsibility of the collective, as their individual load. After this transition had been achieved, however, they retreated to their traditional roles and positions and became largely involved in home and family life. In many other respects female kibbutz members proved to be rather conservative. In retrospect, one can easily minimize the women's "victory" of this stage, although its psychological significance for children and family life can hardly be overstated. Moreover, perhaps the male members and the general kibbutz establishment gave in to the women's desire because it did not seem to affect either the political sphere or the basic values of the collective.

The second major transition of kibbutz society, which is currently being experienced in many kibbutzim, is broader in its scope and goals than the first one. It is clearly male-dominated and -oriented, focusing on issues of values, economy and organization, rather than the nature of family life and education. In the dissolution of the major collective functions (e.g. cooking, shopping, laundry), women's roles in their homes have become even more traditional than before. Today, when extreme changes challenge the community and threaten the interpersonal network among members, women may be more inclined than men to protect the kibbutz from further disintegration, although they seem to be quite passive in working towards this goal. When I examined the attitudes towards the changes by men in Gilgal, I ended up with a mixed result: a minority was vehemently against introducing changes in the old kibbutz structure, while the majority was wholeheartedly for it. Furthermore, while men justified their attitudes with either ideological or economic considerations, women presented their arguments within a discourse of care for each other and a comfortable life.[30] Only the future will tell whether women's voices will be heard when approaching the next turns on the kibbutz road.

NOTES

* I wish to thank all the kibbutz members whose life stories provided the material for this article. My warmest gratitude also to Professor Hannah Naveh for her insightful comments.

1 See Amia Lieblich, *Kibbutz Makom* (New York, 1981) (on Beit Hashita), and *Gilgulo shel makom* (The Metamorphosis of a Place) (Tel Aviv, 2000) (on Gilgal). In my study of Kibbutz Beit Hashita I used the pseudonym "Makom" (place) for the kibbutz. In the meantime the real identity of this kibbutz was made public, and the members of Beit Hashita today no longer feel the need to conceal the kibbutz's real name. However, I have used psuedonyms when quoting individual members. Since both Beit Hashita and Gilgal will be much referred to in this article, the following background details may be helpful. Beit Hashita, in the east Jezreel Valley, was founded in 1928. It is one of the largest kibbutzim in Israel, and at the time of the study, 1978, had a population of over 1,000 members, children and other residents. The people I interviewed there for my study were between 18 and 70 years old. Gilgal, a much newer and very small kibbutz in the Jordan Valley, was founded in 1974, and its population is less than 100. Most of my interviewees in Gilgal were in their thirties. Both of the kibbutzim belong to the Kibbutz ha-Me'uhad movement.

2 See for example Lionel Tiger and Joseph Shepher, *Women in the Kibbutz* (New York, 1975); Melford E. Spiro, *Gender and Culture: Kibbutz Women Revisited* (Durham, NC, 1979); Michal Palgi et al. (eds.), *Sexual Equality: The Israeli Kibbutz Tests the Theories* (Norwood, PA, 1983); Rae Lesser Blumberg, "Kibbutz Women: From the Fields of Revolution to the Laundries of Discontent," in ibid., pp. 130–50; Aviva Zamir, *Mothers and Daughters: Interviews with Kibbutz Women* (Norwood, PA, 1986), and "Metzuyanut shel haverot kibutz betafkidim kalkaliim merkaziim" (Women's Achievements in Central Kibbutz Economic Roles) (Ph.D. diss., Hebrew University of Jerusalem, 1998); Menachem Rosner and Michal Palgi, *Ha-shivyon bein ha-minim ba-kibbutz: Nesigah o shinui mashma'uti* (Gender Equality in the Kibbutz: Regression or Significant Difference) (Haifa, 1986); Barbara Swirski and Marilyn P. Safir (eds.), *Calling the Equality Bluff: Women in Israel* (New York, 1991); Sylvie Fogiel-Bijaoui, "From Revolution to Motherhood: The Case of the Kibbutz, 1910–1948," in Deborah S. Bernstein (ed.), *Pioneers and Homemakers: Jewish Women in Pre-State Israel* (Albany, NY, 1992), pp. 211–33; and Gila Adar and Michal Palgi, *Nashim ba-kibbutz ha-mishtaneh* (Women in the Changing Kibbutz) (Haifa, 1996).

3 Carol Gilligan, *In a Different Voice: Psychological Theory and Women's Development* (Cambridge, MA, 1982).

4 Ayala Gilad, "Ha-kibbutz siyem et hayav" (The Kibbutz's Life is Over), *Ha-Kibbutz*, 7 July 2001.

5 See, for example, Henry Near, *The Kibbutz Movement: A History*, Vol. 1, *Origins and Growth, 1909–1939* (Oxford, 1992).

6 Quoted in ibid., pp. 49–50.

7 Ayala M. Pines, Elliot Aronson and Ditsa Kafry, *Burnout: From Tedium to Personal Growth* (New York, 1981).

8 Eliezer Ben Rafael, *Crisis and Transformation: The Kibbutz at Century's End* (Albany, NY, 1997), p. 61.

9 Near, *The Kibbutz Movement,* pp. 88–91.

10 Ibid, p. 91.

11 Ibid., p. 367.

12 Ibid., p. 370.

13 See, for example, Ben Rafael, *Crisis and Transformation*, and Daniel Gavron, *The Kibbutz: Awakening from Utopia* (Lanham, MD, 2000).

14 All quotations in this section are from Lieblich, *Kibbutz Makom*.

15 Ben Rafael, *Crisis and Transformation,* pp. 61–65; cf. Yonina Talmon-Garber, *Family and the Community in the Kibbutz* (Cambridge, MA, 1972); and Tiger and Shepher, *Women in the Kibbutz.*

16 Eliezer Ben Rafael and Sasha Weitman, "The Reconstitution of the Family in the Kibbutz," *European Journal of Sociology,* Vol. 25, No. 1 (1984), pp. 1–27.

17 Nurit Leshem, *Shirat ha-deshe* (The Song of the Lawn) (Yad Tabenkin, 1991), pp. 3, 28.

18 Hereafter quotations are from Lieblich, *Gilgulo shel makom.* The quotes were translated verbatim.

19 This term refers to the daily afternoon hour (or couple of hours) which parents spent with their children, free of all chores or educational duties and dedicated solely to love, which was intended to compensate for the parents' absence from their children's daily lives.

20 See, for example, Gavron, *The Kibbutz: Awakening from Utopia,* and Ben Rafael, *Crisis and Transformation.*

21 Ibid., pp. 159–88.

22 See Ben Rafael, *Crisis and Transformation,* p. 64.

23 Ibid.

24 Zamir, "Metzuyanut shel haverot kibbutz."

25 Dana Blank, *Nashim be-tahalikhei ha-shinui shel shnot ha-tishim ba-hevrah ha-kibbutzit* (Women and the Transformation of the Kibbutz), mimeograph (Tel Aviv University, Dept. of Sociology, 1995).

26 Ben Rafael, *Crisis and Transformation,* p. 162, Table 6/6.

27 In kibbutz jargon, the secretary is the general administrator of the community — a most distinguished and influential role.

28 Zamir, "Metzuyanut shel haverot kibbutz," p. 178–209.

29 See Hadas Wiseman and Amia Lieblich, "Individuation in a Collective Community," *Adolescent Psychiatry,* Vol. 18 (1992), pp. 156–79.

30 Amia Lieblich, "Ha-kibbutz al saf ha-alpayim: halom ve-gilgulav" (The Kibbutz at the Turn of the Century: What Happened to the Dream?), in Anita Shapira (ed.), *Medinah ba-derekh: Ha-hevrah ha-yisre'elit ba-asorim ha-rishonim* (A State in the Making: Israeli Society in the First Decades) (Jerusalem, 2001), pp. 295–316.

"Career Women" or "Working Women"? Change versus Stability for Young Palestinian Women in Israel

Khawla Abu Baker

The attitudes of young Palestinian spouses regarding women's employment and their other roles as housewives and mothers shape their marital relationships and psychological well-being. In Arab society, as elsewhere, the work or career of women cannot be discussed without relating to dominant attitudes to family, marriage, divorce and other social and cultural contexts and norms. Yet the particularities of the Palestinian society in Israel, living as it does in several interfaces with different norm systems (Israeli Jewish secular society, Israeli women's movements, westernization and globalization in their local version — as well as changing attitudes within Palestinian society itself), produce extra social pressure on the traditional attitudes which now must come to terms or clash with social change and external influence. Whereas 20 years ago a good match and marriage for Palestinian women was socially considered as their ultimate "career," today, among other signs of social change, there are young Palestinian academic women, albeit a small group to date, who do not share their society's traditional views of marriage and notions of "careers." This article aims to track the changes occurring in the attitudes of these few young Arab women that lead them to behave differently from the cultural expectations of their society. It also aims to shed light on the concepts of marriage and being single (divorced or unmarried) among young Palestinian women in Israel, on their expectations from their relationship with their spouses and the influence of marriage on their careers.

The data and examples used here are drawn from the content analysis of 28 therapy cases dealing with couples and 17 therapy cases dealing with married women. All the wives were either students in higher education institutions and universities or professionals. Their ages varied between 20 and 49 years. All the husbands were professionals, and their ages varied between 23 and 52 years. Although the information is derived from therapy sessions and not from interviews directly aimed at investigating attitudes and positions, counseling is nevertheless a social context in which subjects concerning social change are also discussed. Moreover, the contents of therapy sessions are actually a rare opportunity to learn about the attempts to bring about social change in the face of the forces of social stability in the life of Palestinian families in Israel, since interview discussions of such matters are usually influenced by social desirability while discussions in therapy are authentic and mostly uncensured.

Within the changing Arab world, including that of Palestinians in Israel, young career women place themselves in direct confrontation with the traditional norms of marriage and society by introducing different concepts of women's duties or lifestyle. This clash often results in a rapid burnout either in their careers or in their marriages. Since the authority and legitimization these young women refer to are those of Israeli-Jewish and Palestinian career men or Israeli and Western career women, they have to invest much of their energy and time in negotiating the politics of power within Palestinian families, whether their own young ones or their extended families on both sides of the marriage. The problematics and complexity of this sociopolitical context will also be discussed here.

The category of Palestinian career women is an exclusive group. Although about 24 percent of Palestinian women above the age of 15 are registered as being in the work force,[1] it cannot be assumed that about a quarter of Palestinian couples share family roles and duties equally as a result of women's engagement in waged work. Palestinian women have found, as elsewhere, that adding work outside of the house to their lives does not necessarily entail a systemic change in the operation of the household. While Palestinian women share family income responsibilities with men, men refuse to change their traditional social roles and their cultural allowances, and in this they are strongly supported by social, political, historical, cultural and religious norms. Thus, regarding women's participation in the work force two concepts have developed to reflect the tensions and strains which they face due to this social pressure: "working women," which applies to most Palestinian women who work outside of the home, and "career women," which is rarely used either by the women themselves or by Palestinian society, and yet refers to Palestinian women who in some sense model their "work" on the Western liberal notion of "career."

The emerging small group of young "career women" are mostly acquainted with each other through being trained in the same institutions or meeting in the same social groups. They live in towns and villages, mainly in independent accommodations where they are able to maintain their own lifestyle.[2] They are establishing a new subculture in which they are seeking answers to such essential existential questions as family structure, a woman's relationship with her husband, the meaning of motherhood, the type of relationships a woman should have with her extended families, cross-gendered friendship (in traditional Arab culture women are not allowed to have male friends) and the housewife's duties. They are reexamining and redesigning Palestinian women's personal and social concept of self. Since social change is brought about through individuals, this study shows that Palestinian career women pay a high psychological and social price for their desire to restructure self and society.

The Meanings of Family, Marriage and Divorce

According to the Arab psychosocial structure, the perfect and absolute unit is the family, not the individual. Islam, which is the core of Arab culture, considers marriage an essential developmental stage in an individual's life. The prophet Mohammed measured marriage as equaling half of the total religious deeds in a Muslim's life. He commanded all Muslims to marry, saying: "There shall be no chastity in Islam." Parents or custodians have to help those who are not able to marry for financial reasons in order to protect Muslim society from prostitution and other deviations.[3] Leila Ahmed argues that the family laws legislated in Islam reorganized gender relations and authority roles between men and women. This reorganization continues to influence the status of women in Islam in modern times.[4] Marriage contributes to the growth and stability of Arab society through the family unit.[5] Marrying in the Middle East is therefore a universal behavior: about 97 percent of adults are married. The remaining three percent include those who have been widowed and divorced.[6]

It is believed that marriage, as a psychosocial developmental stage, furnishes the individual, male or female, with wisdom and maturity. It is the apparatus of the ultimate change in an individual's status from irresponsible youth to manhood and womanhood. In spoken Arabic a woman is called *bint,* which literally means "girl," until she has sexual intercourse for the first time, immediately after her marriage. Therefore, women who remain single are described in spoken Arabic as "girls" not as women. A 17-year-old young married woman is expected to be psychologically and socially more mature than a 30-year-old unmarried woman. There is no parallel term for young unmarried men in the language.

Arab societies socialize women to regard a marriage opportunity as a "train that passes just once in a woman's lifetime." Each year after the age of 20 is viewed as crucial for a woman with regard to marriage. This is also the period that is vital for career building. It is a commonly held belief that a match is the individual's destiny which God arranges for him or her. An unmarried woman who refuses a good match will be severely blamed, even if she has no inclination towards the match at all. An Arab proverb reflecting the collective social consciousness states that "a shadow of a man is better than a shadow of a wall," meaning that a man in a woman's life is the best social support for her future. Arab women throughout history have suffered from very bad marriages, but have stayed married given that the alternative, being divorced Arab women, is considered the lowest status in the hierarchy of Arab family and society. Old single women, those who were never married, suffer from negative social judgments. The Arabic language reflects these social judgments by describing women's status according to the age at which they marry: young women are called 'azbaa (not yet married). This term is used in most Arab countries for women under the age of 30. For unmarried women over 30 years old the term used is 'aanis (old single woman). Applying this term to a woman implies that she no longer has any chance of marrying. The fact that there is only one word to describe the unmarried status of men, 'azib (bachelor), indicates that they may decide to marry at any stage of their lives.

'Aanis, widows and divorced Arab women, all of whom lack a relationship with an official spouse, are required to abstain from sexual relationships and avoid all social scandals. However, these three types of "single women" are differentiated by the social support they receive and by the deference granted to their situations. Widows are given the most social sympathy, while divorced women and 'aanis are treated as though they are to blame for their status. All three groups of women have great difficulty in finding a spouse of their own age and social status; most will remain without a husband for the rest of their lives.

The rate of divorce among Palestinians in Israel is very low in comparison to that among Jews in Israel and other Western societies. In the 40 years between 1955 and 1995, the divorce rate increased from 0.7 percent to 1.2 percent among Muslim families, while among Christian families it remained at about 0.1 percent.[7] Arab women in the Middle East are blamed for their divorce, since the culture of the Arab family expects a married woman to understand her husband's needs and psychology.[8] A woman who has been divorced is therefore treated as a woman who has failed in her most important mission, and the very term "divorcee" sometimes connotes disgrace and condemnation. Although Islam encourages men to marry divorced women, society mostly relates to them as untouchable.

A divorced woman with children can rarely remarry as long as her children remain in her care. If she wishes to marry, she has to place them in the custody of her own or her ex-husband's mother. As a result of the high divorce rate that existed in the early years of Islam, a woman's relationship with her husband was neither stable nor secure in comparison with her relationship with her children. Consequently, Arab women are socialized to look to their children as a more fundamental, secure and lasting source of love than their husbands. Men are expected to protect their families rather than to love their children, shielding them from any harm or shame. Social norms empathize with men who, for various reasons, are not able to raise their children or show them their affection, while harshly criticizing mothers who decide to relinquish their child custody rights. Fathers are able to move from one marriage to the next, leaving their children in the custody of their ex-wives or their own mothers, while social norms prevent women with children from moving on in the same way.

A divorced woman has no chance of marrying a man who has never been married. Usually a much older divorced or widowed man may see her as a potential marriage partner. Arab society accepts this degradation of a divorced woman's status as a natural result of the loss of her youth. Therefore, the majority of Arab women who file for divorce are aware that this decision entails a sentence to stay unmarried for the rest of their lives, a prospect that convinces the majority of women to accept their bad marriages as their destiny. The alternative is not much better, unless, of course, they suffer from a very abusive marriage. The percentage of single divorced Arab women in Israel is higher than that of men as a result of the remarriage of divorced men to previously unmarried women.[9]

After a divorce, a woman is expected to return to live with her family of origin (the blood family, rather than the family of the spouse). In cases where the woman has custody of her children, she has to accommodate herself and them to the new conditions. The wealth of the woman's family of origin determines whether she may continue living as an adult with children or whether she must return to live as a dependent "child" in her family's home. Divorce, therefore, deprives Arab women of their relative independence as adults, consequently lowering their economic status. For the most part, women who live in all-Arab towns continue to live with their children in their own residences, without being forced to go back to live with their families of origin. It is believed that in comparison to divorced Arab women who live in the villages, these women are more educated and have better access to the jobs available in Arab towns, factors that allow them to remain financially independent. All the women in Al-Krenawi and Graham's study (151 women) reported that their families of origin limited their freedom to make social contacts and forced them to inform their families regarding their movements.[10]

The average age difference between married couples is about 10 years,[11] which preserves the superior status of men in terms of education, profession, income, social and psychological maturity and political power. The age gap institutionalizes gender inequality, and reproduces it in the Arab family. Arab society is very much divided in its opinion about gender roles, which are determined by tradition, customs and social norms. As a result of the changes that have occurred in the last 50 years in Israel as well as in the other Arab countries, such as the rise in the standard of women's education, wage labor has come to be regarded as a quantitative or technical, not a fundamental, change in traditional social values.[12] These changes have not caused a revision in the politics of the distribution of power within the family or in social norms.

A "healthy" family structure continues to be based on the paradigm of men as providers and women as housekeepers. Despite the fact that, as noted above, about 24 percent of Palestinian women in Israel over the age of 15 are enrolled in the civilian labor force, no deviations can be found from the traditional gender roles of men and women among their families. Of the 28 husbands interviewed in this study, none took responsibility for any housework. Six of the 28 earned less than their wives, either because they were in an internship training period or because they were unemployed. Husbands regarded activities such as keeping the baby quiet while the mother cleans, serving themselves food or ironing their own clothes as helping with household chores.

The History of Paid Labor for Palestinian Women

For many years, poor Palestinian women, like all poor Arab women, worked for most of their lives in the fields or as domestic servants in other women's houses. Poverty in the Middle East created generations of land workers and domestic servants who exchanged their labor for food and shelter.[13] Rich women had to avoid paid work in order not to damage their husbands' status as the providers for their families, and such women involved themselves in volunteer work if they wanted to contribute to the community.[14]

Schooling in Palestine was as rare for women as it was in the rest of the Arab world until the 1950s.[15] In the early 1930s and 1940s less than five percent of Palestinian women completed secondary school education, most of whom were Christian. The vast majority of these graduates worked as teachers in girls' schools, while some of them were asked to work in neighboring Arab countries such as Lebanon and Syria. Indeed, the figures of the first Palestinian unmarried teacher 'aanis are still part of the narrative of their communities. The employment contracts during the period of the British Mandate forbade women who married to continue working in the school system. Therefore, families of origin, as well as young bridegrooms, associated a Palestinian woman's marriage with her ceasing to work. This condition suited the Islamic norms which state that a husband should provide for a woman's needs.

Until three decades ago Palestinian society continued to condition marriage on the woman quitting her job. Wealthy bridegrooms had to promise the brides' families that they would let them "sit" at home, meaning that they would be "ladies," not "working women." At about the same time, rich and middle-class families started to allow their daughters to continue to higher education, but for the sake of education, not a career. Palestinian women who embarked upon academic studies, a category that has been always very marginal,[16] found upon graduation better marriage matches but did not form a category of career women.

The compulsory education law legislated in Israel in 1951 turned the Ministry of Education into the main employer of educated Palestinian women, both those who had been trained as teachers and those who had not. Women's jobs became a female issue rather than a family or a social one. "Working women"[17] had to find ways to combine their dual responsibilities: their families and their jobs. The possibility of combining a teaching job, with its short hours, with all the traditional housewife's duties convinced many parents to encourage their daughters to become teachers. Many women who had been trained for other jobs transferred, after retraining, to teaching. As a result, the main profession of educated Palestinian women became only an adjunct of their traditional jobs as housewives. Women teachers use their time together at school to share with each other knowledge of the most efficient ways of managing their housework and cooking duties. It was their duties at home that prevented women from becoming leaders at work.

Nahida,[18] a 35-year-old teacher, refused the job of supervisor so that she could arrive home an hour before her children to prepare their meal. Later, when a very young male teacher accepted the job, she felt very humiliated. She was sure that her husband would not have helped her succeed in the new assignment had she accepted it. She became very passive-aggressive towards him.

While Palestinian women started accepting their new dual roles, as housekeepers and as paid professionals trying to supplement the family income, men did not discuss modifying their roles socially in accordance with these changes. Social discussion during the last two decades has moved from treating women's work as a family shame and making excuses for it to seeing it as a family necessity. Young Palestinian men prefer to marry "working women" who have permanent jobs. However, the social discussion has never raised the issue of changing the role of Palestinian men, especially of those whose wives work in paid jobs.

Despite the fact that families of origin and husbands benefit financially and socially from the work of Palestinian women, they continue to control decisions concerning women's right to work. Families who fear the misconduct of their daughters force the latter to quit their work and stay under their controlling eyes at home. Husbands who judge that their wives are incapable of combining their two jobs, as housewives and as paid professionals, intimidate them and forbid them to work.

Hamid, a 28-year-old farmer, argued with his wife, Siham, a 25-year-old teacher, and told her to quit her job when she asked him to help with the household chores. Siham had two babies and her hands were full with home and professional duties. She was deeply depressed and suffered from chronic fatigue syndrome. Had Siham agreed to quit her job she would have had to accept living from her husband's low income and relinquish any possibility of being financially independent. Although she had to put extra effort into managing her dual duties, Siham found that her job enabled her to make plans for her future. Cleverly controlled by social norms and the traditional division of labor, such "working women" believe that their success lies in the very fact of "going out to work."

The goal of most Palestinian professional women that emerged in the 1970s was to convince their families and communities that they were able to serve in their dual jobs. Women wanted to continue working, despite the harsh responsibilities they thus took upon themselves: first, because work was their primary means of self-expression, and second, because the workplace provided women with an opportunity to meet socially, which is an important component in the culture. For many women, it is the only place where they may meet educated adults with whom they are able to share their ideas. Third, and most important, even though men did not double their responsibilities as women did, they began to respect "working women." Deep down they understood the importance of women's contribution.

Shadi, a young trainee lawyer, physically and psychologically abused his wife who worked as a secretary and was the major breadwinner at that time. Shadi agreed in therapy sessions that he appreciated his wife's work "outside and inside the home." Then he explained his abuse against her as "her fault, since she constantly wants to remind him that she gives him his pocket money, making him feel ashamed of himself as a man."

The second generation of professional women have been raised in communities that were influenced by the first generation of "working women." While the belief that Arab women's main job is "the husband and the children" is still dominant among the second generation, a very small new category of career women who have different ideas is emerging from this group. Among this category one may find young Palestinian women in their mid-twenties and early thirties who are in the process of academic training, are interns, or in the very first years of their career and who are driven by the ideology of career development. They work in jobs such as medicine, the media, art, law, computers, architecture and science. They expect from themselves to work long hours, to compete on the market, to remain up-to-date in their area of profession and to invest in their own career development. This is the first flowering of a Palestinian "yuppie" category in Israel. Palestinian society has integrated young men who belong to this category into the mainstream of political, economic and social leadership, accepting their norms and new westernized lifestyle. However, the case is not the same for young women.

New Expectations from Marriage

Young Palestinian academic career women have been obliged to change their own concept of partnership in marriage in order to combine marriage and work. They would not be able to be lawyers, doctors, community development planners, school principals and so on were they forced to be home before lunch like their mothers and aunts. Change is not easy for this group, since the only role models they have are Jewish and Arab men in the same professions or Jewish and Western women. Change is also not easy for their partners since the model they have for the Palestinian "working woman" is the traditional combination of housewife and "working-until-lunchtime professional."

In Palestinian society it is important that an individual follows the traditional gendered path.[19] When an individual decides to design his or her own personal path, social opposition will follow. Mechanisms such as rumors and public criticism, and social sanctions such as boycott and psychological or physical violence are used against people who attempt to individualize. While these mechanisms are used against both men and women, the intensity, amount of violence involved and the length of time of the sanctions exercised are greater in the case of women. Sawsan had been accepted to medical school. At that time she was already engaged to Basem, who needed money for their forthcoming marriage. He convinced her to postpone the decision to study to a later period. Sawsan started working, had two babies and was eager to go back to school. Basem abused her psychologically and socially, since he had not succeeded in completing his own higher education. Seven years later, Sawsan went back to school without consulting Basem. He complained to her brothers, who beat her severely and prevented her from leaving her home for a month.[20] Basem claimed that a woman who decided to enroll at the university without the permission of her husband might secretly conduct herself in an antisocial manner. Hence she had to be controlled.

Sawsan decided to stay in school. She threatened her brothers and husband to complain to the police if any of them beat her again. They all boycotted her, including her husband who moved to another room in their house. Sawsan had to work for her living and for her education expenses. Meanwhile the arrangement with her husband seemed the best social solution for her career and for her children.

Society expects young Palestinian career women to take the future structure of their families into consideration when they plan their career. Young women doctors or lawyers are challenged by their own families of origin or by their spouses to change their desired specialization so as to fit the traditional role of housewives and mothers. For young husbands and their families of origin and the career women's families of origin this narrative is "normative."

Palestinian career women face aggressive social rejection of their role for two main sociocultural and political reasons. First, a comparison between women's and men's career decisions connotes a discussion of equal rights between the two genders. This debate is the most dramatic in the Muslim and Arab world, leading to a direct clash between the sacred meanings of the Islamic laws concerning gender differences and the secular interpretations of the law. A woman who claims equality may be charged with challenging God's words and His will. Husbands, even very modern ones, are able to use this verdict to control their wives' intentions of enjoying complete equality in their marital life. Second, Palestinians have an ambiguous relationship with Israel and the West. On the one hand, it was the British Mandate, the establishment of the State of Israel and the influence of the Western media on Palestinian culture that brought about an intensive acculturation process from the beginning of the twentieth century.[21] On the other hand, Israel and the West are conceived as the "enemy," as the force planning to erase the magnificent Arab culture. Throughout the history of cross-cultural influence between the Arab world and the West, Arab women have been attacked for adopting Western fashions, manners, ideas and lifestyles. Palestinian career women have been attacked by their husbands, families or friends for "collaborating with the West," which means being "traitors to their own legacy." No similar accusation is used by the society against acculturated or "yuppie" Palestinian men.

Marriages among Academic Palestinians

The group comprising academic Palestinians find their spouses in a variety of ways. They may meet as colleagues in academic institutions or while studying in different institutions, sometimes in different countries. They may meet as colleagues in a work place or be introduced to each other by family or friends. The families of origin of this group are more open to allowing the young to develop a relationship before the official engagement. This is a real change in comparison with traditional family practices which still do not permit the young couple to meet alone before their wedding day. The attitude of young academic couples towards premarital sex varies. While a small group finds it natural to discover their sexual feelings towards each other in the pre-engagement period, the majority, mainly comprising women, find that they are under unwelcome pressure from their partners to agree to engage in premarital sex. The compromise frequently chosen is sexual games without penetration, so that the woman may save her virginity for the wedding night. When hesitancy exists, or when the woman's refusal is clear-cut, the main cause is the attitudes of traditional and religious women towards premarital sex.

In rare situations, parents know that their children, both young women and young men, are engaging in a premarital sexual relationship and condone it. Among the 28 couples in the study, two sets of parents knew about a premarital sexual relationship and showed their consent by allowing their daughter's boyfriend to sleep overnight in their house. But most parents prefer that their children abstain from premarital sexual relations. Religious parents forbid all physical contact in the relationship before marriage, regarding it as a sin and disastrous misconduct. The stance of the parents influences how the women's behavior is judged when marital problems occur. Ghada, the eldest daughter in a religious Christian family, was involved secretly in a sexual relationship with her fiancé, Habib, three months before their marriage. When marital problems started, mainly as a result of Habib's suspicion that Ghada was having an extramarital affair at her workplace, she was not able to share the reason for Habib's suspicions with her family.

Among the couples mentioned above who become acquainted before marriage, no one meets his/her future partner in a natural setting. Those who live on the same campus are far removed from their normal lifestyles in their villages and towns. Such couples live in a kind of utopia, which does not help them learn about each other's attitudes regarding real life. After marriage, the couple usually resides in the husband's community. At this stage, they examine their relationship as a couple for the first time. Any disagreements usually take place at this stage of the marriage, followed by disappointments in cases where the couple does not succeed in bridging the gap between their different points of view.

Maha met Anees in their first year of study at university. They developed their relationship for about a year and a half, and were then engaged for another year and a half. During that period they engaged in a sexual relationship. Anees convinced Maha that they should be independent in their personal decisions and not influenced by their families of origin or traditional social roles. When they married, Anees' father forced him to become involved in the family business, changing all his plans with Maha. Anees was an only son who felt obliged to obey his parents. Maha felt that their life on the campus had been a lie. Anees claimed that a person should adapt to his environment, blaming Maha for being childish and selfish.

Many young Arab women assume that an educated man should hold gendered egalitarian attitudes. The traditional figure of the authoritarian husband is symbolically called in Arabic *si sayyed* (the master). The *si sayyed* is characteristically harsh, brutal and closed, believes in gender segregation and in male supremacy, using all females in his family to serve his needs. Young Arab women see young educated men as being the opposite of *si sayyed*. They are mainly attracted to men who have graduated from European universities on the assumption that a person who has studied in the West must have learned Western norms regarding women's equal rights.[22]

Management of Premarital Problems

Any declared relationship between an Arab couple is regarded as the first stage of preparing to marry and establish a family. Arab society does not condone temporary relationships where both sides declare that they will be together for a while and then move on in their lives, as is common for teenagers or young people in their early twenties in the West. Any relationship between males and females is measured as a potential for marriage. Therefore, a major component of any relationship between the sexes is the consideration of marriage.

Because marriage in Arab society is an agreement between two families of origin, the two sides soon become involved in an intensive social relationship parallel to the one developing between their children. When a disagreement between the young couple occurs, the parents from both sides work towards solving the problem. Only in rare situations, such as when serious incompatibilities are discovered which lead them to believe that the dispute is incurable, do parents encourage their children to break the engagement. Families of origin are often wary of gossip told about them or about their children by the family of the opposite side or by the community. They put all their energy into helping their children accept problems and disagreements as part of the normal relationship between any couple. It is typical for the families of origin to bring forward the marriage date, believing that marriage has the power to cure premarital disputes.

The breaking of an engagement is more likely to be accepted if it has been broken by the man rather than the woman. Men's reasons for breaking an engagement are usually related to difficulties in reaching a satisfactory bond with the fiancée or her family. Young women's reasons for breaking an engagement are usually related to discovering that their fiancé is not the partner they desired. In the majority of cases they will not be supported by the people around them. Older women play a crucial role at this stage, convincing the young woman not to break the engagement with a variety of arguments. They may persuade her that every woman has the ability to change any man according to her design, or they may share stories of their own or others' marriage problems as the life wisdom each woman has to have in order to preserve her marriage. The young woman may be reminded that Arab women appreciate women who suffer silently, trying to solve their problems or accepting them, without making any social noise about their situation, influenced by the *mastura* (tight-lipped) psychology.[23] She may also be warned that the price a young Arab woman may pay for breaking an engagement is to remain unmarried for the rest of her life. She should therefore solve or accept her problems and refrain from breaking the engagement.

These interventions confuse many young women, who decide to remain in the relationship despite all the disadvantages they discover. Mona, a 32-year-old teacher, said that four months after her engagement she discovered that her fiancé, Ahmed, was narrow-minded and wanted to control her. However, because she had agreed to be involved with him in sex games, she was afraid that he would tell others of this, ruining her social reputation. She married Ahmed and their problems have been exacerbated over the last seven years.

Career Husbands' Attitude to Equality in Marital Life

Young Palestinian career men usually have difficulties in understanding the source of marital problems. They regard themselves as being very different from their fathers' generation and from other non-academics of their own age. They maintain a Westernized lifestyle, which is reflected in the appliances and furniture in their homes, their up-to-date fashions, their recreational activities, and so on. They believe that the "freedom they allow" their wives shows the type of norms they embrace. Nonetheless, many of these educated men retain traditional or religious attitudes.

Ahmed, a 35-year-old civil engineer, compares himself with his father, who was a civil engineer and never shared details about his work, his finances or his social life with his wife. The father expected his wife, who was a teacher, to serve and obey him completely. Ahmed claims that he treated his wife Mona in a more democratic way but that she did not respect how he related to her. He believes that Mona wanted to abuse the margins of freedom he was willing to grant her, trying to veil activities or relationships she had. Ahmed compares himself with Mona's brother, an uneducated worker who physically abused his wife for not obeying his orders.

With respect to household chores, it is rare for any Palestinian man, even those who are second-generation academic Palestinians, to grow up sharing full responsibilities for household chores with the females at home. Arab families are for the most part confused by the type of socialization they have to give their male children. Public Arab opinion does not educate men to do any household chores nor does it appreciate men who do, regarding them as "womanly." Young husbands do not share the household chores unless they have been asked or forced to by their spouses. These arguments, which can last hours, or in some cases years, prompt a reexamination of gender roles, duties and status in Arab culture and societies. However, the results of these arguments/struggles are mainly kept in the private realm, which means that the process has no effect on the whole category of working women.

The need to take care of children and household chores is a major factor in the development of Palestinian women's careers. However, its importance is underestimated, since each woman believes that its influence on her career pertains only to her, and is not a general problem.[24] Some academic men offer financial solutions to the dispute over their household duties either by hiring a *woman* to do all chores that the husband is asked to do by his spouse or, alternatively, by supporting the family financially while the wife takes a break from her job for several years to raise their babies. The latter offer may seem a generous one from the husband's point of view; however, it ruins the wife's professional self-esteem and chances of furthering her career. An example of a dual-career family, where the husband was a specialist doctor at a hospital and the wife was a lawyer, highlights how the solutions themselves can become the major problem in a couple's life. Majeed convinced his wife Mervat that she could not claim equality in developing her career since that would involve spending most of her time at work and leaving their two children unsupervised. After two years of constant aggressive arguments, she was convinced to work from home, a decision that was not good for her career, causing her to lose many of her clients who did not feel comfortable coming to see her in her home. Mervat suffered from depression and ended up cutting off her relation with her estranged husband, although continuing to live under the same roof for the last four years.

When young academic Palestinian career men compare themselves with other men, they judge their own behavior as being very democratic and egalitarian. They use the term "I allow my wife" without being aware that it is precisely this kind of thinking that is a symptom of controlling intentions. They defend their stance, saying that they are neither understood nor appreciated for the changes they have brought about in their families. An accountant furiously asked his wife, a young nursing student: "Did your father allow you to have a driving license? Did he allow you to obtain a private car? Do your brothers or father do any chores at home?" When she answered "I didn't choose either of them as my spouse," he answered, "You do not appreciate what you have been offered in this marriage. You do not want to be the wife of somebody who respects you; you do not want to be free within marriage, but rather on the loose on your own."

The main reaction of academic husbands, who see themselves as reacting democratically to their wives' complaints, is anger, frustration and the belief that the wife is "looking for problems." When they discover that their wives are serious about solving the equality problem or alternatively, want to end the marriage, they are too proud to accept part of the responsibility for the situation. Some refuse to be involved in counseling in order to emphasize that the wife is the one who needs to correct her marital behavior.

Mechanisms of Controlling Social Change

Social change involves the details of daily life. In therapy for couples people negotiate components of their tendencies towards social change versus social stability. It is important to pay attention to mechanisms that help or hinder these opposing tendencies.

Traditional Meals

Because most restaurants in Israel are too expensive for the majority of Palestinian families, who are mainly middle and low class, most families cook their own daily meals. Career women are more accustomed than others to eat out or to buy their meals, which is unusual behavior for traditional Arab women, who spend hours every day preparing every meal from scratch. Keeping all the traditional dishes on the daily menu of Palestinian families is one of the mechanisms used to control women's time, energy, creativity and career development.

The first generation of "working women" never complained publicly about having to prepare food. They were proud to convince their environment that they were capable of combining "home and work." In order to succeed with their goals, they worked without break from dawn to late at night, without being able to develop their careers further. The new generation dares to spend more money on prepared food and invest longer hours at work. This reality is new for the first generation and their sons, the husbands of the new generation. Criticism is usually expressed against "the younger generation who do not want to work hard." Husbands who "agree" to eat out or to buy prepared meals use their consent as another way of claiming that they are "helping" and supporting their career wives.

Children

An Arab couple is expected to start having children immediately after marriage. Over the last 30 years, the average number of children in the Palestinian family in Israel has decreased from five to three. Women with career expectations, but who were brought up in traditional families or are married to men with a traditional orientation, will be under pressure to have two to three children within the first five years of the marriage. Career women who put their career development first postpone motherhood for an average of five years. This latter group faces personal questions, criticism, and interference in their own personal decision. Most people assume that a medical problem is preventing pregnancy. Husbands who agree to delay having children believe that they are offering important help to their wives. In Arab families, it is difficult to find a couple who prefers career development at the expense of not having children at all.

When children are born to a young career couple, it is mainly the women who take care of them — one or both grandmothers, other female relatives or women who work in child-care centers. The career mother has to orchestrate babysitters. A young student who had one baby immediately after marriage and then twins within another year became a mother of three before she finished her degree. Her husband continued with his plan, developing his new career as a lawyer, while the wife's mother, who was a teacher herself, took care of the three babies. The student's sisters and aunts were an important part of the team who brought up the babies. It was very hard for the student to focus on her studies since orchestrating all the details was more than she was able to handle. Her mother suggested taking the babies to live with her, freeing her daughter psychologically to concentrate on her degree.

Gendered Judgment of Professions
The status of professions is judged by the gender of the professionals rather than the importance, rarity or other rewards of the profession itself. Thus, the job of a husband who is a teacher is appreciated more than that of his wife who is a doctor. In the reverse case, if the husband is a doctor and the wife a teacher, the higher status is accorded to the man's profession Since all professions occupied by women continue to be regarded as "women's work" without the added social rewards men win for their professions, women are placed in a frustrating double bind.

Young Career Women vs. Young Working Women: Two Case Studies

Each of the following cases of two women who turned to therapy represents one pole of the scheme: the very career-oriented young woman who puts her own career before her marriage, and the society-oriented young woman who puts social norms and traditional marriage before her career. An analysis of both cases will follow.

Nuha
Nuha was a 27-year-old young woman married to Saleem, a 32-year-old wealthy medical specialist. She was brought up in a democratic home in which both parents worked. Her mother, an energetic and dominant woman, maintained all the traditional female roles as a housewife. The parents allowed Nuha to study towards a degree in art and photography in Western Europe. She met her husband two years before graduating during one of her visits home. Saleem studied medicine in another West European country. His father was a wealthy doctor and his mother was a retired teacher. Although his mother had worked as a teacher for about 30 years, she bore the main responsibility for housekeeping and child care. Her wealth enabled her to hire constant help from other women in her village.

Nuha and Saleem visited each other at their different universities several times during the first year and phoned each other regularly. During the subsequent year they became engaged and married immediately after graduating. They lived in a town near Saleem's village. Saleem finished his internship and started his specialization. Since it was difficult for Nuha to find a satisfying job close to her home, she had to go to work in one of the big cities in Israel. Meanwhile Saleem convinced her to try alternative jobs as options to her career, which she did. However she became very frustrated, feeling that she was not fulfilling herself in her field. Saleem's plans were to inherit his father's prosperous clinic in the town.

Saleem worked long hours and rarely arrived home early. In addition, he loved to socialize with his friends whom he would meet after work for sports' activities or eating out. Nuha wanted him close to her. She wanted them to cook meals and clean together, to have an egalitarian lifestyle. Saleem suggested hiring a housekeeper. Nuha never cleaned or cooked in her home, nevertheless she became withdrawn. Three years after their marriage, Nuha was constantly between jobs, trying to adapt. Without planning, she became pregnant. After a very difficult period of hesitation, she decided to keep the baby, despite her feelings that her relationship with Saleem was unsatisfactory and not developing in the direction she wanted. During the pregnancy she continued to feel lonely. She talked with Saleem several times, stating that the pregnancy was for both of them. She asked him to be a partner in the stages of pregnancy, including joining an antenatal exercise group for couples. Saleem claimed that his busy program at work and with his friends prevented this.

When Nuha gave birth, Saleem took two weeks off from work. However, he spent all the time with his friends who dropped by to see the baby. Nuha was furious. Both his mother and hers tried to convince her that Saleem's behavior was very "normal." They compared him with their own husbands and other men his age, highlighting his abilities and his unique career future. They said that they knew of no other man who took two weeks off when his wife gave birth.

Four months after the baby's birth, Nuha came to counseling. She wanted to discuss the idea of divorce, which was growing in her mind. She did not want to discuss the issue with her parents or friends, since she was sure that everyone would try to convince her that she had been wrong to make her career, her emotions and her own idea of marriage her priorities. Now, having a baby was an additional case against her. After three months in counseling Nuha came to the conclusion that she would not be able to change Saleem's norms. He was developing as a promising doctor in his field. He started working a few afternoons a week in his father's clinic and became more distant from his home. Saleem refused at this stage to participate in counseling. When Nuha asked him to join her he answered:

> I have no problem as a husband. I work, I'm not an alcoholic, I never shout at you or beat you, I never asked you to cook or to clean. I always

give you money. I gave you total freedom; I never asked how you spend your time when you are not working! Why should I go to counseling? Who among your friends lives your life? You need counseling. You need to get real.

Nuha discussed amicable divorce with Saleem. She decided to take her baby and move to one of the big cities in Israel. She rented an apartment and started a new job. Relatives and friends tried to convince her to change her mind, reminding her that her income would never enable her to live the type of luxurious life she was used to with Saleem and that she would find it difficult to remarry as a divorced woman with a child.

Nuha was convinced that the type of life she lived with Saleem made her feel like a slave in a harem. She was sure that he loved her, but believed that he did not know how to show her his love and respect. He had learned from his father to connect love with money. However, she wanted a real egalitarian relationship, which he had never learned to offer. His long working hours, his traditional family and his attachment to his bachelor friends did not give him the opportunity to focus on his marriage and on the meaning Nuha wanted for their relationship. His own attachment to his career unintentionally prevented Nuha from developing hers.

Fadwa

The Islamic family court referred Fadwa and her husband Shadi to couples therapy in an attempt to solve their problems. 22-year-old Fadwa was studying to become a high school teacher, and Shadi was a 29-year-old physiotherapist. Three months before the couple came to therapy, Fadwa had filed in the family court for an allowance for her and her baby. Fadwa was staying with the baby at her parents' home, having been forbidden by Shadi to go home after they had a big argument. When Fadwa and Shadi met in therapy they were both full of rage and the desire for revenge.

Fadwa accused Shadi of trying to control her. She felt that she had had more freedom before she met him than after marriage. Her parents both worked as teachers and were very active in the community. She had been brought up to be very active, participating in youth camps and being a member of a performing group.

Shadi was the son of divorced parents, a matter that caused him great shame among his friends, since divorce is very rare among Arab couples of his parents' age. Shadi was the first in his extended family to receive an academic education. Most women in his family did not finish high school. When Shadi studied in Western Europe, he experienced double changes in his life: while learning and adopting many aspects of a Western lifestyle, he also became very religious. Upon graduation and returning back home, he became more traditional and religious in his daily lifestyle. He became convinced that women's freedom and equality in the Western countries destroyed the family's stability. Shadi wanted to marry an educated "working woman" who could share financial responsibilities so that he could focus on establishing his career.

A friend arranged the meeting between Shadi and Fadwa. Shadi, as a religious person, insisted upon making their engagement official. A religious ceremony took place; they were registered as wife and husband.[25] Fadwa wanted to postpone this stage, since she needed more time to get to know Shadi. She did not realize that Shadi was under stress: he wanted to have sexual relations with her but since he was religious he wanted to refrain until he had the religious legitimization. Fadwa, however, refused to have sex before the actual official wedding ceremonies. Shadi's pressure ended in their having "sexual relations without penetration." Fadwa felt that Shadi was using the opportunity to drive her to or from her university in order to have a few moments in which to force sexual relations on her. The people around her had the impression that Shadi encouraged Fadwa's education and that this was the reason for his willingness to drive her to and from school. Fadwa tried to terminate the relationship. Her parents warned her of the social reaction that could be expected, especially since officially she would be regarded as a divorced woman if she broke the engagement. They convinced her to give herself another chance. The two families of origin decided to start immediately with the preparations for the wedding, believing that the "roof" over the couple would improve their relationship.

Fadwa refused to have sex with Shadi for four months after marriage. He beat her up several times. She was too ashamed to share her reality with her parents or any of her friends. The relationship between the two became very violent, physically and psychologically. Fadwa heard from old women that a man who is sexually frustrated becomes very violent. She forced herself to start having sex with him and immediately became pregnant. Fadwa was a brilliant student who wanted to maintain her accomplishments. Also she found out that focusing on her degree kept her mind off her marital disappointment.

Although Shadi worked long hours, he was frustrated by the long hours that Fadwa was away from home. He argued that none of the women in his family ever left her home all day long as Fadwa did. She failed to convince him that he should not make comparisons between her lifestyle and that of women in his extended family. Shadi beat Fadwa, accusing her of disrespect of his extended family.

When Fadwa's parents' mediated in the dispute, Shadi complained that Fadwa was not doing her housewife's duties at home. Fadwa complained that Shadi never took care of any of the household chores. Shadi said that he was helping by buying his food and ironing his clothes, "jobs that wives should do for their husbands." Fadwa's mother started cooking for the couple. She asked her younger daughters to clean their sister's home during the weekends. When Fadwa gave birth, her aunt took care of the baby, so that Fadwa could continue to focus on her degree. Shadi felt that Fadwa's family had too a great an influence on her life and too much free access to their home. He asked her to put the baby in the care of his stepmother. Fadwa refused. She was beaten brutally, and subsequently left to go to her parents with her baby.

In individual therapy, Fadwa confessed that she had never loved Shadi. She had built a stereotypical idea that young academic men who lived in Western countries were kind and respectful to women. She never questioned Shadi's belief system before their engagement. She never discussed their duties as a couple. Although she was very busy with her school assignments, she never asked him to help her with household chores. When he blamed her for not fulfilling her household duties, she never challenged the idea. Fadwa's dream was to have a husband who believed in an egalitarian lifestyle. The role model she had grown up with was that of her mother who was able to juggle her jobs as teacher and housewife.

Fadwa suffered much stress during her stay with her parents. They made it clear to her that if she decided to get divorced she would have to go back to live with them; she would not be allowed to live by herself. Also they convinced her that her chances of remarrying would be minimal. Her parents were concerned for their reputation in their community and for the influence of Fadwa's divorce on the marriage chances of their other daughters.

After two months in therapy, Fadwa decided to go back to live with Shadi. He presented his conditions, aimed at limiting Fadwa's sense of independence, freedom and equality. Fadwa became totally submissive. She explained that her decision was determined by several factors:

1. She had learned that it was easier for her to live with one violent person instead of living in fear of the unpredictable social violence exercised against divorced women;
2. she had witnessed several couples in her surroundings who lived in a kind of detached relationship, though remaining legally married for many years;
3. Fadwa experienced restrictions in her parents' home that she had never experienced before. She preferred to have their support and remain a married woman rather than to suffer from their restrictions as a divorced woman;
4. Fadwa concluded that she should change her opinion regarding her profession. She reflected that "I don't want to be a career teacher building other people's lives while I ruin my own. I should be flexible and be a teacher like everyone else: work a few hours a day and be able to take care

of my daughter too. I don't want my relatives to bring her up while I bring up other people's children."

Fadwa was convinced that she would be more secure developing her career as a married rather than as a divorced woman. Shadi concluded the therapy sessions by stating that "Fadwa learned a lesson from this experience. Now she has to use this wisdom with her husband for the rest of her life."

Conclusion

Young Arab career women, although still a very rare phenomenon, are reconstructing the meaning of marital relationships as well as Arab women's concept of self. While in therapy, they dare to voice their personal dreams as well as their social rights.

Wives and husbands use different terms of reference to examine the social change they are looking for. Wives compare their husbands with Western men, concluding that Arab husbands are still more traditional, conservative and fanatical. Husbands compare themselves with their parents, concluding that they are very democratic and revolutionary.

Social change in Palestinian society does not proceed in a straight line. Adopting traditional norms or lifestyle or returning to religion is very acceptable to all categories of society. Yet, it has a differential influence on each gender. A young, democratic, egalitarian career Arab husband may rebel against the social change he went through, declaring that he is "returning to traditions." He will then gain the respect and support of his extended family and community for conserving the social norms without losing his option for a career. A young, democratic, egalitarian career woman who decides to rebel against the social change she went through will lose the margins of freedom she succeeded in gaining. Hence, young Palestinian career men are able to combine traditional norms with a modern lifestyle without jeopardizing their personal freedom, while young career women are not able to do so. They will pay a high price in their career life if they try to combine traditional norms with a modern lifestyle.

Social change in the last 150 years has always been both a private and a public matter. At the end of the nineteenth century ideological and social movements, led by men and women in Egypt, Lebanon, Syria, Iraq and Palestine, discussed ways of changing the status of Arab women through education, work and political participation. However, the political stability that most Arab states achieved by the mid-1950s shifted the focus of their societies to other existential problems such as infrastructure, economic affairs and foreign policy, rather than to gender equality issues. In particular, the revival of the Islamic movement is a new and important factor in this respect.

Public discussions on the status of women tend to become a conflict between fundamentalists, who claim to be protecting traditions and religion, and westernized elements, who claim to be protecting democracy and equal rights. Thus, at the beginning of the twenty-first century the situation of women, as individuals, as groups and as a class, has not changed. Although a few studies have been published by Arab men regarding the status of Arab women, the struggle is still considered a purely female rather than a social issue. In Arab societies, women's movements fight for equal social rights, while movements struggling for social equality are not developed enough to bring about change in the relationship between the genders.

The main difference between academic and non-academic women lies in the type of profession attained by the academic woman, rather than in career development or lifestyle. Some Arab families stop supporting their daughters' education financially when the latter become engaged to marry. This behavior reflects these families' attitude to women's education as an economic investment that helps men — whether the fathers or husbands — attain a better income and higher social status, rather than as an investment in the women themselves. Women's education in Arab societies is not yet perceived as an investment in building a woman's personality, career and self-esteem. The majority of Arab men prefer to marry educated women for their future expected income, not for their knowledge or minds.

Marriage causes a greater social and psychological change for Arab women than for Arab men. First, while women have to move to the husbands' communities, acclimatize to the husband's lifestyle and build social relations with the husband's relatives, men stay in their own communities, being required to visit the wives' extended family only on social occasions. Second, when women move from one location to another, they give up most of the past relationships that they developed before marriage. Women who insist on continuing to live as they used to before marriage will be judged to be psychologically and socially immature. In some cases their behavior will provide legitimization for divorce. At the same time, men are allowed to continue developing the relations and lifestyle of their bachelor days. And finally, women have to interrupt their career development on several occasions during their lives: when they move to their husband's community, when they have children and when their extended families are in need of their help.

Palestinian society may have changed its opinion on the waged labor of women, but not its norms regarding men's participation in household chores. Since women are solely responsible for household chores and baby care, ambitious women who anticipate developing a career are severely restricted. The social ecology[26] under which Palestinian women live, together with the psychological stress of divorce, forces many young academic women to lower their professional expectations from developing a career to merely being "working women."

The rapid psychological burnout of career women causes them to underrate the role of profession and work in their lives. As a result of poor ego strength and a lack of extended family support, they move from the standpoint of career women, which they adopted before marriage, viewing their profession as a main element in their personality and life, to a new standpoint after marriage that perceives the profession merely as a means of earning an income and spending a few hours every day in the company of educated adults. This group of young professional women adopts the attitude that the first generation of "working women" had towards their work and professions.

Women who place their career development before their unhappy marriages are often those who experience burnout in their marriages and find refuge in developing their careers. They have ego strength that enables them to survive difficult decisions, often without the support of their extended families or communities. They are condemned by their society for being selfish and not behaving according to expected social norms. Their personal life experience is used in various ways by different groups within Arab society. Some point to their strength and uniqueness as leading career women, while others point to their responsibility for ruining their families.

The support of the family of origin, which is always very important for Arab individuals, becomes crucial when a person experiences psychological or social stress. Marital problems cause ongoing psychosocial stress, especially when none of the expectations of marital relations are met in real life. Families of origin prefer to convince their daughters to preserve the marital relationship, trying to save them from harsh social criticism, marginality and loneliness.

Social change is measured by changes individual people accomplish. Detailed everyday politics reveals initiators of change, their carriers, their limitations, and the psychological and social causes of the whole dynamics. Details of such negotiations of change are very rare since they usually take place in the private realm. When politics of social change are shared in the public realm they are usually presented in a summarized form, packaged in a socially desirable wrapping. A full narration of therapy and counseling sessions provides examples of detailed negotiations, thus giving a deeper insight into the nature of the politics of power within young Palestinian families and the process of social change within this society.

Education and profession — as elsewhere — have always functioned as levers for change in the status of Palestinian women. Yet, in order to gain access to education and career building, and in order to be able to sustain a career on a professional level, a wider change in the social norms regarding gender roles in Palestinian society is necessary. Women, both as individuals and as a group, have brought about a substantial change in their own lives and in that of their communities. They now have to affect the social perception of the "working woman" and replace it with that of the "career woman."

NOTES

1 *Shnaton statisti le-Yisrael* (Statistical Abstract of Israel), No. 51 (Jerusalem, 2000), table 12.7.

2 About 5 percent of Palestinians in Israel live in extended families where two families or more live in the same household. See ibid., table 2.19. Other types of collaborative households exist among young couples in the first years of their marriage, mainly to support them financially.

3 See 'Abd-Allah al-Buchari, *Sharh al-Imam al-Hafith Ahmad Ben 'Ali Bin Hajar al-'Asqalani* (Interpretation of the Imam al-Hafith Ahmad Ben 'Ali Bin Hajar al-'Asqalani) (Beirut, 1986), p. 22.

4 Leila Ahmed, *Women and Gender in Islam: Historical Roots of a Modern Debate* (New Haven, 1992), Chap. 2.

5 See John, L. Esposito, *Women in Muslim Family Law* (Syracuse, 1982), pp. 13–48.

6 Philippe Fargness, "The Arab World: The Family as Fortress," in André Burguière et al. (eds.), *A History of the Family*, Vol. 2, *The Impact of Modernity* (Cambridge, 1996), pp. 339–74.

7 Khawla Abu Baker, *Mishpahah ve-ribud ba-hevrah ha-palastinit betokh Yisrael* (Stratification and Family Structure in the Palestinian Society in Israel), to be published as a unit of the Open University, Tel Aviv.

8 See the advice pre-Islamic mothers gave their daughters before marriage in Walther Wiebke, *Women in Islam from Medieval to Modern Times* (Princeton, 1995). It is important to note that this advice is still taught in Arabic textbooks, influencing the socialization of young adolescents, males and females.

9 *Shnaton statisti le-Yisrael*, No. 51, table 2.19.

10 Alean Al-Krenawi and John R. Graham, "Divorce among Muslim Arab Women in Israel," *Journal of Divorce & Remarriage*, Vol. 29, No. 3/4 (1998), pp. 103–19.

11 See Ahmed, *Women and Gender in Islam*, Chap. 2

12 See the study by Majid Al-Haj, *Social Change and Family Processes* (Boulder, CO, 1987). See also Halim Barakat, "The Arab Family and the Challenge of Social Transformation," in Elizabeth W. Fernea (ed.), *Women and the Family in the Middle East: New Voices of Change* (Austin, 1985), pp. 27–48.

13 See Beth Baron, *The Women's Awakening in Egypt: Culture, Society, and the Press* (New Haven, 1994).

14 The Koran states "Men have authority over women because God has made the one superior to the other, and because they spend their wealth to maintain them." See *The Koran*, 5th rev. ed. (London, 2000), 4:34, p. 83. For the history of volunteer work in Palestine among women, see Khawla Abu Baker, *Be-derekh lo slulah: Nashim araviyot ke-manhigot politiyot be-Yisrael* (A Rocky Road: Arab Women as Political Leaders in Israel) (Ra'anana, 1998); see also idem, *Mediniyut ha-revahah ha-hevratit veha-hinukhit bekerev ha-okhlusiyah ha-aravit be-Yisrael* (The Social and Education Welfare Policies toward the Arab Citizens in Israel) (Jerusalem, 2001).

15 Education in the Middle East was segregated. The first formal school for girls in Egypt was opened in 1829, but education became compulsory only in 1952. The picture was similar in other Middle Eastern states. For detailed information, see Samira Harfoush-Strickland, "Formal Education and Training in Non-Traditional Jobs," in Suha Sabbagh (ed.), *Arab Women: Between Defiance and Restraint* (New York, 1996), pp. 67–70.

16 The proportion of Palestinian female students in Israeli universities is about 4.4 percent in undergraduate studies, and about 1.7 percent in graduate studies. They constitute 50 percent of the Palestinian students in Israel.

17 I deliberately use the term "working women" since 100 percent of women over the age of 40 described themselves as such and not as "career women."

18 All real names have been changed to maintain confidentiality. Couples in this study are all Palestinians, Muslims or Christians who live in Israel.
19 For a detailed description of the structure of the society and its influence on mental health, see Marwan Dwairy, *Cross-Cultural Counseling: The Arab-Palestinian Case* (New York, 1998).
20 For further readings regarding cultural opinion on women battering in Palestinian society, see Muhammad M. Haj-Yahia, "Wife Abuse and Battering in the Sociocultural Context of Arab Society," *Family Process*, Vol. 39, No. 2 (2000), pp. 237–55.
21 For the influence of the acculturation process on the marital lives of acculturated Palestinians, see Khawla Abu Baker, "Acculturation and Reacculturation Influences: Multilayer Contexts in Therapy," *Clinical Psychology Review*, Vol. 19, No. 8 (1999), pp. 951–67.
22 See Dwairy, *Cross-Cultural Counseling*.
23 See Khawla Abu Baker "The Meaning of Tight-Lipped Arab Women in Marital Problems," unpublished lecture, 2nd Conference on "The Psychology of Meaning," Vancouver, July 2002.
24 For the influence of family duties on decisions of pioneering Palestinian women, see Abu Baker, *Be-derekh lo slulah*.
25 According to Islamic traditions in the Middle East, an engaged couple can have the religious ceremony in which they are declared husband and wife immediately, so that their meetings have religious legislation. The wedding ceremony, after which the couple will cohabit, may take place months or years later.
26 For a comprehensive understanding of the meaning of "psychological ecology," see U. Bronfenbrenner, "Toward an Experimental Ecology of Human Development," *American Psychologist*, Vol. 45 (1977), pp. 513–30; for the development of the concept for social and cultural contexts, see C.J. Falicou, "Learning to Think Culturally," in H.A. Liddle, D.C. Breunlin and R.C. Schwartz (eds.), *Handbook of Family Therapy Training and Supervision* (New York, 1988), pp. 335–57.

Normalizing Inequality:
Portrayals of Women in the Israeli Media

Dafna Lemish

The media texts are one of the prime sites of society via which it is possible to study the position of women in Israeli society. This is an arena for our society to present itself, define our identity for us, establish the parameters of consensus and relegate what is perceived as unconventional to the margins. The media

> set up a symbolic frontier between the "normal" and the "deviant," the "normal" and the "pathological," the "acceptable" and the "unacceptable," what "belongs" and what does not or is "Other," between "insiders" and "outsiders," Us and Them. It facilitates the "binding" or bonding together of all of Us who are "normal" into one "imagined community"; and it sends into symbolic exile all of Them — "the Others" — who are in some way different — "beyond the pale."[1]

Since the second wave of feminism, media have been at the center of much of feminist critique for their role in legitimizing and reinforcing capitalist-patriarchal ideology, excluding and marginalizing women's voices and contributing to gender inequality and discrimination. The media's portrayals of social life have been accused of being a central mechanism serving to fixate the gendered separation between the public sphere of the open, rational, political world of men and that of the private sphere of the closed, emotional, care-giving world of women.

The issue of gender representation has been the topic of much discussion and debate in feminist media studies.[2] It consists of at least two complementary perspectives: women's representation in the media (the presence of women, as well as women's issues and perspectives, in the public discourse) and the portrayals of women in the media texts (the way they are represented). Kaplan defined this issue in her distinction between "self," the reality experienced by a woman, and "image," the image of that reality in the media.[3] This distinction raises many epistemological questions regarding the nature of reality: What is women's current reality? How can one define its multifaceted nature and the transitions it has been going through in both historical as well as cultural variances? What is the "right" representation of women's current reality? How can we aim at representing the multi-realities of diverse female-worlds?[4] These questions are relevant also to the study of media audiences, their uses, gratifications, pleasures and social contexts of consumption; as well as to the means by which their voice is heard or silenced, highlighted as significant and important, or as trivial and marginal, and the like.

The purpose of this article is to examine the portrayals of women in the Israeli media through an integrative overview of various studies conducted by Israeli researchers, including my own accumulative work. What can we learn from the examination of the media about women's place in Israeli society at the turn of the century?

Portrayals of Women in the Israeli Media

The integrated examination of the content of the Israeli print and broadcast media engaged in documenting reality (such as newspapers, news programs, current-events programs, talk shows and social programs) and in entertainment (such as quiz shows, soap operas, children's programs) demonstrates the perception of the marginality of women in Israeli society. While men are presented as the "normal" majority of society, women are presented as the minority "other" — the exception, the incomplete, the damaged, the marginal, and sometimes even the bizarre. This way of framing women by the media was defined by Tuchman as "symbolic annihilation," achieved through processes of condemnation, trivialization and the absence of women from the media.[5]

An examination of the Israeli media reveals fundamental principles of patriarchal thinking, including relegating the feminine to the private sphere; restricting presentation of females to the physical functions of sex and reproduction; and placing women within the world of emotions, where rational thought is lacking and behavior uncultivated. Advancing the perception of the marginality of women in society finds expression in all of the media, to the extent to which women are shown at all: they are limited primarily to traditional roles related to the private sphere or, if in the public sphere, in such traditional caring roles as volunteering in service activities, education, health and welfare. Women's personality traits are depicted as being fundamentally different in nature from those of men: they are less logical, ambitious, active, independent, heroic and dominating. By contrast, they are portrayed as being more romantic, sensitive, dependent and vulnerable.[6] The following pages examine these claims in detail based on analyses of the content of the Israeli media, both by quantitative as well as semiotic research methods.

Representations of the "Real World"

The main body of research of women in the Israeli media has dealt with them as subjects of the news, current events and politics, as depicted on television and in the print press. Various studies conducted have dealt with a number of complex issues such as the degree of feminine presence in the genres, women's placement in the framework of the various programs, the way they are presented, and the traits attributed to them. In the very first study in this area, an analysis of Israeli news programs broadcast in 1988, Tidhar found that men appeared six times more than women, and that men aged over 50 spoke directly to the camera four times more than women in this same age group, while women younger than 20 appeared six times more frequently than their male counterparts.[7]

There were also notable differences in the roles of interviewees on news programs and talk shows: women appeared in dependent roles more often than men — such as "the wife of ..., the mother of ..." — while men more often appeared in professional positions. Representatives of the public were exclusively men, while women represented the volunteer sector. Ariel's study on the patterns of introducing women in Israeli television, newspapers and magazines suggested complementary findings: while men, in print and broadcast, were introduced with their professional credentials, women were introduced in terms of their sexual and family identities. Written descriptions of men presented them as independent people working outside the home, while women were presented as immature, dependent on others, unemployed outside the home, and addressed by their first names.[8]

Israel was among one of 71 countries in which the images of women and men were examined on a random day, 18 January 1995. Using a uniform research tool, the content of the hard-news pages of the newspapers and the news reports on radio and television in each country were examined. The findings reinforced what was known from previous studies: most of those interviewed or mentioned in the news were men (91 percent on television, 90 percent on the radio, and 85 percent in the newspapers of that day). Subjects dealing specifically with the world of women — such as health, employment, discrimination, and the like — were all but absent from the sphere known as "news" (10 percent on television, 8.5 percent on the radio, and 0 percent in the newspapers of that day).[9]

Of particular importance was the finding that the most common role for women in the Israeli news was as victim (of violence, accidents and disasters). Women as victims accounted for 67 percent of all women as seen on television, 57 percent of those mentioned on the radio and 72 percent of those named in newspapers. The preference of the media for dealing with women as victims (over creative or active women, for example) is a double-edged sword.

On the one hand, the media create public awareness of violence against women, thus advancing the social debate and remedies. On the other, the tendency of the media to eroticize, trivialize and sensationalize (for example, excessive detailing of the acts of sex and violence, exaggerated use of color headlines and emotional rhetoric, invasive pictures, and the like) depicts the phenomenon as a private battle of passive, unfortunate women, instead of as a structural social problem of power relationships and inequality. The media discussion makes extensive use of the "institutional" voice in covering these subjects — the responsible policeman, the prosecuting judge — reinforcing the impression that "everything is under control," while ignoring the female voice of the victim and her environs. One way or another, the media continue to perpetuate the impression of females as weak, passive and in need of male protection.

Another comparative study examined the image of women in the print and broadcast media in 41 countries on 7–8 May 1995. This study found, as well, that in Israel women comprised less than 10 percent of the central figures in the news and that they were almost entirely absent from the public sphere with regard to domestic politics, foreign policy, defense and security, economics, commerce and religion.[10]

A study of the portrayals of female immigrants from the former Soviet Union sheds additional light on the issues. Analysis of the content of the Hebrew press between 1994 and 1997 demonstrated that these women immigrants were presented primarily in the context of the sex industry in Israel: prostitutes, call girls and escort girls. As such, they were depicted as the "other" of Israeli society. They were to be located in the margins of Israeli society among those in poverty and criminal society. Their Jewishness was called into question, and they certainly did not behave as was expected of Jewish women and mothers: they were often single mothers, they had abortions, they drank alcohol, and so forth. This manner of coverage demonstrates the process whereby women citizens who are part of the collective "us" are portrayed as "others" who are foreign to Israeli society and are undermining morals and good social order.[11]

Of particular interest is an examination of the status of the wives of prime ministers in the Israeli press. Analysis of the media coverage of Leah Rabin, Sonia Peres and Sarah Netanyahu revealed that, while each developed a different pattern of behavior vis-à-vis media contacts, all three had placed the value of the family in first place, while compromising on or giving up their own careers (in pure female professions: nurse, teacher and psychologist, respectively). All three had played the role of "first lady" through some form of public volunteer work, an activity generally reserved for action by women of means and not financially rewarded. Press coverage of these women placed particular emphasis on their private spheres: their personal appearance, descriptions of their home, furnishings, the domestic atmosphere, renovations, holding dinner parties, and the like. Over the years, in fact, the wives of Israeli prime ministers have been portrayed as totally conforming to the traditional profile of women in Israeli society. None presented themselves, through the media, as models for the advancement of the status of women.[12]

Coverage of women in competitive sports is another unique area that has been examined.[13] Since sport is an area dealing with the physical world, it offers grounds for examining how the physicality of the male body is presented as a paradigm of superiority over female physicality. For example, although "sports" is an inclusive concept, it is used to refer to the coverage of masculine activities. Hence coverage of sports activities in which women engage is depicted as "other" — "women's sports." Coverage of sports activities in which Israeli women were engaged is negligible. For example, in one study reported by Bernstein, it was found that only five percent of the items in newspaper sports sections were devoted to women athletes, and even those were small news items not accompanied by photographs. Pictures of women in the sports sections usually portrayed them in dependent roles, as "the wife of …," "the girlfriend of … ." Coverage of women athletes addresses, among other details, their external appearance, thus diminishing their athletic achievements and reducing them, as other women, to their sexual functions.

The inequality in how women and men are portrayed by the media is so deep that it is even perpetuated in election campaigns by parties officially committed to social equality. Lemish and Tidhar found that promotional campaign broadcasts — which are the "calling cards" of the political parties and their public image — of the 1988 and 1996 elections deviated only slightly from the familiar images: across all parties, women appeared on average in 13 percent of promotions in 1988 and 17 percent in 1996, and had the following characteristics: they were younger than the men; they tended, more than men, to be presented without being identified or without definition of professional credentials; they appeared as lay persons from the street; and they were depicted with more emotional messages then men. They received less camera exposure during their appearances and tended to be shown more in mixed groups with men. A qualitative analysis of these images highlighted how during the 1988 campaign pretty young women, dressed in the height of fashion, opened and closed the broadcasts of the large parties, provided continuity between segments and "assisted" the public to reach the "right" conclusions. In this role, they did not express any personal political opinions but rather narrated the party line. Most of the parties did not permit women to present the parties' position on such central issues as peace, security and the economy. The little exposure given to women politicians focused on familiar women's areas — education, health and welfare. Relatively anonymous women were chosen to speak about the Israeli–Arab conflict.

Each was presented in her dependent role; that is, their claims and the justifications for them derived from their roles as "friend of...," "mother of...," "grandmother of...." In these roles, the women represented the civilian home front and wondered aloud about the ramifications of the possible death (or about death which had already occurred) of the men in their lives.[14] Thus they were relegated to the private aspect of the public sphere.

During the 1996 campaign, the "motherhood" strategy was particularly evident. Women-as-mothers was the dominant message of most of the parties, both in terms of the content presented and as a vehicle facilitating other messages. Mothers appeared with babies on their laps and children at their sides. As mothers, they spoke of their children, while the camera continually panned to the children. In this role, they spoke of such subjects as peace, the future, education, equality, personal security, poverty, religion, retirement, minorities, and army service. Bereaved mothers spoke in the names of their children. Even such a senior woman politician as Limor Livnat (who later became the only woman minister in the Netanyahu government and is now Minister of Education in Sharon's government), in her personal appeal to the electorate, drafted her children, Shir and Yair, who were afraid of going on their annual school trips because of the absence of peace and security. It seemed that only women's roles as mothers could legitimize their appearance on screen and the message they were conveying.

Analysis of deviations from these expected norms is particularly interesting. In 1988, of all the campaign broadcasts, there was only one which presented a woman who was not a politician, not in a dependent position, not reading a prepared script, but expressing her personal opinions on general political topics. This exceptional woman was a high-school student from a northern development town representing the right-wing Likud Party. It is interesting to note that this "extraordinary" appearance engendered extensive public reaction in the mass media and became one of the "trademarks" of that year's campaign. Using the political opinions expressed by a teenage girl — moreover, one from a peripheral town (four deviations from the "norm" of male, adult, Ashkenazi, middle-class) — was, it would seem, still an exceptional strategy in the Israeli media. In general, though, the trend for change was found among small, marginal political parties with records of interest and action in the fields of human rights and women's rights: Ratz (later to become Meretz, headed at the time by acclaimed human-rights leader, Shulamit Aloni) and Hadash, the Arab-Jewish Progressive-Democratic Party. In this case, the media, as in many other instances in the history of social-political transitions (as, for example, in the case of the movement for withdrawal from Lebanon in 1982, or the anti-war movement during the Vietnam war in the early 1960s in the USA), echoed the early signs of possible change in the existing social reality, rather than leading this new trend themselves. It seems that the media tend to break the spiral of silence and give a voice to alternative perspectives when they sense that the public is ripe to break through consensual views.

In her study of women in local politics in Israel, Herzog demonstrated the different ways via which the media fixated on these women's roles in the private sphere rather then their public agenda, portraying them as interlopers trying to achieve the impossible.[15] These themes were highlighted through the relegation of the discussion of women in politics to women's magazines and the women's sections in the national and local newspapers (instead of political-news sections); through excessive emphasis on the fact that the candidate was "first of all a woman"; through a depiction of the involvement in politics as threatening femininity and as being in conflict with self-fulfillment in the home and family frameworks; and through the emphasis on extraordinary women as being the exception to the rule.

Unique conflict situations, such as the uprising in the occupied Palestinian territories (*Intifada*) from the late 1980s, sharpen the problematics of the images of women in television news. When society is drawn into the whirlpool of a major social-political conflict, people's lives naturally tend to become more politically oriented. Such situations have particular effects on women. On the one hand, as members of society they must recognize their lives in the face of threats to social, political, economic and/or physical existence. On the other hand, under such circumstances, women tend to become more active in the public sphere, traditionally occupied by men. However, in an analysis of the content of news of the Palestinian uprising over the course of several years, it was found that the *Intifada* was framed as a male issue on all levels: only five percent of the figures who appeared on screen were women, and 18 percent appeared in mixed groups. The decisive majority of those interviewed were men, while the minority of women interviewed appeared in dependent positions more than in any professional capacity. Only women who expressed extreme political views were identified by name and role, emphasizing the marginality of their perspective. Further, substantial differences surfaced between the images of Jewish and Palestinian women: while Jewish women were presented stereotypically, in a manner familiar with other studies of the news, the Palestinian women were presented more as being active side-by-side with men, without a clear gender distinction.[16] This supports Ridd's argument that despite the fact that war and conflict are male territory, women are capable of actively penetrating it when the situation is perceived as an extreme and temporary crisis, such as the Palestinian struggle for independence.[17] Hence the power of the image of Palestinian women with firearms, or leading violent or mournful demonstrations.

It should be emphasized that the unique contribution of both Jewish and Palestinian women — each group independently on its respective side, as well as through joint actions — has not earned media coverage. Editors of television news, as revealed by research about the *Intifada*, chose to ignore women's political movements that deviated from the national consensus and sought to offer alternative ways to resolving a political crisis. For example, there was a startling absence of coverage of Women in Black, a protest movement against the ongoing occupation which challenged the Israeli social and gendered order, raised questions about it and proposed alternative action.[18] In contrast, another political-protest movement which objected to the presence of the Israeli army in Lebanon — Four Mothers — emphasized the fears of mothers for the fate of their children and openly exposed speaking with the "force of the womb." This movement has enjoyed relatively broad media coverage, and its success in changing the national agenda can be attributed to the positive role attributed to motherhood by Israeli society. Perceived as the ultimate female sacrifice for the national collective, this role accords legitimacy to the female voice in the public sphere, whereas expression of women's political opinion as equal members of society does not earn comparable recognition.[19]

The aggregate picture requires our asking about "intention": is there a media policy that intentionally prevents the voice of women from being heard? We were able to confront this question with the outbreak of the Gulf War in 1991, when women disappeared from the Israeli airwaves. In-depth interviews conducted with senior personnel in broadcast organizations revealed that this disappearance was more the result of outright unconscious discrimination than a conscious policy.[20] For these men, women in general were perceived as being less professional and unreliable during a period of distress because of conflicts with their roles as mothers and their emotionality. Similarly, policy makers also relied on an assumption (which has never been proven empirically) that the public, comprised of both men and women, perforce prefers the "authoritative" voice of a man (naturalized and cultivated preference). Here, too, there was one woman who was an exception that proved the rule: Orly Yaniv, who anchored a news program throughout the war. As a good-looking female figure, non-argumentative and non-threatening, she fulfilled her role as a supportive, non-aggressive interviewer and represented the "person in the street," rather than the "expert" professional person.

A clear example of the invisibility of discrimination against women broadcasters during the Gulf War was illustrated by the following quotation from a senior radio editor:

> I made the manpower decisions, so I say it with full responsibility: The decision, who will broadcast what was not made according to the broadcaster's sex. It was MY decision [about] who can stand a difficult

and stressful situation. I made my decisions accordingly. I think the considerations were purely professional. We purposefully chose a small group of men, only four, so that the population will identify with them and get used to them.... The women broadcasters are mothers; they have children. There were women who stayed home or went away. There was a feeling that 6 million people were listening, and the smallest mistake could have cost many dangerous self-injections of antropin shots [the antidote for biological- and chemical-warfare materials]. There was the fear that the broadcaster will lose control during the broadcast. Imagine he hears that a Scud missile just hit the street where he lives. He is the source of authority at that moment. You can't replace him if his voice is shaky and he sounds panicked. My decision was practical: Who could we trust under such conditions. There was no discrimination.[21]

Evidently, only women were perceived in terms of being the mothers of children (private sphere); only with regard to women was there concern that they might panic (emotionality); only on them was it impossible to rely (childishness, lack of professionalism). All of this is anchored in the eyes of the above speaker as a pure, rational and professional perception.

Advertising

Advertising is of primary interest in discussion of gender representations because it is an essential mechanism for advancing capitalism and Western patriarchal interests and therefore serves as a mobilizing force preventing the possibility of change. Chief among the criticisms leveled by feminists against advertising in Israel is that it frequently and blatantly depicts women as sexual objects. Semiotic analysis identified the ways in which exposed parts of the female anatomy are displayed, provocative body movements, enticing facial expressions, tantalizing glances, finger movements, self-caressing, emphasis on the lips, and the like, as well as extensive use of lingual and para-lingual movements. In all of these ways advertising frequently reduces women to their simple sexual functions.[22]

In spite of the many ways in which advertising in Israel was transformed with the introduction of commercial television in the early 1990s, only a few changes have taken place in portrayal of women in advertising over the last 20 years. Research findings comparing advertisements which appeared in Israeli newspapers and magazines in 1979 and 1994 showed that women continue to be depicted as sexual objects, in provocative positions, in inferior status relative to men, via use of body parts to reinforce the headings and draw attention.[23] Women in advertisements frequently continue to be shown touching themselves and the product in a provocative manner; they are degraded, more than men, and exhibit less control over themselves.

Female sexuality is often woven into advertising through the use of devices hinting at violence. Thus, for example, the following motifs also associated with pornography were found in Israeli advertising: fragmentation of the female body (presenting parts of the body disconnected from the whole); bondage (portraying women in restraints or with some form of physical limitation on their freedom of movement); forced physical contact (advertisements depicting men using physical force on women); symbolic violence (advertisements portraying women in association with violence, even if expression is not actually given to the violence); and potential violence (advertisements which present women in situations known to the viewer as being potentially violent). In most of these advertisements the woman appeared to be ignoring the violence, indifferent to it or even enjoying it. What is more, women were even depicted as encouraging sexual violence: they were dressed and posed provocatively; undressed or exposed parts of their bodies in manners intended to be provocative to the viewer. They exuded a willingness to initiate sexual relations under any circumstance and at any price.[24] The objectification of women in advertisements is also expressed in how extensively they are used as objects rather than subjects having their own existence: as fruits — colorful, juicy and tempting to eat; as packages (such as perfume bottles); as animals — identified with the untamed, the natural, the impulsive, the uncivilized.

A quantitative study that examined commercials on Channel 2 during the years 1993–96 revealed consistency in the discriminatory characterizations of women.[25] Women, more than men, were identified with lower-value and lower-status consumer products, particularly those associated with housekeeping, or those for improving one's external appearance. These products are a priori identified with female stereotypes, as has been discussed before, and therefore serve to reproduce the boundaries of female representation. Such commercials project a differentiated status of men and women: men in commercials were depicted, more often, in the work world, while women in Israel were still presented in the domestic domain or without context. The rewards promised by advertisements centered on external appearance for women, while those for men dealt with practical benefits. Commercials directed at men or using men most often portrayed them as a "professional" source of information guided by rational thought, while those directed at or using women usually presented them on the "personal" level, characterized by emotional considerations. Most women in commercials were significantly younger than the men (75 percent were younger than 30, while 52 percent of the men were above 40), reinforcing the value placed on women's appearance and adherence to the "beauty myth."[26]

With regard to the image of sexuality, significant differences were also found between men and women. Many more women than men were presented partially dressed or nude (31.5 percent in comparison with 14.7 percent); and employment of voyeuristic camera work was seven times more frequent for women than for men. Use of women's body parts, only, was almost double that of men. Three times as many commercials using women were based on sexiness than those in which men appeared. This finding also included advertisements in which girls were the lead characters.

Madonna or Whore

The Israeli media often perpetuate both sides of the dichotomy reserved in patriarchal culture to women: the "Madonna" on the one side and the "whore" on the other. As "Madonna," the Israeli woman is cast in the role of the mother — the one who gives birth, nurtures, raises, sacrifices herself, and — finally — the one who mourns her dead son. This image also includes the extension of the private roles into the national sphere. As "whore," she is pressed into the mold of the sexual object, the essence of whose existence is tantalizing/threatening the masculine and whose ultimate fate is to be punished as a victim of violence and exploitation. Here, media content legitimizes the dehumanization of women and regards them as objects lacking a consciousness and an individuality.

An illuminating example of social perceptions of women's role in Israeli society can be found in a number of visual projects related to the celebrations of the country's 50th anniversary of independence in 1998. An examination of women's images presented in albums celebrating Israel's jubilee clearly reveals women's place in Israeli society: the attention devoted to women altogether is negligible, and when they are included, it is their social function that is portrayed, as that of the sacrificing mother or wife. Similar evidence can be found in the highly praised television series *Tkumah* (Revival, referring to the revival of a Jewish state). This production used leading mainstream historians and television professionals in an effort to present as multifaceted a picture as possible of the country's history. Yet, for the most part it ignored women. Various segments of the series were devoted to all of the possible societal divisions — Ashkenazi and *Mizrahi*, secular and Orthodox, veterans and new immigrants, settlers in the occupied Palestinian territories and members of Peace Now, Jews and Arabs. Only half of the country's populace — the women — hardly appeared on the television screen. Ignoring, perhaps refusing to include, documentation of the role of women in the establishment and development of the State, as foundations of the collective memory and national self-identity, is greater testament than anything else presented to date of the symbolic annihilation of women. "If you're not there, you don't exist," says a popular commercial. Simply, the women are not "there," in the world presented by the media.

Extraction from Invisibility?

Yet, as in other developed countries, studies are finding evidence of "creeping" change in the images of women in Israel. Lately, more than ever, women have been appearing more as professionals, in addition to being the keepers of the private sphere. This gradual transition to a more liberal model can be attributed to real changes in society and to the cumulative influence of the feminist revolution. Simultaneously, however, it can be further understood by taking into consideration two complementary factors. First, a major portion of the changes involves showing women more in the manner perceived as masculine (independent and powerful, for example, as typified by a number of women politicians and female journalists holding senior positions) or presenting men in ways that are usually perceived as feminine (as sexual objects in advertisements, or as bereaved fathers or tearful soldiers, for example). Neither of these strategies allows for expression of the unique female experience, female worldview and values, female ways of thinking and politics, as is evident, for example, in the discourse surrounding the Israeli–Palestinian conflict. Second, if we address the contents of the media, such as advertisements, not as an unequivocal reflection of reality but as expressions of a consumer society, the image of the "new" woman can be interpreted as utilizing the feminist discourse for the sake of advancing consumerism at the expense of women's advancement. Recognizing and mobilizing the growing economic power of women in Western society has, according to some theorists, brought about a backlash in the form of a new enslavement: to an unattainable ideal of beauty, to exalting the preservation of eternal youth and to nurturing an inferior self-image which is in constant need of improvement.[27]

The question of representation is central not only in a discussion of media content (where it has been studied extensively) and media audience (to which the feminist interest has shifted recently), but also to the study of media-related professions (where research is sorely lacking). The end of the twentieth century has witnessed the growing feminization of media professions in Israel as in the rest of the world, facilitated not only by social, but also by technological, economic and statutory changes in media professions. For example, the flexibility facilitated by the new technologies — fax, computer, Internet, cellular phones and the like — allows easier juggling of career and domestic expectations. The "new-journalism" trends of "soft news" reportage and personification of the news are more favorable to women's traditional writing styles and interests. The tightly competitive market takes advantage of women presenters of news as a "bait" attracting diverse audiences. However, against expectations, this process has not rocked the gendered, fundamentally patriarchal political-economic ownership; neither has it been successful in transforming the professional norms and value systems of media operations. Furthermore, as research has been documenting, the presence of women at the production end of texts does not necessarily guarantee change in contents: do women in the media professions represent and present women differently from men? Do they define differently what is newsworthy? Do they bring different perspectives to the worldview presented on the screens, the airwaves and the printed pages? These and other questions have been central to feminist media studies which analyze the work of professional women in media organizations as located within social, economic and organizational contexts, and not as a personal change by a particular female celebrity.[28]

The claim that the growing feminization of the media industry in Israel will bring about significant change in the hegemonic worldview presented in the media texts is a hotly debated proposition in Israel, as it is elsewhere.[29] To what extent will the increased presence of women in this field affect or shape professional norms, blur the boundaries of the dual perceptions of reality, shift the public interest to areas which are less exposed, change the accepted distinction between information and commentary, and the like? Moreover, what are the values attributed to these possibilities? Two doctoral dissertations struggling with these issues have just been completed: the first, focusing on print-journalism, and the second on radio-journalism.[30] Both present a complicated and unsettling picture of the institutional constraints and professional socializing mechanisms. Anecdotal evidence coming from the advertising world is not encouraging either. The significant growth in the number of women employed in advertising has not been accompanied by concomitant changes in the symbolic representations of women in advertisements. It seems these female advertisers internalize the value system that perpetuates the low status of women and accept these standards, in their struggle for professional survival and success.

Within this tension between the domination by conservative images and trends toward change, a number of women stand out in expressing women's voices in the media. Each of these women, however, has been perceived more than once as having paid a price for daring to do so; for example, by giving up having children or by adopting a "masculine" professional character. Recently, a number of additional women have begun to assume prominent roles as anchorwomen as well as field reporters and press-commentators in normally male areas, including politics, defense, crime, sports and economics. A weekly feminist TV program on the commercial channel has achieved a respectable audience share and seeks to contribute to the cultivation of a new definition of "women's issues" in the public mind.

In spite of these hints at possible change within the Israeli media, a realistic assessment of the picture of the world presented by the media still leaves women in the margins of the social, economic, cultural and political processes, as has been documented in many other studies worldwide. Attempts of feminist grass-root organizations engaged in media-watch and social change efforts (in areas such as portrayals of women in advertising) to voice criticism have met strong consensual opposition by the media organizations themselves which deny their own contribution to the discrimination of women.[31] Here, we might say that Israeli women find themselves torn between their multiple identities and loyalties. As a result, they have difficulties elevating the feminist struggle to the top of national as well as their own priorities. "This isn't the appropriate time to bother society with banal questions about images in the media or the femininization of poverty," the national conscience seems to argue, "when we still have to fight a battle for existence against our external enemies." Opposing the national consensus threatens women because it shakes their sense of belonging to the collective and the fundamental assumptions both on which they were educated and about which they are expected to educate the younger generation.[32] Thus, accepting the underlining hegemonic militarist perception of patriotism as defining Israeli society and remaining silent is an additional price that women pay for the continuing state of political conflict.

The exclusion of women from the public sphere, including the forums of political, cultural and economic power, is achieved through processes of negation of self-identity, abrogation of rights, and repression. Women's achievements in all realms of life are ignored or overshadowed by a stereotypically limited range of roles. This contributes further to the invisibility of women as a group within both societal and individual consciousness. Analysis of media representations should therefore be understood in the broader perspective of the discussion of women's cultural imaging. It bears the need to question whose images are portrayed, and what their meanings and consequences are.[33] Both senders and receivers of media messages may be perpetuating these stereotypes, consciously or not, out of an interest in maintaining the status quo of gender power relationships. The media did not invent women's inequality and victimization, and they cannot be held solely responsible for the existence of discrimination. Yet, the images they present can reinforce and legitimize a patriarchal worldview by glorifying the situation and/or by presenting it as the normal or expected state of affairs. The Israeli context presents unique challenges to understanding the universal discrimination of women. The traditional national emphasis on family and childbearing perpetuates woman's place in the private sphere and puts her in conflict with her activities outside this realm. The centrality of the army, the ongoing struggle for defense and occupation, and the system of masculine values associated with them (such as war, conquest, repression, exploitation, violence and rape) have grown to dominate the public sphere and serve to marginalize women.[34] Indeed, participation in the public discourse that gives unequivocal preference to questions of "national security" impinges on women's ability to take part in the central political sphere.[35] Religious interests take priority over egalitarian principles in the Israeli legislative process. What is more, the court system has chosen, by its lack of intervention, to prefer cultivation of the Jewish rather than the egalitarian nature of the state.[36] In this context, the media portrayals of women serve as one additional socializing mechanism for maintaining discrimination and for normalizing inequality in the public eye.

NOTES

1 Stuart Hall, "The Spectacle of the 'Other'," in idem (ed.), *Representation: Cultural Representations and Signifying Practices* (London, 1997), p. 258.
2 See, for example, Helen Baehr and Ann Gray, *Turning It On: A Reader in Women and Media* (London, 1996); Pamela Creedon, *Women in Mass Communiation: Challenging Gender Values* (Newbury Park, CA, 1989); Lana E. Rakow (ed.), *Women Making Meaning: New Feminist Directions in Communication* (New York, 1992).
3 Ann Kaplan, "Feminist Criticism and Television," in Robert C. Allen (ed.), *Channels of Discourse* (Chapel Hill, NC, 1987).
4 Keya Ganguly, "Accounting for Others: Feminism and Representation," in Rakow (ed.), *Women Making Meaning*, pp. 60–81.
5 Gaye Tuchman (ed.), *Hearth and Home: Images of Women and the Media* (New York, 1978).
6 Chava E. Tidhar and Dafna Lemish, "Women in the Intifada: A Television News Perspective," in Akiba A. Cohen and Gadi Wolfsfeld (eds.), *Framing the Intifada: People and Media* (Norwood, NJ, 1993), pp. 142–59.
7 Chava E. Tidhar, "Women in Israel's Broadcasting Media and on Israeli Television," in Yoshiro Kawakami (ed.), *Women and Communication in an Age of Science and Technology* (Tokyo, 1988), pp. 112–28.
8 Mira Ariel, "Female and Male Stereotypes in Israeli Literature and Media: Evidence from Introductory Patterns," *Language and Communication*, Vol. 8, No. 1 (1988), pp. 43–68.
9 Media Watch, *Global Media Monitoring Project: Women's Participation in the News* (Toronto, 1995).
10 Anat First and Donald L. Shaw, "Where Have All the Women Gone? The Presentation of Women in Foreign News: A 1995 Multi-National Study," paper presented to the annual conference of ICA, Jerusalem, Israel, 1998.
11 Dafna Lemish, "The Whore and the 'Other': Israeli Images of Female Immigrants from the Former USSR," *Gender and Society*, Vol. 14, No. 2 (2000), pp. 339–49.
12 Dafna Lemish and Gili Drob, "'All the Time His Wife': Portrayals of First Ladies in the Israeli Press," *Parliamentary Affairs*, Vol. 55, No. 1 (2002), pp. 129–42.
13 Alina Bernstein, "British and Israeli Coverage of the 1992 Barcelona Olympics: A Comparative Analysis" (Ph.D. diss,, Centre for Mass Communication Research, University of Leicester, England, 1997).
14 Dafna Lemish and Chava E. Tidhar, "Still Marginal: Women in Israel's 1996 Television Election Campaign," *Sex Roles*, Vol. 41, No. 5–6 (1999), pp. 389–412.
15 Hanna Herzog, *Gendering Politics: Women in Israel* (Chicago, 1998).
16 Tidhar and Lemish, "Women in the Intifada."
17 Rosemary Ridd, "Powers of the Powerless," in idem and Helen Callaway (eds.), *Caught up in*

Conflict: Women's Responses to Political Strife (Houndmills Basingstoke, 1986), pp. 1–24.

18 Sara Hellman and Tamar Rapaport, "'Eleh nashim ashkenaziyot, levad, zonot shel aravim, lo ma'aminot be-elohim, velo-ohavot et Eretz Yisrael': Nashim be-shahor ve-itgur ha-seder ha-hevrati" ('These are Ashkenazi Women, Alone, Whores of Arabs, Don't Believe in God, and Don't Love the Land of Israel': Women in Black and the Challenge to the Social Order), *Teoriyah u-Vikoret*, No. 10 (1997), pp. 175–92.

19 Dafna Lemish and Inbal Barzel, "Four Mothers: The Womb in the Public Sphere," *European Journal of Communication*, Vol. 15, No. 2 (2000), pp. 147–69.

20 Dafna Lemish and Chava E. Tidhar, "Where Have All the Young Girls Gone? The Disappearance of Israeli Women-Broadcasters during the Gulf War," *Women and Language*, Vol. 22, No. 2 (1999), pp. 27–32.

21 Ibid., p. 29.

22 Dafna Lemish, "The Ripple Effect: Pornographic Images of Women in Israeli Advertising," in Stanley G. French (ed.), *Interpersonal Violence, Health and Gender Politics* (New York, 1997), pp. 285–95.

23 Anat First, "Nothing New under the Sun? A Comparison of Images of Women in Israeli Advertisements in 1979 and 1994," *Sex Roles*, Vol. 38, No. 11–12 (1998), pp. 1065–77.

24 Lemish, "The Ripple Effect."

25 Gabriel Weimann, "Migdar u-firsomet: Nashim ve-gvarim be-tashdirei ha-pirsomet ha-televiziyonit be-Yisrael" (Gender and Advertising: Women and Men in Television Advertisements in Israel), *Megamot*, Vol. 40, No. 3 (2000), pp. 466–85.

26 Naomi Wolf, *The Beauty Myth: How Images of Beauty Are Used against Women* (New York, 1991).

27 Ibid.

28 Liesbet van Zoonen, *Feminist Media Studies* (London, 1994); Creedon, *Women in Mass Communication*.

29 Yehiel Limor and Dan Caspi, "Ha-feminizatziyah ba-itonut ha-yisre'elit" (Feminization in the Israeli Press), *Kesher*, No. 15 (1994), pp. 37–45; Cynthia Carter, Gill Branston and Stuart Allan, *News, Gender and Power* (London, 1998).

30 Einat Lachover, "Ha-havnayah ha-migdarit shel ha-itonut ha-ktuvah be-Yisrael" (Gender Structure in the Written Media in Israel) (Ph.D. diss., Tel Aviv University, 2001). Aliza Lavie, "Radio ve-migdar be-Yisrael" (Radio and Gender in Israel) (Ph.D. diss., Bar Ilan University, 2001).

31 Dafna Lemish, "Gender at the Forefront: Feminist Perspectives on Action. Theoretical Approaches in Communication Research," *Communication: The European Journal of Communication Research*, Vol. 27, No. 1 (2002), pp. 63–78.

32 Yvonne Deutsch, "Israeli Women against the Occupation: Political Growth and the Persistence of Ideology," in Tamar Mayer (ed.), *Women and the Israeli Occupation: The Politics of Change* (London, 1994), pp. 88–105.

33 Lana E. Rakow, "Rethinking Gender Research in Communication," *Journal of Communication*, Vol. 36, No. 4 (1986), pp. 11–26.

34 Deutsch, "Israeli Women against the Occupation."

35 Mayer, *Women and the Israeli Occupation.*

36 Frances Raday, "The Concept of Gender Equality in a Jewish State," in Barbara Swirski and Marilyn P. Safir (eds.) *Calling the Equality Bluff: Women in Israel* (New York, 1991), pp. 18–28.

Women of the Wall:
Radical Feminism as an Opportunity for a New Discourse in Israel

Leah Shakdiel

It seems I am a descendant of mute women.
It seems there is in me a beehive of words I will never enounce.
It seems I am condemned to be spread daily in the sweetness
of their formless honey, to be bitten with the needle of their speechlessness.
Gathered-in, distorted notes, will come, will come, and open up my choking throat.
Whispering, storming, sub-wombian waves, will come, will come, and break
through the dam of shame.
My deserted, saddened voice, frozen in the silent pole, will come, will come,
will burst and flood and sip into the abyss of earth like hot burning foaming red
lava.
My whole, my voice will come, fierce immense tall strong and echoing forward
silencing all
those whispering mouths:
"The honor of the king's daughter is heard inside only."
Smadar Falk[1]

Thomas Kuhn taught us that paradigms change when they no longer reasonably explain phenomena that defy them, while at the same time a new theory develops in the margin of the known discourse that offers a better explanation for those phenomena.[2] I will try to examine one such phenomenon which remains inexplicable by the current paradigm for the analysis of Israeli society — "Women of the Wall" (WoW). I think that tackling problematic phenomena such as WoW has the potential to produce a new perspective, which cuts across the boundaries of current social categories. In other words, this group can serve as a litmus paper that diagnoses the changing Israeli society, if we understand its history as a chain of noisy interactions with active "chemicals" that are usually invisible.

I should disclaim the following in the beginning: I do not belong to the WoW group, but I am a close friend of some members, share many of their ideals, and care a lot for their struggle, though I feel ambivalent about the site they chose for action (namely, the Western Wall in Jerusalem).[3] Over the years I have also shared with them my critique of some strategies they adopted. I wrote this article from this standpoint, mingling the private and the public, the personal and the political, theoretical research and political action. I thank group members for the information and the ideas they shared with me; the conclusions drawn are mine alone.

Background: Group "Herstory"

At the very end of 1988, in the Hyatt Hotel in Jerusalem, the First International Conference of Jewish Feminists was held, 15 years or so after the sprouting of Jewish feminism in New York.[4] Jewish women had worked for the women's rights movement since its beginnings, and many Jewish women who had been active in various political movements since the nineteenth century have had a feminist agenda; however, the term "Jewish feminism" marked a new development within what is known as "the second wave" of feminism — no longer contained within the struggle for equality with Jewish men, they now committed themselves to changing both Judaism and Jewish society in light of the feminist vision.

Some participants in that conference in Jerusalem have been Modern Orthodox activists from North America, feminists who had been involved since the 1970s in organizing women's *tefilla* (prayer) groups (WTGs) in their communities.[5] These groups are motivated by the urge to change the place of women in public prayer from a passive audience to active participation, albeit within the limits of Orthodox Halakhic policies — that is, the accepted interdiction in those circles to hold mixed-sex prayers. No longer willing to remain an addendum to men's prayer, behind a partition, these women hold separate prayers for females only, where they can experience active roles such as leading group prayer, organizing the event, reading aloud from the Torah scroll for all present, or being honored with various parts of the ritual (*Aliyah* — stepping up to empower the reader to read for them, opening the Holy Arc for taking out the Torah, holding the Torah up following the reading, etc.). Many of these women are familiar with prayers in a women-only group, the daily routine in the single-sex schools they attended; nonetheless, the novelties these prayer groups introduced — reading from the Torah scroll, as well as reading the Book of Esther from a scroll on Purim — are welcomed with tears of revolutionary excitement. These are adult women, often recognized scholars in various Jewish studies, finally included in an experience that is considered basic and universal in the life of every Jewish boy from his bar mitzvah (when he turns 13) onwards — looking at the inside of the holy scroll from up close, in the very center of the prayer group and not in the margin.

These women prayer groups meet on Simhat Torah, a holiday marked by calling up to the Torah every male present in the synagogue, a custom that emphasizes the redundancy of females; on Rosh Hodesh, the beginning of every Jewish month, as a new expression for a forgotten women's monthly holiday; and for celebrating bat mitzvah, the coming of age for girls who turn 12 in the same way this event has been marked for boys in recent times. Some women also wrap themselves in a prayer shawl during these services, though they make sure to wear shawls with feminine designs that distinguish them clearly from the traditional ones used by men. It is worth noting that at the time (1988) there was only one such prayer group in Israel, in the Yedidya congregation in Jerusalem;[6] this prayer group derived its practice from the custom imported to Israel in the 1970s by an immigrant from the US, Pnina Peli.[7]

One of the proponents of this new practice in the Jewish world who came to Jerusalem for the 1988 conference was Rivka Haut from Brooklyn, New York. Haut had already edited a newsletter named *The Women's Tefillah Network*, which since then has become an electronic forum, WTN, that enables the groups to stay in touch, consult with each other, and evolve towards a "movement" with some loose guidelines. The most radical groups function just like an all-male quorum of ten (*minyan*); the most traditional ones make a point of considering their reading from the scroll as Torah study only, meticulously avoiding imitating rituals reserved for males; and the mainstream includes the majority of the groups, those who enable women to say the blessings over the reading (thereby marking its status as fulfillment of a *mitzvah*, a ritual obligation), but omit the three "sanctifying texts" that can be shared in a male quorum only (*Barkhu, Kaddish, Kedushah*). The Network has given rise to a group of Modern Orthodox rabbis who support this new practice and are willing to provide Halakhic guidance to specific issues.[8] I think that the most important achievement of the WTN is the legitimacy it has created in certain Orthodox circles for the seeming oxymoron "religious feminism," first propagated by Rebbetzn Blu Greenberg from New York.[9] Eventually, this gave rise to two organizations that hold large-scale periodical conferences: the Jewish Orthodox Feminist Alliance (JOFA) in New York (founded by Blu Greenberg in 1997), and the Religious Women's Forum "Kolech" (Your Voice) in Israel (founded by Hannah Kehat in 1999).

That winter of 1988, in Jerusalem, Rivka Haut initiated another novelty: women's prayers at the Western Wall, with a Torah scroll and prayer shawls.[10] At the time, Israel was undergoing a governmental crisis over the "Who is a Jew" issue, and Haut thought she had two advantages. First, as a diaspora Jew, she was free of the sharp dichotomies that typify Israeli discourse concerning religious issues and had experience in cross-denominational negotiations. Second, as a feminist she was used to the solidarity of "sisterhood," and therefore free of the rivalries that paralyze male politics in general. This self-image, by the way, is characteristic of other WoW activists even today.[11]

Haut and other Orthodox feminists who lobbied in the conference halls for the new idea convinced the others who joined them to hold the planned prayer service at the Western Wall within the Halakhic parameters of most Orthodox WTGs, while sharing roles among all denominations. A scroll was borrowed from the Reform movement in Jerusalem, and on Thursday morning, 1 December 1988, a big group of women, mostly American tourists, arrived at the women's section of the Western Wall, crowding around the scroll to protect it, singing softly the popular "Oseh Shalom" verse ("He Who makes peace in his Heavens will make peace upon us and all of Israel"), while being accompanied by reporters and photographers. The video sequence documents their excitement and anxiety, how they hurried to leave the site following the service, while the onlookers were beginning to show curiosity and protest.[12] Haut records that on this occasion the women escaped unharmed, but the violence was already beginning to set in (insults and curses were yelled, men shaking the *mechitza* (the partition separating the men's and women's sections) threateningly), in spite of the explicit admission by Rabbi Yehudah Getz, who was serving at the time as the *Memuneh al ha-Kotel*, the official supervisor of the holy site on behalf of the Ministry of Religions , that the women were not violating any *Halakhah*.

Some participants from Jerusalem, mostly immigrants from the US, decided on the spot to turn the event into a tradition, to be held every Rosh Hodesh with a Torah scroll, as well as every Friday (when the service does not include such reading). Following Psalms 97:1, they started calling themselves "Shirah hadashah" (new song), though they have been known in Israel as Kvutzat Neshot ha-Kotel, in accordance with their official English name, Women of the Wall. They soon became victims of repeated violence from Ultra-Orthodox women and men alike — they were pushed around, beaten up, chairs were thrown at them. They naturally demanded that the police protect them, but were stunned to learn that they were the ones accused of disrupting public order, and not those who attacked them: police officers stood by and did nothing to stop the violence, and special female law enforcement workers were hired by the Ministry of Religions to drag them away, in spite of their quiet behavior and only passive resistance.[13]

The group's impression that the media in Israel were biased against it was substantiated by research that compared media coverage of various struggles conducted by women around the same time.[14] In spite of their cross-denominational ideology and practice, they were consistently presented as "American Reform." Otherwise, their issue was cut to fit the prevailing "media concepts" in Israel — women as silenced and invisible, and when mentioned at all the interpretative context can be either "feminists as provocation" or "women as victims of violence (preferably with dramatic visuals)." The steadfast prejudice of reporters resulted in gross factual mistakes in the coverage with regards to "who was who", "who said what," and "what happened." The only newspaper well disposed for accurate coverage of the group's issue over the years has been the English-language *Jerusalem Post*. These findings were indirectly corroborated by subsequent research, even though the media were not exclusively the focus of research.[15]

The WoW group has also failed to rally support from Israeli women's organizations: their struggle was and is still considered weird and objectionable. The only known politicians who have been prepared to lend their name to the cause are Reform group member Anat Hoffman (Jerusalem City Councilwoman, Meretz Party), and ex-American Meretz MK Professor Naomi Chazan, whose background is traditionally Jewish. The lasting core of the group is very small, and its activities attract mostly Jewish feminists who are only temporarily in Jerusalem — tourists, overseas students, academics on sabbatical.

Early on, the angry women decided to seek legal support for their cause. Rabbi Getz, drawing his authority as supervisor of the site from the 1967 Law of Protection of Holy Sites and the 1981 Rulings for Protection of Sites Held Holy by Jews, issued that same first winter a formal prohibition for women to wrap themselves in prayer shawls and read from a Torah scroll while they pray at the Western Wall. Later he even added a prohibition for women to sing aloud during the service at the Wall. On 21 March 1989 the group appealed to the Supreme Court demanding that their right to pray at the site according to their customs be upheld against the authorities (Rabbi Getz, the Ministry of Religions, the Chief Rabbis of Israel, and the police).[16] This appeal resulted in an interim order to the police to defend the praying women, as long as they abided by the instructions of Rabbi Getz.

Since contacts with Jewish feminists in the diaspora have been maintained throughout, the group's activities actually have two facets. On the one hand, these are Israeli citizens struggling for their rights (free expression, organization, ritual, religion). On the other hand, they are also Jewish women who work on importing ideas about Jewish feminism that originated in the US — empowering women's voice in the public sphere, including public religious ritual.[17] Their friends in North America organized the International Committee for Women of the Wall (ICWOW) which joined the legal struggle;[18] it should be noted that the latter is the only organization that grew out of the conference in Jerusalem in 1988, which naturally ended with many declarations concerning future action in various fields.[19] On 11 November 1989 ICWOW members gave WoW an expensive gift for which they had raised funds — a Torah scroll, which relieved WoW of the need to borrow scrolls from benevolent "radical" synagogues. ICWOW also arranged women's prayer services abroad, as publicized acts of supporting the WoW's struggle in

Israel. The American Jewish Congress, the organization behind the 1988 conference in Jerusalem, extended its support for the group, in administration and finances, so that the need to establish a separate formal organization for the group (*amutah*) did not arise until recently. Throughout all these years Haut and others have also tried to make this issue central to the activities of the WTN at large, but with only partial success: there is no consensus among WTN members about WoW, and most of them prefer to concentrate on building local prayer groups and networking with other groups for mutual support.

During these years, the Western Wall has been in the public eye for another reason: the Reform and Conservative movements have tried repeatedly to struggle for their right to hold egalitarian mixed-sex services in the site. Even their attempts to hold such services in the back of the official prayer area, and only twice a year (on Shavuot and Tishah be-Av), have ended with violent reactions of Ultra-Orthodox men, curses, spitting, flinging dirty diapers at worshipers, bullying and blows. The authorities have time and again tried to tie WoW's struggle with this one, by promoting the same solution for all appeals to hold "non-normative" prayers in the area: sending the groups to hold their services along the Wall but not in the officially designated prayer area — either in the tunnel (to the north) or in the open (to the south) — which actually means praying in areas of intense archeological interest to site visitors. These suggestions were rejected by WoW and by the Reform movement, whereas the Conservative movement did work out an agreement with (then) Government Secretary Yitzhak Herzog and moved its services to the southern area, under Robinson's Arch. At any rate, it seems that confounding the struggle of a multi-denominational women's group for single-sex prayers in the existing women's section and in accordance with Orthodox *Halakhah* with the struggle of the non-Orthodox for mixed-sex prayers in an area that cannot possibly be part of the existing division of the space, makes it even more difficult for Israelis, including official authorities, to understand WoW's agenda accurately.

The procedures of the Supreme Court have lasted over a decade already, and there seems to be no end in sight. Judge Aharon Barak rejected the appeal on 21 August 1989. On 31 December 1989, the Minister of Religions and the Minister of Justice jointly issued a ruling that accords stronger legal status to the restrictions on WoW's prayer practices that Rabbi Getz had publicized earlier. Every once in a while the Supreme Court issues decisions that tell the authorities how to find speedy solutions to the problem, but the phrasing of those decisions lends itself to different interpretations, so that the mood of WoW members, as well as their supporters and their opponents, continues to fluctuate between optimism and pessimism accordingly. On 26 January 1994, for instance, the Supreme Court decided to set up a governmental committee in charge of solving the issue. This decision was read on the one hand as Judge Elon's opinion that WoW should be directed to hold services outside of the currently designated prayer area,[20] with the aura that has always surrounded Elon's written opinions, as the only rabbi then on the Supreme Court, and the occupier of the traditionally designated slot in the court for a scholar in Jewish law. On the other hand, others have stressed the explicit statement in the decision that invites WoW to appeal again to the Court's aid if the problem is not solved in the committee's negotiations.[21] Indeed, the ensuing "work" on the issue dragged on, and WoW appealed again to the Court with the demand that it forced the State to institute acceptable prayer-service arrangements in the site.[22] The most recent scandal to date occurred following the publication of the Court's decision in this case (this time it was unanimous, and with explicit sympathy to WoW's cause) on 22 May 2000, which instructed the authorities to find a solution to the problem in no later than six months. One week later, the Knesset ratified the first reading (of the three-stage process required for passing new laws) of a proposition to inflict imprisonment of seven years on women who pray in the Western Wall area with either prayer shawls or tefillin (phylacteries), blow the shofar there (!), or read there aloud from a Torah scroll. For a short time it looked as if WoW was enjoying unprecedented public support for their courageous and just struggle against the outrageous farce promoted by the "forces of darkness," but the scoop faded fast, and when the Attorney General appealed to the Court to reconsider the case in a nine-judge forum (as opposed to the previous three-judge quorum), the Court granted the government its wish, and this time no deadline for solving this issue was specified.

To date (2002), the only explicit achievement of WoW's Supreme Court struggle is the 1989 temporary compromise. The group is allowed to hold services in the archeological garden up the stairs to the west of the Wall area; ironically, these are the ruins of a church built by the crusaders in 1127 CE, Saint Mary of the German Knights. The women start by praying *Shaharit* (the morning service) and *Hallel* (additional psalms for Rosh Hodesh) in the back of the women's section, and this includes singing aloud. Only then do they go up the stairs to the relatively secluded space off the main street, where they take out the Torah scroll as well as their prayer shawls, and some even put on their tefillin at this point. Over the years, a few bat mitzvah girls from Israel and abroad have marked the celebration in this framework. The violence directed at the women has died out — protest shouts are heard occasionally, but it seems that the "regulars," Ultra-Orthodox men and women, have gotten used to WoW's monthly presence in the early morning.

An important side effect of the publicized legal struggle is the development of the Halakhic discourse concerning WTGs, in Israel and not only in the US. The journal *Tehumin*, generally considered as reflective of Chief Rabbinate positions, naturally chose to start addressing the issue with an article by the Jewish law expert who wrote the relevant part of the defense docket for the State; the title — "Women's *Minyanim* at the Wall" and not "a women's prayer group at the Wall" — is not completely innocent, as it reflects the ongoing policy of WoW's opponents to unite its unique cause with non-Orthodox practices.[23] Only in "response to the first article" did the journal publish an article by Shmuel Shilo, the Jewish law expert who had written the relevant part of the original appeal, together with another Halakhic response by a woman, Rivkah Lubitch, who thus made history by breaking into this male rabbinical bastion, and Shochetman's "response to the responses" which left the last word with the Chief Rabbinate.[24] Other articles in Modern Orthodox journals exposed for this audience the existing Halakhic options to hold women's group prayer services under certain conditions.[25] During the 1990s this new practice spread considerably throughout Israel, but whether this is a belated impact of earlier similar developments in US Jewry or a direct result of WoW's struggle is hard to ascertain.[26]

The Usual Explanation: War of the Daughters of Light against the Sons of Darkness

A "Protestant" Struggle in a "Catholic" State

> A Group of men began screaming at us, rhythmically, cursing us, warning us, shouting asur — forbidden, pigs; and tameh — unclean. For them, the sight of women reading from the Torah was more than they could bear. I lifted my eyes from the words of the Torah for a moment to glance at them. They seemed garbed in darkness, in intolerance. I forced my eyes back to the Torah scroll, to the holy black letters suspended on the white parchment. We women assembled were like the letters of the Torah, each one individually different, yet creating meaning in our unity, surrounded by the whiteness of the ancient stones.[27]

Haut's report, quoted above, is pervaded with emotional contrast between her pure religious experience, as a prayer in communion with God in the holy site, and the dark primitivism of the "black" men across the partition. This description fits well with modern Jewish Enlightenment literature, which has documented since the eighteenth century the struggle against Jewish clericalism, in the apocalyptic genre of "the children of light in war with the children of darkness." The very use of the terms "tolerance vs. intolerance" plants the discourse well in this context.

Yet, this literature deals generally with the process of secularization — the modern, humanistic spirit of reason, facing the future and progress, clashes with the evil ghosts of institutionalized religion, as it clings to the past and violently suppresses all openings for free thought and life. Can this discourse then encompass also a clash between a new group of religious people and the ruling religious establishment? We are familiar with this dynamic in Judaism of earlier times, such as the sects that split off from Jerusalem towards the end of the Second Temple period, or the outburst of hasidism in Eastern Europe in the eighteenth century. But can we apply this model to contemporary Israel? Maybe this is what Rabbi Getz, the Western Wall Supervisor, meant in his letter to WoW on the first of Tammuz, 5749 (summer 1989):

> My dear and respected sister,
> I welcome you as you come to the Western Wall, remnant of our Temple. You are now in the holiest approachable site for our people in these times …
> I beseech you, dear sister, to help me protect the holiness of the site from desecration, God forbid, *and not to change anything in our people's tradition of many generations.*
> And I bless you with the blessing of the High Priest Eli to Hannah [the prophet Samuel's future mother]: "And may the God of Israel grant you the wish you put forward to Him."[28]

Hannah's prayer at the Shilo Tabernacle was a ritual innovation right in the religious center of that time, and Eli, the supreme religious authority then, became convinced of the appropriateness of her act only after she had insisted and begged (1 Samuel 1). Moreover, the Babylonian Talmud already mentions her prayer as the primary source of many laws that Jewish men must abide by when they pray (Tractate Brahot, 31). Rabbi Getz, then, understood at the time the revolutionary potential of WoW as a change within religion — neither easy nor welcome, albeit not impossible. Could the other actors in the arena, including WoW members, also conceptualize the issue in this way?

I think that WoW members can be characterized as "Protestant Jews," according to the distinction introduced by Akiva Ernst Simon, and not only because most of them have immigrated to Israel from the US.[29] They all belong to the minority among Israeli religious Jews who have internalized the social contract that considers religion as completely voluntary, as well as the discourse of rights and liberties that comes with it — freedoms of religious practice, expression, organization and religious pluralism. Within the conceptual framework of "Protestantism" it is possible to include the struggle of a group who claims it has more faith in God and purer religious feelings than the fossilized established "church" and its followers. Do Israelis have the appropriate cognitive map that can take in this worldview?

The responses of the Israeli media point at the difficulties involved here. The issue has been covered in the news as a violent clash between the Ultra-

Orthodox and their victims, and not enough attention was paid to the need for accurate identification of the victims. WoW has had the image of American Reform Jews, because in Israel not only the Ultra-Orthodox but also many secular Jews look upon Reform Judaism as a brand of secularism. I choose to exemplify this with a quote from an article on a totally different subject:

> The Shimshon Center is located at the eastern tip of the Hebrew Union College campus, on a hill in the western city, across from the Old City walls, David's Citadel and the Jaffa Gate.... The most prominent visual element in the Shimshon Center is the multi-purpose hall that towers about three stories above the roof of the building, proclaiming its existence from afar with provocative transparency.... Without knowing the secrets of worshiping God, certainly not according to Reform tradition, it seems that a transparent hall is not exactly the place for intimate communion of humans and their Creator, but rather a kind of loud proclamation, externalization and exhibitionism.[30]

Indeed, the hegemonic Zionist narrative creates for Israeli society a conceptual and interpretative framework founded upon processes of secularization from the Enlightenment onwards, a linear continuum with slots for all of us, from the primitive to the complex, from the early to the progressive, from the fossilized to the dynamic. This applies as a matter of course to the secularization of the public sphere: modern politics takes pride in its exit from the private sphere, in fortifying it as the realm of rights and freedoms, and in protecting it from invasions of the authorities. The transfer of religion to the private sphere is the inevitable consequence: every attempt of religious groups to compete for control in the public sphere is conceptualized as "a cultural war" at best, if not as "dangerous corrosion of the foundations of state and society." Religion is likened to an unreliable wild animal — it must be "domesticated," kept inside clearly designated borders, as limited as possible. The image is no coincidence, since this is how modernism treats "nature" in general: humans control it with the various sciences, and therefore it can only reside within culture in its interpreted, fenced in, domesticated expressions. This logic is all the more spelled out in Israel, because the task of Zionism was to turn a people defined by its religion into a people defined by its nationality as conceived in modernity — that is, to educate the Jewish masses towards a new reality.

So "provocative transparency," visibility, externalization and exhibitionism cannot go hand in hand with religious faith, which "naturally" belongs indoors and not outdoors. This assumption leads easily to the conclusion reached by many that WoW members are not sincerely motivated by the urge to worship God, but rather engage in a kind of weird provocation, a nuisance that disturbs the public peace, another outbreak of "the Jerusalem syndrome," a passing episode of anthropological value only.

Status Quo

Moreover, Israelis feel exhausted by the ongoing struggles of "the religious" for control of the public sphere, both in its geographic and in its political sense. In Simon's terminology, Israelis are familiar only with struggles of "Catholic" religion with the "Catholicism" of secular Zionism — that is, its claim to be all-embracing and universal. Much like the Thirty Years War in Europe, these religious feuds end periodically in status quo agreements that signify defeat and giving in to the enemy, always with reluctance. The arena is conceived as a split between two binary camps and not more; such a perspective has room for "Protestant religion" only as a polite, tame renter of a sublet apartment in the house of secularism, never as an assertive contestant in the public sphere.

One of those status quo agreements relates to the Western Wall Plaza in Jerusalem since 1967. The site was entrusted to the Ministry of Religions, on the assumption — based on the political reality in Israel — that this ministry would forever be in the hands of whatever religious party was included in any government's coalition. No one was particularly surprised when the Ministry of Religions soon organized the space just like an Orthodox synagogue, with a partition between men and women that leaves about two-thirds of the visible part of the wall to the men; later on, an underground section to the north, under Wilson's Arch, was added. This partition not only separates the sexes physically, it also marks the gender hierarchy accepted by Orthodoxy, between male hegemony in religious ritual (public prayer with all its signifiers) and the secondary status of the women's section (private prayer only).

Every attempt to tip the existing status quo in religious–secular relations in Israel is conceived as triggering dangerous explosives. In such circumstances it is necessary to assess the relative power that the challenging party can rally: how many seats in the Knesset? How many vital junctions in the country are threatened? How will the proposed change influence the daily lives of the secular? Admittedly, these criteria indicate that no small group, especially no small women's group, can compete successfully with the big drama-generating issues in this field: conscription of Yeshiva students, the closure of the Bar Ilan Road in Jerusalem on the Sabbath, the imprisonment of Shas Party leader Aryeh Deri.

Constitutional Revolution

During the past decade, many have thought that the decline of the collectivist discourse in Israel — socialism as well as Zionism — is twinned with the rise of the Liberal Democracy discourse of individual rights and freedoms, especially since the "constitutional revolution" led by the President of the

Supreme Court, Aharon Barak. Does this change mark improved prospects for WoW? After the Court decided in 1994 that the government should set up a committee that must solve the problem within six months, one group member, Bonna Haberman, wrote as follows:

> In the letter appointing the committee, the principles of freedom of religious practice and access to the holy site were emphasized.... We are looking for a clear affirmation of pluralism as a constitutive part of religious practice in Israel, which includes women. For Women of the Wall, the January verdict is one milestone in a long process of educating the political, judicial, religious, and social sectors, both in Israel and abroad, about women's religious and spiritual activism.[31]

Haberman integrates here two movements of European history — the Protestant revolution (tolerance to the plurality of officially recognized religious groups), and the democratic revolution (individual rights and freedoms) — and expresses her view that it is both possible and necessary to educate all Israelis and diaspora Jews to acknowledge the value of a women's group that embodies all of this at once. Was her optimism realistic?

This assessment of the situation is reflected in a change in the legal strategy of WoW. The first petition in 1989 emphasized arguments in favor of freedom of religious practice at the Wall, whereas the explicit feminism of the group was not mentioned at all.[32] The second petition in 1995, orchestrated by law professor Frances Raday, who served inter alia as the legal advisor to the Israeli Women's Network (IWN), already brought out the claim to women's equality. Several critical studies had already proved that the commitment to forbid gender discrimination, as included in the 1948 Declaration of Independence, is only a baseless myth.[33] Nonetheless, the impression during the 1990s was that Israel, or at least its judicial discourse, was finally ready to ratify at least some liberal feminist policies, that is, practices that indicate the alignment of women's status with that of men. Did this strategic change in the struggle produce any additional value?

During this second stage, WoW's activities were documented in a video which is mainly used for public relations and fundraising abroad.[34] On the one hand, the video includes the previous arguments: the Ultra-Orthodox who monopolize the Wall feel threatened by the demand to concede one hour a month for a different ritual; there is no religious freedom in Israel; the authorities portray WoW as some grotesque provocation, in an anti-Semitic style, in order to de-legitimize it. On the other hand, the video shows WoW members as they discuss sexist Halakhic practices such as men daily thanking God for not having made them women; and Raday explains that the egalitarian inclusion of women in an individualistic and pluralistic world increases the threat of WoW and therefore also the opposition to it. The meeting held in the presence of the camera is conducted in English. Could the same discourse, which sounds quite elementary in the English language, have occurred in Israel in an equally smooth manner if it had been conducted in Hebrew?

If the constitutional revolution is only as successful as the transition from the discourse of conflicting collectives to the discourse of civil rights, then it has failed so far. Israelis largely cling to the dichotomous model of reality, and tend to interpret *public* events in the terminology of "the secular vs. religious cleavage" (whereas extensive research of *private* beliefs and practices displays enormous complexities).[35] It is even possible to argue that the constitutional revolution has worsened the situation so far: it seems that the religious tend to oppose it, and classify all its supporters automatically as secular. Due to the contrast between the Israeli electoral system (universal suffrage without prior registration, a Knesset that reflects the raw citizenry with no mitigating mechanisms) and the way judges are appointed by the judiciary itself, the motion to invest the Supreme Court with constitutional properties has funneled the religious feuds in the past decade into a war between this institution and the Knesset. How well can WoW fare then if it expects the Supreme Court to settle a controversy over religious ritual?

All three judges of the second court case expressed unequivocal support of WoW's right to hold services at the Wall (2000), and this seems to confirm that the expected change has indeed happened and liberal democracy is on the rise in Israel. However, as Shmuel Berkovits points out, this change resulted directly from the new policy of "judicial activism."[36] It is an unprecedented case in Israeli legal history, where the Supreme Court stretched its authority without really substantiating the need for such a move, and insisted that the Court and not the government should settle issues of freedom to pray in a holy site. This is in sharp contrast to the Court's own earlier policy on similar issues — it used to reject petitions of Jews to hold services on the Temple Mount. And indeed, the government as well as the Knesset reacted immediately and found ways to circumvent the Court's decision.

It looks then as though WoW's supporters as well as its opponents continue to appropriate its struggle into the general discourse of cleavage between the two familiar camps. They only differ on the question on which side of the frontline these women belong. WoW's supporters prefer to contain it in the "kosher" religious camp, whereas its opponents see it as anti-religious dangerous heresy.

The inclusion of WoW within the religious camp is expressed first and foremost in the rich discussion of the issue and its corollaries in journals of religious Zionism in Israel and Modern Orthodoxy abroad. There is no parallel discussion in other Israeli publications, whereas in the US WoW's struggle is considered of relevance to Jewish and Israeli politics in general. Downsizing the issue to the religious realm, and more specifically to the Modern Orthodox realm, goes well with the traditions of secular modernism. As long as religious strife is played out in the inner court of the religious, it is tolerated, mainly because this arena has no bearing on the lives of the secular. Let the women settle the controversy with the rabbis, and/or the Ultra-Orthodox, in the Wall's very plaza, since we had conceded it long ago and they go there as they please.

Susan Sered compared three struggles of religious women in Israel who tried to enlist help from the Supreme Court to advance their public status: women's election to municipal Religious Councils, women's election to forums that elect state-official rabbis, and women's group prayer at the Wall. Her research also shows that WoW's issue was narrowed down to the religious realm. In all three cases, the women involved made a point of presenting their struggle as "rebellion" and not as "revolution," that is, as a complaint about injustice in dispensing existing procedures and not as an attempt to bring about fundamental turnover of the social and political order.[37] This finding, incidentally, is corroborated by research on Orthodox WTGs in North America, who appear to exercise the same restraint in the course of their struggle for legitimacy in their communities.[38] Sered then shows that in the first two cases this is indeed how the struggles were perceived by all, whereas in the case of WoW the religious establishment reacted fiercely to events that it perceived as an attempted revolution of the foundations of culture. By and by it transpires that this research too found that the case unfolds in the arena of religious politics, while other Israelis respond from the standpoint of onlookers from outside.

The response of the Knesset to the Supreme Court decision in 2000 indicates that the dichotomous discourse was not even questioned. When religious Members of the Knesset (MKs) were asked off the record how come they had voted in favor of imprisoning Jewish women who dared to pray according to *Halakhah*, they simply said, "No one intends to put this law into effect, the vote is meant to express our protest against Supreme Court policies in general." This, then, is still the "grand narrative." And for its sake it is even conceivable to "export" to the secular camp a group of women who hold Halakhic prayer services, as if the whole thing is only artificially resuscitated by the Supreme Court.

Summary
This discussion may explain why WoW has such a hard time rallying public support. In a society that instinctively gravitates towards the modernist dichotomy of religion and secularism around every new issue, WoW is perceived as too religious for the secular and too secular (that is, too

"Reform," or too "Protestantly Jewish") for the religious. However, this does not explain why the issue has dragged on over so many years, or the difficulty faced by Israeli society as it attempts to resolve an issue that it formally considers small and negligible so that it can cross it off its agenda. It seems that the phenomenon of WoW outgrows the limits of the present discourse and cannot be addressed within the accepted paradigm for analysis of Israeli socio-politics.

A Different Reading:
Do Women Belong in the "Founding Rock of Our Very Existence?"

While the secular enlightened discourse continued its efforts, as analyzed above, at drawing the lines around legitimate religiosity in Israel (in Ari Elon's words, "riboni" vs. rabani," that is, the sovereign vs. the rabbinical),[39] new research has been brought forward that deals critically with the symbiosis between the two. It is claimed that Jewish religion was "nationalized" by Zionism, and that this project of political co-optation is at the center of Israel's social and cultural problematics.[40] This approach goes beyond a critique of Judaism as a religion, a culture, a politics, and demands that we apply the same analytical tools to the civil religion that arose out of modernism and its political project, the Zionist nation-state. It is in this scholarly context that I want to point at a missing link connecting that critical discourse with feminist critique of Judaism, Zionism and Israel. Likewise, I want to subject to this perspective not only Judaism as a patriarchal religion and culture, but also the sexist patterns that modernism produced as it proceeded to reinterpret the sociopolitical nexus it pretended to usurp but ended up inheriting.[41] This is the real challenge that WoW presents; I think that this missing link explains the cognitive dissonance that bars us from understanding this group on the basis of the paradigm which is commonly used for examining relations of religion and state in Israel.

War and Peace
On December 1988 Israel did not only face a crisis concerning the "Who is a Jew" issue. It was the end of the first year of the first Palestinian uprising in the territories occupied for 21 years, the year a new word — Intifada — entered the Hebrew language. One member of the planning committee of the international conference in Jerusalem was Letty Pogrebin, a well-known Jewish feminist from New York and a long-time activist on behalf of peace in the Middle East. In her autobiography she devoted the last two chapters to the possible interactions of Jewish feminism and the Israeli–Palestinian conflict, the first of which deals with the feminist conference in Jerusalem. This chapter describes not only the birth of WoW. Pogrebin reports that together

with another committee member, Lilly Rivlin, she struggled to include the issue of peace in the conference agenda, but they had to settle for an academic session titled "Women, War, Peace." They found, however, support for their position in the Israeli organization "Shani" (Israeli Women against the Occupation), whereupon they jointly prepared a "post-conference conference" for Friday, 2 December 1988, under the title "Occupation or Peace: Feminist Response." That other conference ended with participants joining the weekly protest of Women in Black in a central Jerusalem street junction.[42]

Not a trace of all this can be found in WoW's "official" published record of that week.[43] The video that documents Jewish feminism of those years includes separate sequences of both demonstrations (the one at the Wall, and the one in the street junction), as if they did not happen within two days, nor took place in the same city; as if they did not grow out of the same conference.[44] After all, these are two different issues, each of them attracting different Jewish feminist women. I have a personal confession to make here: I too participated in the big conference, but when invited to join the prayer service at the Wall, I expressed my reservations. I did, however, participate in the conference on Friday as one of the panelists, and also joined the street protest it ended with.

Are these two issues really mutually exclusive? One possible explanation may be found in research on Women in Black,[45] a group with some elements resembling those of WoW. Both groups involve educated, middle-class, Ashkenazi women, "rich in personal resources" and experienced in political activity. Both groups concentrate on producing "a minimalist public event" which gets reproduced regularly and amasses momentum, thereby shaping "a symbolic bordered site" with "new interpretation of the social order," challenging political patterns and popular images.[46] Sara Helman and Tamar Rapoport stress that the effect of such a group hinges on the economical minimalism of its actions — concentrating on one thing and insisting on it for a long time — in spite of the frustration expressed by some participants who have failed in their attempts to convince others to stretch the ideological agenda further.

Susan Oren included in her research interviews with women who had reservations about joining WoW because, just like me, they had different political priorities. But mostly I find support for Helman's and Rapoport's thesis in interviews with those, as quoted by Oren, who were initially hesitant but joined WoW later. These women ended up intentionally separating their political activities on behalf of peace, which they continued elsewhere, from their activities in WoW, which they perceived to be focussing on something else. Moreover, whereas Women in Black created "a symbolic bordered site" in a previously neutral arena, WoW had even more of an interest to separate their actions from all other issues — their site had already borne a heavily symbolic baggage, which they had to lift from the public mind in order to succeed in their unique "public event":

> I still don't see myself as a Kotel [Wall] person. It strikes me that people view it as a symbol beyond the symbolism that it has, that it's a remnant. I think there's almost an element … that people worship the Wall rather than what it symbolizes in the place, which is one of the things that bothered me over the years.[47]

> I want to note that praying with WoW has changed my attitude to the Wall. In the course of the 1980s I had undergone a process of gradual alienation from this place. Coming there I had felt increasingly estranged, uncomfortable, for reasons I will not go into here, I will only say that it had to do with changes in the daily life at the Wall. Participation in WoW has "given me back" the Wall.[48]

This article is written during a continued bloody "situation" of unsettled security since October 2000. Palestinians call this second uprising "The Al-Aqsa *Intifada*," and not only because it was triggered by Ariel Sharon's entrance to the mosques' area (he was then leader of the opposition in the Knesset). Rather, the inter-religious conflict over the Temple Mount/El-Haram a-Sharif embodies the heart of the territorial dispute between the two peoples.[49] A peripheral news item concerning the joint visit by Supreme Court judges and WoW, in order to check closely on possible prayer service arrangements, disappears shortly under piling reports of another issue: stone throwing and gun shots, Muslims digging up their own archeology thereby destroying Jewish remains underneath, heated declarations on both sides about eternal holiness and *casus belli* and indivisible area control, waving flags, stamping civilian fighters (theirs) or soldiers (ours).

The Wall's status in the context of national security has unquestionably been at the center of Israeli and Jewish consciousness ever since the liberation of Jerusalem in the Six Day War, and the photograph of the overwhelmed paratroopers who reached it then, looking upwards, has since decorated every patriotic assembly held to honor the city. No wonder then that Levy Zini chose the title "We Got the Wall" (*Ha-kotel be-yadeinu*) for his documentary even in the year 2000 — this is a well-known code in Israeli discourse which has blended us into one "generational experience" since 1967. Zini filmed mostly men — praying aloud in various ways (this includes the voice of the Muezzin that travels over the loudspeakers from the mosques above), celebrating bar mitzvahs, soldiers in uniform carrying guns, policemen looking into a "suspected object," beggars. Most women appear cast into the role of onlookers, enablers of the male experience: mothers carrying refreshments for bar mitzvahs, teachers leading schoolboys to the prayer site, mothers, sisters and girlfriends watching soldiers being sworn in. They exist in the margins, hold individual silent prayers behind the partition, and watch from the sidelines an exclusively male drama. One interviewee, writer Yochi Brandeis, who was brought up Orthodox but is no longer religious, basks in her nostalgia over the impact of collective male prayer at the site. All this is mixed with a voice-over report of "the Reform WoW": they are heard singing the Rosh Hodesh additional prayers and then "Oseh Shalom," a verse from the Psalms which serves as lyrics for a popular prayer for peace, but they remain unseen. The camera focuses on the Ultra-Orthodox men yelling at them, on the policemen dragging away some of those men, with the voice-over coming on again saying "WoW left the Wall at the conclusion of a rowdy event."

Even Rabbi Getz, the site Supervisor in 1989, in the letter quoted above, did not limit his comments to matters of religious practice, but found it necessary to allude to the 1967 war, as the constitutive myth of Israeli Zionism ever since, when he wrote to WoW: "Remember that in this very generation young Israeli men shed their blood and sacrificed their youth, so that you can approach it [the Wall] safely and peacefully." Does a group of women have any chance of changing the symbolic content of such a site, all maleness and war? The problem is emphasized in the following quotation from a totally different context:

> According to the commercials … we immediately feel a strong urge to get up and act, to do bungi-jumps, to ride a horse, liberate the Wall, something like that. And we won't settle for simply liberating the Wall, we must do it in a white bikini.[50]

The liberation of the Wall in 1967 as a historical event has become, then, a metonymy for every important "act," for asserting oneself, for leaving a mark on the world at large, that is, for victory in war; it is the ultimate male "act." Pogrebin insisted on juxtaposing this aggressive militarism with direct feminist critique, but not at the Wall — whereas WoW chose the exact opposite, to produce a regular event at the very site, an event that clearly breaches the discourse that organizes and controls all occurrences there.

The Civil Religion Is Catholic

On the surface, Zini's documentary video deals with daily life at the Wall plaza, brings out the variety of simultaneous events, and the plurality of voices in the interviews. However, the subtext throughout is none other than the message of national Jewish unity as centered on the Wall. Even the few interviewees who express a mental distance from the site, interpret their attitude in the context of their personal post-nationalist, universalist politics, thereby affirming the main content of the Wall as a symbol. A decade of

WoW's activity there has not changed at all the perception of the site as observed and analyzed by Danielle Storper-Perez and Harvey Goldberg in 1984–85:

> Much goes on at the Wall which is neither the subject of ancient doctrine nor of modern administrative regulation, so that only an ethnographic approach, focusing on actual behavior, and attempting to view the Kotel as a "Total social fact," can begin to make inroads into understanding this contemporary shrine whose religious and national meanings intersect with many aspects of social life.... While the Kotel takes on a multitude of specific meanings in relationship to this medley of cultural categories, it also represents the totality of Jewish peoplehood, fragile as their interrelations may be in the flux of routine life.... There thus are expressed at this site a multitude of patterns in which pan-Jewish sentiments and identities congeal with the more particular objects of the life cycle and ritual calendar.... The very fact that the Kotel plaza, as a ritually important space, is available to everybody at all times, points to its attributes as a shrine that transcends the interpretations and claims of any specific group.... Along with the uniformity embodied in established Kotel roles and their incumbents, is an active, but partially predictable, diversity.... The heterogeneity of the Jewish people, brought together in a single space, is captured, condensed, and highlighted.... Each must admit, happily or begrudgingly, that he or she is part of a larger national whole.... The person is able to link his [sic] existence to wider identities.... All the Jewish communities and ethnic groups, all the religious tendencies — including the Lubavicher Hassidic "mitzvah tank" ... are present. Individual and collective, communal and national can be found, compounded with one another.... It is possible to view the Kotel as a physical space, suffused with history, in which the story (or stories) of contemporary Israel are condensed. A clearly circumscribed area in the midst of an eminently Middle Eastern setting, the Kotel proclaims Israel's deep roots in the past, even as its newly expanded plaza and the care with which it is guarded are evidence of the political will which created and maintains the new state. ... Official and informal pressures placed upon visitors to the Wall to act in accordance with its sanctity provide the framework for the range of mutually reinforcing religious, national, and ethnic expressions, which characterize its ambience.[51]

Storper-Perez and Goldberg complement this "social ecology" and "sacred geography" with two more aspects of the Wall which they describe extensively but do not analyze at all, they simply seem to take them for granted: the organization of the space as the only synagogue imaginable, which is

Orthodox, and the totally unproblematic place women occupy willingly in the margins of the hegemonic "stories" taking place there at all hours. The hegemony is bordered by "extremists" on the right (Jews claiming their right to hold prayer services on the Temple Mount itself) and on the left (followers of Professor Yeshayahu Leibovitch who argue that the sanctification of the Wall as a national-religious shrine is idolatrous). Zini's video, years later, repeats the same perception of the hegemony, and can only brand WoW as "Reform," a momentary dissonance.

Zali Gurevitz and Gideon Aran show that, in contrast to Eliade's theory concerning the cosmological meaning of holy sites ("axis mundi," where heaven and earth touch), Judaism has limited this perspective since antiquity, by removing holiness from concrete human lives so that it is embodied instead in the Torah scroll. Jewish holy sites then should be analyzed first and foremost from an anthropological perspective. Even the Temple was the political center of government, and only as such did it become also the center of national religious ritual.[52] The "Catholic" religion we are looking into is therefore the civil religion, above all. The meaning of the Temple substitute, the remnant of its outside Western Wall, has been constructed over the years along the same lines of nationality and civil society politics.

The Western Wall became a famous Jewish concept in the twelfth century, when the Muslims turned it into a permanent site for Jewish prayer services; they were anxiously strengthening their hold on the Temple Mount by removing both Christians and Jews to arranged ritual places away from the mosques. Suleiman the Magnificent, the sixteenth-century Sultan, officially reaffirmed the right of the Jews to pray there and instructed his court architect to design the site accordingly.

In the course of the nineteenth century, Jews started bringing with them to the prayer area chairs, tables, Torah scrolls and other ritual objects, and their awakening interest in settling in the land included attempts to purchase the place. These actions changed the attitude of the Muslims towards the Wall. They started claiming that the "El-Buraq Wall" is holy to Islam, by retroactively "moving" to it the tradition concerning the exact spot where Mohammed had tied his magical animal El-Buraq, on which he had flown at night, with the angel Gabriel, to the Haram a-Sharif. They also appealed successfully to the Sultan to limit Jewish activities at the Wall.[53]

When the land came under British rule, the Mandate charter included a commitment to ensure free access and freedom of religious practice in the holy places. The Jews lobbied with the British in order to expand their rights at the Wall, so that the site could become a real synagogue.[54] On 23 September 1928, the Eve of Yom Kippur, they placed there a folding partition (a wooden frame with curtains), for separation between men and women, while preparing for the "Kol Nidrei" service that evening. The British police commander, pressured by the Muslims, instructed the Jewish attendant to remove the partition. The next morning, when he saw that it had not been done, he ordered his men to destroy it. A fight broke out: the officer later described the screaming women who attacked his men as "agitated ladies, just like a demonstration of suffragettes." Even though during Turkish rule Jews had been allowed to bring prayer furniture on the High Holidays, this time Muslims regarded this to be a more severe act. They now considered this as an attempt at shaping the site as a synagogue in the context of Zionist efforts to establish a national home in the land of Israel under the auspices of the British Mandate. To them the incident seemed to be in line with continued attempts by Jews to purchase the Wall area from Muslims, and with the founding of "The Committee for the Wall" by Professor Joseph Klausner of the Hebrew University. The political status of the Jerusalem Mufti was on the rise, while Jabotinsky (as well as Chief Rabbi A. I. Kook) scored points in the Zionist movement: the linking of religious strife to national conflict sparked fire on both sides. What followed is better known: the feud at the Wall deteriorated into the 1929 pogrom.[55]

The British set up an investigating committee, which reinstated the status quo at the Wall: the site was recognized as holy for both religions, but as a place for prayer services for Jews only, within the limits of the 1928 White Paper. This became law in 1931, and remained the status quo until 1948, when the Jordanians conquered the Old City of Jerusalem and no longer allowed Jews to pray there.[56]

Immediately following the liberation of the city by the Israeli army in 1967, Moshe Dayan, then Minister of Defense, set up status quo arrangements for the Temple Mount that left the area of the mosques under Muslim control though accessible to members of other religions. This necessarily left the Wall area as the holiest Jewish-Israeli site, supervised by the Ministry of Religions (whereas the area to its south was entrusted to the Ministry of Education and Culture, for archeological digs and eventual tourism). A few months later, all important rabbis, Ultra-Orthodox and Zionists alike, published a Halakhic prohibition on going up to the Temple Mount, in an attempt to hold active Jewish messianism in check and avoid provoking the Muslim world into Jihad. This rallied overall support to Dayan's policy, with the exception of the relentless "Ne'emanei Har ha-Bayit" (Temple Mount Loyals), whose numbers increased in the 1990s when the Israeli government seemed to respond too meekly to increased Muslim Palestinian activity there.[57]

Immediately following the Israeli conquest in 1967, a large plaza was cleared of houses, and all was ready for the final institution of a stately Jewish-Zionist shrine in the form of an outdoors synagogue. Mass prayer services are held there (such as the large-scale priests' blessing during Pesach and Sukkot), reinforced by attributes of "national sanctity": archeological digs that leave intact only the Jewish narrative of the area, the transfer of military ceremonies to the site, inclusion of a photographed close-up with the Wall in the itinerary of visiting heads of state.

Shmuel Berkovits notes that the 1967 law (Protection of Holy Sites) that underscores the status quo at the Wall does not include the definition of the term "holy site," but only authorizes the Minister of Religions to institute rulings for its implementation, as was done for the Wall (though not for the Temple Mount) in 1981. He argues that as long as there is no statutory definition, the secular law should be read as referring by default to religion and religious law for relevant decision making.[58] In 1994, while ruling on the first WoW petition to the Supreme Court, the Deputy President of the Court, Professor Menahem Elon, stated that the prayer site at the Western Wall is "the holiest synagogue in the world of Judaism," that "the nature of the site customs should be set according to the widest common denominator of the people praying there, which is the generations-old custom," and therefore the petitioners could not be allowed to hold their services there, since they offended all of this. As he put it, "the local custom and the status quo are one and the same." Judge Levin disagreed, but the Court President Shamgar joined Elon's ruling, which left that interpretation intact,[59] until the unanimous ruling on the second petition in May 2000, which caused the Knesset to anchor Elon's 1994 reading explicitly in the language of the law, as noted above.

I have surveyed this history at length so as to substantiate my claim that the site where WoW act is not only reserved for religious ritual. Rather, the Wall epitomizes the changes that the Jewish notion of nationhood, and eventually nationality, underwent in the last millennium. At first, the people were defined by its "holy teachings" (in Rabbi Sa'adya Ga'on's words, meaning the Jewish law), tolerated as a "people of the Book" in the bosom of Islam, and therefore relegated to prayer services in a visibly marginalized site and format. Zionism, much later, translated religious traditions into the pattern of modern nationalism striving towards territorial sovereignty, which in turn encouraged the development of symbols with a highlighted territorial dimension.[60] Finally, Zionism matured into a nation-state that sanctifies its civil religion with a mix of symbols and rituals both old and new.[61] Pierre Nora supports this argument by pointing to a causal relationship between the decline of spontaneous familial and communal memory in the modern age and the complementary rise of national "lieux de mémoire" (sites of memory) that enable the weaving together of personal lives into new collective bonds.[62]

WoW's activities then are not only addressed at the religious and the Ultra-Orthodox, those who pray at the Wall, the rabbinical establishment, the religious parties. They are addressed at the hegemonic Israeli ethos — and since Israel is at the center of collective consciousness of organized Jewry abroad, it is possible to include here also the hegemonic Jewish ethos in the diaspora: as expressed even by the polemic inside the Reform movement concerning the necessity to engage in a struggle to undo the Orthodox monopoly of prayer at the Wall.[63]

A "Catholic" Civil Religion in an Ethnocratic State
Of all the terms suggested to mark this hegemonic national perception, I prefer Oren Yiftachel's "ethnocracy." He uses it to designate a regime centered on the "ethnos" (and not the "demos," the citizenry) as the main political principle, even though many democratic elements can be detected in it at the same time.[64] Israel, a modern nation-state created by the Zionist movement, is defined as a Jewish state in its Declaration of Independence. This enables the different groups included in the Jewish "ethnos" to take part in the project of Judaizing the territorial space while excluding the Palestinians. It also enables the construction of a hierarchical system of unequal resource distribution on an ethnic basis, even within the Jewish people. Yiftachel notes that ethnocracy is characterized inter alia by diffused borders: Palestinian citizens of the "demos" are only second-class members of the collective, whereas all diaspora Jews are potential Israelis (as defined by the Law of Return), and have a share in "the state of the Jewish people" (e.g., through the Jewish Agency and its rights in land ownership and settlement). This process gained force since the Six Day War, due to the discriminatory arrangement applied in the "liberated territories" — Jews settling outside of the international borderline of Israel ("the Green Line") have full membership in the collective, in contrast to their neighbors who are "conquered," and many of whom are "refugees."

The so-called dichotomous struggle between democracy and theocracy takes place then against the background of the existing social and political order, which is held in place by the ethnocratic perspective shared by most of the religious (including most of the Ultra-Orthodox) as well as most of the non-religious in Israel (the traditional and even many of the secular). Amnon Raz-Krakotzkin shows that this background is made invisible by the popular discourse concerning the breach between the religious and the secular. In this way the "enlightened secular" manage to blame the general problem of Israel on the "parochial religious." In Freudian terms, it appears like an obsession with the unimportant, coupled with the projection, or the suppression, of the main problem, which becomes a silenced, half-conscious, sanctified taboo: one ethnocratic half is perceived as "democratic" whereas the other ethnocratic half is "theocratic."[65] Elsewhere, he brings out the Jewish-Ashkenazi nature, and therefore also the colonialist and orientalist nature, of this problematic process, because it is based on exclusion, silencing and marginalizing of Palestinians as well as *Mizrahi* (Eastern) Jews.[66]

I argued above that the Western Wall epitomizes more than any other site the ethnocratic nature of our society: in every historical period, the Jewish prayer arrangements there demarcated the respective political status of the Jewish people ("Judea Captiva," "Ahal el-Dama"). Since the creation of the "national home" mechanisms under the British Mandate, following the Balfour Declaration, these prayer arrangements have reflected the status of the Zionist and Israeli ethnocracy. This may explain why Israel, a modern state, finds it so hard to separate between the religious and the political elements in the conflict over the holy sites, and consequently fails to stabilize a status quo that will pull the two parties apart — two indispensable phases of conflict management in holy sites.[67] The Israelis and the Palestinians alike melt religion and nationalism into one mold, and all inner struggles in each of those communities take place in this "melting pot."

Moreover, this analysis works well not only for the leaders' formal politics, but also for the practices of the different groups that participate in constructing the meaning of the Wall as an ethnocratic site: their attitudes to the Wall reflect in fact their respective attitudes to the State of Israel as the embodiment of Jewish ethnocracy. Some are satisfied with things as they stand, whether or not they define themselves as religious, even if they actually happen to visit the site infrequently (bar mitzvah, school trip, guests from abroad, basic training ceremony of a son). Others, mostly secular, have long lost interest in the Wall and what it stands for, so that their indifference to the place expresses their democratic, universalist, post-ethnocratic views. Groups who struggle to change the existing arrangements do so within the general assumption concerning the national role of the site, even when this role is founded in the religious act of prayer: "Ne'emanei Har ha-Bayit" want to expand Israeli sovereignty to the Temple Mount vis-à-vis the Palestinians, who reinforce their hold (in competition with the Jordanians) in order to push back the territorial limits of Israeli ethnocracy.

The ethnocratic ethos, then, diffuses the borders demarcated by the usual identity discourse, e.g. between "left" and "right": the conceptual infrastructure of these two camps unites them both as "the national camp." I choose to exemplify this border diffusion with another group that is often juxtaposed to national Zionism — the Ultra-Orthodox — as expressed by Avishai Stockhammer:

> The Western Wall has turned not only into the center of the country after the war, but also the center of the world. All feet led to it and all eyes were lifted up to it. It was not only the peak moment of spiritual catharsis in the middle of the Six Day War, when the Wall was liberated, and the tough paratroopers, the conquerors of Jerusalem, embraced it — and wept. It was a permanent phenomenon, that the secular started seeing Jews praying. It must have been the opening point of the age of *hazarah bi-tshuvah* [return to religion], which gave rise to a whole generation of "returnees," numbering by now many thousands who have integrated completely into the ranks of Ultra-Orthodox Jewry everywhere.[68]

Other researchers claim that the attitude of the Ultra-Orthodox to the State of Israel has changed over the years, from opposition and self-exclusion to active nationalism. However, Stockhammer, an Ultra-Orthodox political activist, argues that they had always seen religion and nationalism as one, and had opposed Zionism because of its Modernist view that religion is only an issue of the private sphere. This explains the devotion of the Ultra-Orthodox to the Jewish character of the public sphere in the State of Israel, in the state symbols and its calendar, in the non-religious state schools and state bureaucracies. Stockhammer adds his voice to the slogan of Israel's 50th anniversary, "together in pride, together in hope": "Indeed, in spite of all the shadows in the State, there is a lot in it to be proud of."[69] If Raz-Krakotzkin is right and the "secularization" is actually the sanctification of the state, then this may explain how the reconnecting of the Ultra-Orthodox to Zionism is enabled by the very moment when this suppressed narrative explodes to the surface, in 1967.[70] That is why Stockhammer anchors his entire social perspective in a specific historical moment, in the liberation of the Wall in the Six Day War. This event takes on eschatological dimensions, because it brings together secular Zionism, as epitomized by the weeping paratroopers captured in a poem by Haim Heffer, an icon of the 1948 war, to which Stockhammer refers in the article cited above, and the mystical vision of the Temple as the site where spirituality flows out into the world. The Ultra-Orthodox then do not participate in the post-1967 flourishing Israeli ethnocracy for instrumental reasons only, because for the first time since the destruction of the Temple their freedom of ritual practice at the Wall is finally secured by the army and the police. The embodiment of Jewish nationalism in this very site — that is, public prayer service with all its attributes — enables the sanctifiers of secular Zionism to experience transcendental union with traditional religious holiness as represented by the Ultra-Orthodox worshipers, and this union paves the way towards universal redemption.

The ethnocratic infrastructure common to so many Jews may explain why the existing status quo arrangements at the Wall are perceived by most Israelis as an authentic, sovereign expression of Jewish-Israeli nationalism, to the point that every attempt to disrupt them meets with vigorous opposition.

Women in Men's Ethnocracy

Israel is a common name among Israeli men. It is first mentioned in the Bible, when Jacob "Sarah" (fought) with God all night. Then he received the name "Israel" – "for you have fought with God" (Genesis 32). For a woman, the name is Israela. But Israela is a rare name, because our women do not fight with God...

My intention is to try and develop a dialogue on the status and roles of women in Israel, to try to unveil the myths and rituals, so that Israeli women can see and be seen without the distorting shadow of ideology and mythology. In such a dialogue Israela [a rare name for Israeli women, even though Israel is a common one for men] may succeed in recognizing her struggle. If she reaches this recognition, she will find in herself the strength to "fight," to struggle with her image, and then, at the end of the road, she will become Israeli in her own right.[71]

As Lesley Hazleton points out, the ethnocratic Israeli partnership is gendered. In spite of the deeply set rivalry between those devoted to secular Zionism and the followers of Jewish religion, in spite of their different lifestyles, they are in agreement concerning the secondary place of women in the "polis" under construction. On the one hand, the Israeli ethnocracy is tribal in essence, and therefore also patriarchal. On the other hand, just like other "modern" societies, it gave birth to new brands of sexism and machoism, in spite of the rhetoric of commitment to gender equality.[72] Women's struggle for equality in the Israeli ethnocracy is therefore double; they have to act on two parallel fronts: against the legacy of the discrimination of women in religion, as well as against the oppression, the violence and the exclusion from seats of power and so-called "neutral" resources. In contrast to the tendency to blame the inferior condition of Israeli women on religion and the religious,[73] I find it more accurate to emphasize the collaboration of both sides on this issue, as they use different but complementary practices, because there is only one camp here, the ethnocratic camp. WoW chose to take on this double political alignment, in a specific site that unites the parties participating in the production of its double meaning, religious as well as national.

Judith Baskin analyzes the separation of women from the main collective arena of rabbinical Judaism. From the many sources she quotes to support this analysis, I choose the following two quotes from the Talmud:

Rabbi Eliezer said to him [to his son]:
"May the words of Torah be burned rather than be given to women."
    Talmud Yerushalmi, Tractate Sotah, 3/4.
Rabbi Yohanan said:
"We learned to be cautious of sin from a maiden."
… For he heard of a maiden who prayed fervently, and said:
"Master of the world! You created heaven and You created hell,
You created the virtuous and the evil ones.
Let no man fall unwittingly because of me."
    Talmud Bavli, Tractate Sotah, 22a[74]

These teachings exemplify, according to Baskin, the basic Jewish perspective on the place of women in the natural Godly world order — they do not participate in Torah study, and their prayer is expected to support the male community from the outside. Breaching these norms interferes with creation itself, desecrates purity and warps the righteous. Women are therefore dangerous, and they have to be controlled by physically separating them from holiness, just as they are excluded from centers of public activity in secular patriarchal societies.

I would like to note further that there is no need to lock women up hermetically at home; it suffices to exalt their roles in the private sphere, and at the same time to limit their presence in the Temple (and in later historical periods, in the "mini-temple," the synagogue) to the periphery of "the women's auxiliary" (*ezrat nashim*). The name of this space marks not only the act of distancing women from the center, but also its subordination to men's ritual — women's spirituality is assigned to the role of "man's fitting helper" (cf. Genesis 2:18). The lack of symmetry transpires also through the daily practice that constructs the women's section as penetrable by men — they pass through if they need to — whereas the men's section is completely closed to women.

According to Baskin, the effort to reproduce on earth a social order that reflects the divine, leads to perceiving man as normal and woman as a deviation from the normal, by definition. This perspective, however, did not fade away when secular politics of religion succeeded Torah scholars and rabbis.

The production of modernism as a multifaceted project can be understood as the melting of forces into one coherent, "scientific," "rational" essence, as distinguished from various kinds of "otherness." Hence the centrality of the new meaning accorded to "male" vs. "female" as binary stereotypes applied to political structures (e.g. the nation-state),[75] and subsequently also to Zionism and the ethnocratic State of Israel. Patterns from the pre-modern past (in the case of Zionism, "the exile," "the diaspora") are portrayed as weak and effeminate, whereas the new force is male, defining itself through its release from femininity.[76] A hierarchy of oppression and colonialization arises, within which real people (women, for instance) are trapped in hegemonic concepts, in "a history of victors." This feminist analysis then shows how modernism was constructed through the subjugation of women worldwide, and further points at the cardinal role, both concrete and symbolic, assigned to women throughout the rise of modern nationalism in general and Zionism in particular. The term "chauvinism" first signified the perspective that attributes "natural" superiority to "our" people, and therefore justifies a hierarchical regime where "our" people rule over others; small wonder it was expanded later to include the perspective that attributes "natural" superiority to "our" sex, and therefore justifies the politics of ruling over "the other," or "second," sex.

Several scholars have stressed the link between the concrete societal ethos that constructs gender in all arenas and the myth that nourishes it.[77] Yvonne

Haddad and Ellison Findly, in the preface to their anthology titled *Women, Religion, and Social Change*, warn against the attempt to separate "society" from "culture" in the analysis of political change. Such compartmentalization, they claim, renders it impossible to discuss the role of women as active historical agents. Janet Bauer too argues that the usual male discourse often constructs women as passive, victimized objects who can only "react," at best, or as a symbolic category, "woman." The same point was made by Sered: "woman," unlike "women," is a cultural symbol, and just like other symbols she is perceived as an indivisible resource — it is only possible to compete by controlling her, all of her.[78]

This is how Hazleton exposes the specific Israeli narrative: "Zion" is the wife and the mother, and the sons, the pioneers, return to her so as to redeem her by "knowing" her, thereby realizing the pictorial vision of the prophets (e.g. Isaiah 62). They are thus reborn as men and heroes, liberated and strong, in contrast to their passive and effeminate fathers in exile. They return to the historical womb in order to fertilize it, and create "her" revival, which is also their own revival. Israeli women (the Jewish ones of course, the Palestinian women are completely invisible) are required to identify with this male saga, cornered into a "choice" between imitating male roles and adopting the role of "the real woman," she who dedicates herself to the ritual of fertility. Nitza Berkovitz complements this analysis, by showing how the State of Israel constructs motherhood as the preferable track for the inclusion of women (once again, the Jewish ones only) in the citizenry. Yosef Ahituv completes the picture by surveying the obsession with bodily modesty typical of religious Judaism as it deals with modernity.[79]

If Jewish manhood needs to be purified of effeminateness as it rises towards national sovereignty, then it stands to reason that grounding that sovereignty in the Wall plaza requires first and foremost the establishment of a partition that separates women and hides them from view (in 1928, and then again in 1967), thereby freeing collective Jewish manhood, not only for prayer but also for a variety of national rituals. Hazleton notes that these men gave in to tears only for a brief historical moment (and even then it was only the rank and file, not the top command), a "window of opportunity" for gender maturity that was shut immediately and left gender dichotomies intact. The liberation of the Wall became the metonymy of national homecoming, except "the united people," an ethnocracy of the religious and the secular, are all male. Even Leftists prefer fraternizing with Palestinian men to the inclusion of women, Jewish or Palestinian, in this newly found solidarity.[80]

Can Radical Religious Feminism Decolonize Jewish Nationalism?

> Given that secular feminists have not yet successfully challenged
> cultural patriarchy (the ethos and structures that support male
> advantage and control in various spheres of activity), that they are often
> no more successful in putting gender issues before communal (ethnic or
> national) ones, that they recognize the variety of women's
> circumstances may require different strategies for liberation or justice in
> different situations, and that religious communities have traditionally
> offered women some cultural/religious power at different moments in
> their life cycle — perhaps we should take a closer look at religious
> feminism. ... Perhaps religious and secular women can, at that point,
> reclaim the democratic impulse to recognize, discuss, and confront the
> common forms of patriarchy that will, most certainly, remain.[81]

The variety of WoW's activities yields different meanings in accordance with
the different discursive directions suggested in the above quotation from Janet
Bauer.

By turning to the judicial system for support, WoW joined the secular
discourse of liberal democracy, and therefore cannot escape the problems that
this strategy entails: Jewish-Ashkenazi exclusivity, and an antireligious
struggle concealed in the rituals of secular nationalism. As I noted earlier, a
"pure" model of liberal feminism would have produced a group that contents
itself with the demand to align their rights and freedoms with those of the men
praying at the Wall. Such a group would have soon pushed to the fore the
Reform and Conservative members, and their struggle would have soon
blended into the struggle of these non-Orthodox denominations, for mixed-
sex egalitarian prayers, under the leadership of male rabbis.

Other group actions point elsewhere, within the range demarcated by
Nitza Berkovitz as a differentiated track for republican (rather than liberal)
participation in the citizenry of the Israeli ethnocracy, meaning, joining the
collective by winning the right to fulfill duties of "female soldiering" and
thereby contribute to nation-building.[82] A women's group that insists on
holding prayer services as a forum representing the entire Jewish people, in the
main national site, proclaims its intention to participate actively in the
definition of the collective good.

It is worth noting that Berkovitz discusses motherhood as the alternative
track for civic participation into which women are forced by the patriarchal
state. Another study describes women (religious-Zionist girls) who are
educated by the male establishment of their social sector, through continuous,
mutually compatible experiences, towards contribution to the nation as an
extension of their future role in the familial home sphere.[83] This model of

collective female national activity can be traced in the special women's prayer service by the Wall on the 29th of Sivan 5647 (1887), marking Queen Victoria's jubilee, for "she removed the bars separating nation from nation" and was favorable to the Jews.[84] Indeed, singling women out periodically in this fashion, as a separate social category, fits Victorian politics, which excelled in refining gender hierarchies in the service of colonialist modernism.

This unique event foreshadows the history of the Wall half a century later. It reminds us that earlier already, under Ottoman rule, Ashkenazi Jewish settlers enjoyed the protection of European consulates ("the Capitulations"), thereby situating their collective identity on the side of Western Christianity, and disregarding the immediate concrete Eastern, Muslim context. Women accepted unconsciously from their men the role of demarcating the borders of the collective and its territorial politics, and with that "baggage" came the politics of colonialism and orientalism. At that point Jews had not yet succeeded in placing a real partition separating women from men at the Wall, but the separate prayer service in honor of a woman, a queen, already fits into the pattern. The modern bureaucracy of patriarchal organizations — churches and synagogues, but also political parties and the like — gives such female "orders" the title "sisterhoods," busy and faithful helpers who know their place in the hierarchy.

The oral and written rhetoric of WoW, as well as their behavior in public as recorded by the media, appear at times to fall inadvertently into either one of the two traps described above: co-optation into the religious–secular cleavage (including the struggle for legitimacy of Jewish-religious pluralism); or into the maintenance of Jewish national sovereignty in the Wall plaza ("Judaizing the space")[85] through Orthodox women's prayer uniting Israelis, diaspora Jews, even settlers, of all denominations, in the "auxiliary" of "the second sex." At this point I want to clarify my standpoint once more: I have often advised WoW to emphasize these aspects, in words and photographs, as the strategy most likely to "succeed," as long as they define "success" in terms of winning legitimacy to holding service prayers their way in this Israeli-Jewish site.

Can WoW skip these traps and emerge with another message? Consider, for instance, the hermeneutic dilemmas involved in the reading of this new prayer:

> May it be Your will, our God and God of our mothers and fathers, to bless this prayer group and all who pray within it: them, their families and all that is theirs, together with all women's prayer groups and all the women and girls of Your people Israel. Strengthen us and direct our hearts to serve You in truth, reverence and love. May our prayer be as desirable and acceptable before You as the prayers of our holy foremothers, Sarah, Rivkah, Rahel and Leah. May our song ascend to

Your Glorious Throne in holiness and purity, like the songs of Miriam the Prophet and Devorah the Judge, and may it be as a pleasant savor and sweet incense before You.

And for our sisters, all the women and girls of Your people Israel: let us merit to see their joy and hear their voices raised before You in song and praise. May no woman or girl of Your people Israel or anywhere else in the world be silenced ever again. God of Justice, let us merit justice and salvation soon, for the sanctity of Your name and the restoration of Your world, as it is written: Zion will hear and be joyful, and the daughters of Judah rejoice, over Your judgments, O God [Psalms 97:8]. And as it is written: For Zion's sake I will not be still and for Jerusalem's sake I will not be silent, until her righteousness shines forth like a great light and her salvation like a torch aflame [Isaiah 62:1].

For Torah shall go forth from Zion and the word of God from Jerusalem [Isaiah 2:3]. Amen, selah.

Rahel Jaskow, "Prayer for Women of the Wall," 2000

This text smoothly joins the tradition of the "Tekhines literature" of Jewish women in Europe as of early modern times — in Yiddish (from Holland in the West to Poland and the Ukraine in the East) and Hebrew (Italy) — in genre and style, and also in its intention to be added to the accepted male prayer book, most of which obligates women too. Chava Weissler, the best-known scholar of the Yiddish *Tekhines*, tries inter alia to identify their authors. She argues that most of them were written by men for women and for "men who are like women" (i.e. lack proper Jewish education), as a means of appropriating female fermenting literacy, and their religious motivation was to bond their personal lives with the collective whose borders are marked above all by Jewish prayer. Nonetheless, Weissler goes out of her way to recover here and there a text written by a woman. Through meticulous comparison with similar male texts she portrays the author as a Torah scholar, who masters Jewish writings of different periods, as well as the hermeneutic methodology peculiar to the genre. Weissler's research traces a portrait of a "proto-feminist" woman, wise enough to resist patriarchal bondage and seeking to empower all Jewish women through her version of the *Tekhine*, including the majority of women who did not have enough Jewish education to tell the difference between its several available versions.[86]

The above "Prayer for WoW" was surely authored by a woman, and the text testifies to her extensive Jewish education. Generally speaking, it resembles many national (and religious-Zionist) prayers, but it includes some feminist additions, more explicit than the ones recovered by Weissler in earlier materials. Jaskow skips earthly politics, the Supreme Court and the media, and addresses God directly, as the God of our foremothers and not only our forefathers, appealing to Him for justice and salvation. She rejects outright the notion of "sisterhood" as an institution set up by men for women, as a pale imitation of their male "fraternity" (known in Israel as "Re'ut," warriors' love for one another, "sanctified in blood," according to one popular 1948 song by Haim Gouri). Instead, she relies on the two-fold meaning that radical feminism endowed this term with when it appropriated and reinterpreted it. On the one hand, "sisterhood" means diachronic solidarity with women of the past, who are thus elevated out of their invisibility and marginality. On the other hand, there is the synchronic solidarity with all contemporary women, not only Jewish. Jaskow's rejection of the male "divide and rule" politics reaches its peak in the explicit protest against the violence involved in silencing women wherever they are. Her text does not seek to construct Jewish women as "equally kosher" when compared to Jewish men; rather, it situates them as leaders in all areas, in prayer and song, in family and community, in the dispensation of justice and in national redemption.

Jaskow's prayer then yields more than the previous two narratives can contain. WoW's agency as historical subjects transpires also through Helman and Rapoport's analysis of "Women in Black," when they note that their researched group does not translate political protest into the creation of an alternative to the social order it undermines.[87] WoW, by contrast, adopted from radical feminism not only the commitment to question the very epistemology that underscores "objective" perceptions of reality and to expose them as male, but also the organizational strategy for building their sample utopia right here and now. They founded a "consciousness-raising group," an originally Marxist mechanism reinterpreted by radical feminism as a viable small "community" in all its aspects.

WoW is, first of all, a new discourse community that transgresses and therefore transcends existing codes and paradigms, as exemplified for instance when one group member discusses why the group's perception of spacial categories such as "interior" and "outside" clash with existing notions. She actually points at the fact that life in the group over the years has been conducive to the development of some theoretical innovations that need to be expressed. This life includes, beyond the periodical public event at the Wall as discussed above, also regular meetings not only designed for political strategizing, but also for social purposes typical of full-scale intimate communities, sharing an exclusive calendar and life-cycle rhythm — after all, WoW deviates from the norms in these areas by designing their own rituals.[88] As Plaskow emphasizes, Judaism, unlike Western modernism, is organized around the concept of "covenant," which creates community and people as collectives wherein individual identities are incessantly created and recreated, interpreted and reinterpreted. Life in such a context helps in fighting off the pressures towards reification and essentialization of the individual.[89] This understanding of Judaism goes well with feminist theories concerning the interaction between individuals and communities, notes Plaskow; in other words, when WoW combines Judaism and feminism, they constitute their group as a concrete preview of alternative peoplehood. Theirs is also a religious community, and as such it embodies a paradigm breach in the history of Judaism, with their innovations in the study of canonized texts and in ritual,[90] and in this sense WoW follows precedents in ideological pioneering such as the hasidic group (*edah* or *havurah*) or the kibbutz.

Above all, WoW is a political community: in Berkovitz's terminology, they constitute the republican meaning of their civic activity. They reject the "choice" between participating in the collective as either "male-soldiers" or "female-mothers," and present instead an androgynous model — praying with some explicitly male ingredients such as the prayer shawl and the Torah scroll, but within an overall design that is clearly feminine. Hazleton highlights the contrast between feminism, adopted by few Israeli women, and femininity, an identity preferred by most of them; I propose that WoW proves, as emphasized by Bauer, that a feminist group can empower women by empowering womanhood. Plaskow too writes along these lines: feminism that arises when women choose consciously their group difference as identity, can lead to real equality, better than liberal feminism, that makes group difference invisible in order to open the way for equal opportunity but has no power to prevent gender blindness from serving as cover-up for gender discrimination.[91]

It is in these practices of WoW that I see the revolutionary potential of the group to change not only existing religious patterns but also "secular"-national patterns of Israeli ethnocracy. Perhaps the very impression of political innocence they leave is crucial in enabling them to produce an event of resistance that undermines the social order, to shape an anarchistic project that cannot be fully interpreted within existing narratives. Otherwise put, in Raz-Krakotzkin's terminology: WoW imports radical feminism to Israel from the exilic diaspora, in order to use it as an Archimedal point for their critique on Israel. Radical feminism is their tool for demarcating a different "horizon" than the one drawn by colonialist Zionism. And the moral validity of this "horizon" is universal, an attribute it owes, paradoxically, to the particularism of the conscientious cultural identity of the people who produce it, as Jews and as women.

Finale: A Decolonized People Is a Feminist People

Early on in the affair discussed in this article, in 1990, the "high priestess" of radical Jewish feminism, philosopher and theologian Judith Plaskow, published a short piece that expressed her reservations about WoW. At the time she saw their struggle as limited to the liberal claim to women's equal rights and freedoms, whereas she was already beyond that point in feminist theory. That same year she also published her most important book, *Standing Again at Sinai*, where she expounded her critique of the Jewish world, women and men, phrased succinctly in her short article: "To name the real issue as that of the power to define what Judaism is and will become.... [To move] far beyond the language of rights to the language of transformation."[92]

By 1999, in the title of another article already cited, Plaskow already worded the goal of this national transformation as "A Feminist People of Israel." The new cultural politics that she preaches there resembles the "horizon" marked by Raz-Krakotzkin; whereas he directs it explicitly at Zionism and the State of Israel, she deals with the Jewish people wherever they live. Since this 1999 article does not mention WoW at all, I suggest that this study is an attempt to respond to her complaint in the 1990 article, with the tools of her own thought.

The story of WoW brings together a variety of themes in a bordered-in, focused site. It is a story about women in a men's world, about female Jews in Israel, about the alienation of newcomers among veterans. It is a story about Jerusalem as the epitome of the Israeli–Palestinian as well as the inter-religious conflict. It is also about religion in a regime that does not separate it from state matters, about dangerous tensions between lawmakers and judges, and about tradition and creativity. Last but not least, it is a story about violence and hatred but also about song and prayer. The aggregation of all these materials in one affair turns it into an easily excitable cord of exposed nerves that are connected to all members of the body, both national ("ethnos") and civic ("demos").

Looking at the issue as a religious controversy, in a society perceived as torn between the religious and the secular, is too narrow. It is a perspective that fails to explain the resilience of this affair to proposed solutions over too many years, nor the passion it is met with. The most important impediment of this perspective is its inability to provide a satisfactory analysis of the involved social segments as they align themselves around WoW. By contrast, applying the lenses of "ethnocracy" sheds more light, not only on this particular nervous cord, but also on the entire "body" of Israel. This explanation combines the analysis of Israeli culture from the perspective of radical feminism with other critical theories that study it at this time. And this combination is necessary, because even when women bring about substantial social change, they may remain invisible, while revolutionary men get all the credit.[93] Or, in other words:

> This intricate waltz of religion and social change ... is adding a seldom-asked question: What has been the role of women during this process? The question is important, for women are the great "sleepers" of history.

Often as much ignored by the religious and political establishments of their own times as they have been by modern Western historians, women have often provided the unpredicted balance of support that determines whether a new direction "takes."[94]

NOTES

* The original Hebrew version of this essay was written for the Forum for Research of Non-Secular Perspective of Israeli Society of the Van Leer Institute, Jerusalem. The author wishes to thank them for their support.

1   "Kol kvodah" (All Her Honour), *Moznaim*, Vol. 73, No. 11 (Summer 2000), p. 51.
2   Thomas S. Kuhn, *The Structure of Scientific Revolutions*, 2nd enlarged ed. (Chicago, 1970).
3   Leah Shakdiel, "Amdah na'arah mul ha-kotel, ve-gurshah" (A Girl Was Standing at the Wall and Got Chased Away), *Hadashot*, 27 April 1989.
4   Martha Ackelsberg, "Introduction," in Liz Koltun (ed.), *The Jewish Woman: An Anthology*, *Response*, Vol. 18 (Summer 1973), pp. 7–11.
5   Rivka Haut, "Women's Prayer Groups and the Orthodox Synagogue," in Susan Grossman and Rivka Haut (eds.), *Daughters of the King: Women and the Synagogue* (Philadelphia, 1992), pp. 135–58.
6   Deborah Weissman, "'Et la'asot la-shem — haferu minhageihem' (al ma'amad ha-ishah be-kehilat Yedidyah)" ("It's Time to Do for God — Let's Disrupt Their Customs" [On Women's Status in Yedidya Congregation], *Amudim* (Journal of the Religious Kibbutz Movement) (Fall 1999), pp. 23–5.
7   Pnina Peli, "Celebrating Simhat Torah in Jerusalem," in Grossman and Haut (eds.), *Daughters of the King*, pp. 271–3.
8   For the best known among them see Avraham Weiss, *Women at Prayer: A Halakhic Analysis of Women's Prayer Groups* (New York, 1990).
9   Blu Greenberg, "Judaism and Feminism," in Elizabeth Koltun (ed.), *The Jewish Woman: New Perspectives* (New York, 1976), pp. 179–92.
10 Rivka Haut, "The Presence of Women," in Grossman and Haut (eds.), *Daughters of the King*, pp. 274–8.
11 See Haviva Ner-David, "Israel: Building," in idem, *Life on the Fringes: A Feminist Journey toward Traditional Rabbinic Ordination* (Needham, 2000), pp. 226–40.
12 Francine Zuckerman, *Half the Kingdom*, documentary video, 60 minutes (1990).
13 Susan Lynn Oren, "Claiming Their Inheritance: The Emergence of Religious Activism among Israeli Women" (Ordination thesis, Hebrew Union College, 1992), Chap. 2, pp. 89–135.
14 Ronit Kampf, "Ha-hipus ahar ha-beki'im: Ha-interaktziyah bein kvutzot meha'ah shel nashim levein ha-itonut ha-yisre'elit" (Seeking Breakthrough in the Wall: Interaction of Women's Protest Groups and Israeli News Coverage), *Patu'ah*, No. 3 (March 1996), pp. 4–23.
15 Susan Starr Sered, "Women and Religious Change in Israel: Rebellion or Revolution," *Sociology of Religion*, Vol. 58, No. 1 (1997), pp. 1–24.
16 *Anat Hoffman et al. vs. the Supervisor of the Western Wall et al.*, Supreme Court Case no. 257/89.
17 Ner-David, "Israel: Building."
18 *Susan Alter et al. vs. Minister of Religions, et al.*, Supreme Court Case no. 2410/90.
19 Letty Cottin Pogrebin, *Deborah, Golda, and Me: Being Female and Jewish in America* (New York, 1991), p. 326.
20 Shmuel Berkovits, "Ha-ma'amad shel har ha-bayit veha-kotel ha-ma'aravi ba-mishpat ha-yisre'eli" (The Status of the Temple Mount and of the Western Wall in Israeli Law), in Yitzhak

Reiter (ed.), *Ribonut ha-el veha-adam: Kedushah u-merkaziyut polit be-har ha-bayit* (Godly and Human Sovereignty: Holiness and Political Centrality of the Temple Mount) (Jerusalem, 2001), pp. 183–240.

21 Bonna Devora Haberman, "Nashot [sic] HaKotel: Women in Jerusalem Celebrate Rosh Chodesh," in Susan Berrin and Jason Aronson (eds.), *Celebrating the New Moon: A Rosh Chodesh Anthology* (Northvale, NJ, 1996), pp. 66–77.

22 *Anat Hoffman et al. vs. Director General of the Prime Minister's Office*, Supreme Court Case no. 3358/95.

23 Eliav Schochetman, "Minyanei nashim ba-kotel" (Women's Minyanim at the Wall) [on Supreme Court Cases no. 257/89 and 2410/90], *Tehumin*, No. 15 (1995), pp. 161–84.

24 Shmuel Shilo, "Tfilat nashim be-tzavta be-rahvat ha-kotel" (Women Praying Together at the Wall's Plaza), *Tehumin*, No. 17 (1997), pp. 160–64; Rivkah Lubitch, "Al tfilat nashim be-tzavta" (On Women Praying Together), ibid., pp. 165–7; Eliav Schochteman, "Od le-she'elat minyanei nashim" (More on Women's Minyanim), ibid., 168–74.

25 Ohad Oppenheimer, "Kri'at nashim ba-torah" (Women Reading from the Torah), *Me-Aliyot* (journal of Birkat Moshe Yeshivah in Ma'aleh Adumim), No. 19 (1997), pp. 168–92; Aryeh A. Frimer and Dov I. Frimer, "Women's Prayer Services: Theory and Practice," *Tradition*, Vol. 32, No. 2 (1998), pp. 5–118.

26 Dinah Safrai, "Minhag hadash ba la-kvutzah" (New Custom in Our Kibbutz), *Amudim* (Fall 1995), pp. 46–7; Tamar El'or, "Leah's Tallit," and "Is It a Feminist Revolution?" in idem, *Next Year I Will Know More: Literacy and Identity among Young Orthodox Women in Israel* (Detroit, 2002); Bambi Sheleg, "Mitzvah sheha-zman gramah: Bitti tikra ba-Torah" (A Time-Bound Mitzvah: My Daughter Will Read from a Torah Scroll), *Nekudah*, No. 222 (1999), pp. 36–41, and responses in ibid. and no. 224; Merav Mazeh, "Feminism: From Theory to Action or the Other Way Round: The Women's Prayer Group of Afikim Ba-Negev Congregation in Yeruham" (unpublished seminar paper, Hebrew University of Jerusalem, 2001) (in Hebrew).

27 Haut, "The Presence of Women," p. 276.

28 Letter appended to Supreme Court Case 257/89, *Hoffman et al vs. the Supervisor et al.* (emphasis in the original).

29 Akira Ernst Simon, "Ha'im od yehudim anahnu?" (Are We Still Jews?) [1952], in *Mivhar kitvei Akibah Ernst Simon* (Selected Writings of Akira Ernst Simon) (Tel Aviv, 1982), pp. 9–46.

30 Esther Zandberg, "Disneyland reformi" (A Reform Disneyland), *Ha'aretz*, 2 November 2000.

31 Haberman, "Nashot HaKotel," p. 75.

32 Sered, "Women and Religious Change."

33 For example, Barbara Swirski and Marilyn P. Safir (eds.), *Calling the Equality Bluff: Women in Israel* (New York, 1991).

34 Faye Lederman, *Women of the Wall* (1999), documentary video, 40 min.

35 Shlomit Levy, Hannah Levinson and Elihu Katz, *Emunot, shmirat mitzvot ve-yahasim hevratiim bekerev ha-yehudim be-Yisrael* (Beliefs, Religious Observance and Social Relations among Jews in Israel) (Jerusalem, 1993); and idem, *Yehudim yisre'elim: Dyukan: Emunot, shmirat masoret ve-arakhim shel yehudim be-Yisrael 2000* (Portrait of Israeli Jews: Beliefs, Traditional Observance and Values of Jews of Israel) (Jerusalem, 2002).

36 Berkovits, "Ha-ma'amad shel har ha-bayit," pp. 202–3.

37 Sered, "Women and Religious Change."

38 Ailen Cohen Nusbacher, "Efforts at Change in a Traditional Denomination: The Case of Orthodox Women's Prayer Groups," *Nashim*, Vol. 1, No. 2 (1998–99), pp. 95–113.

39 Ari Elon, "Mah le-ma'lah mah le-matah? Rak ani ani ve-atah (midrash riboni)" (What's Up, What's Down? Only I, I and You: A Sovereign Midrash), in Yehoshua Rash (ed.), *Kazeh re'eh ve-hadesh: Ha-yehudi ha-hofshi u-morashto* (Observe and Innovate: Free Jews and Their Legacy) (Tel Aviv, 1986).

40 Charles S. Liebman and Eliezer Don Yehiya, *Civil Religion in Israel: Traditional Judaism and the Political Culture in the Jewish State* (Berkeley, 1983); and Yitzhak Reiter, introduction to idem (ed.), *Ribonut ha-el*, pp. 5–20.

41 Amnon Raz-Krakotzkin, "Galut betokh ribonut: Le-vikoret 'shlilat ha-galut' ba-tarbut ha-

yisraelit" (Exile within Sovereignty: A Critique of the Concept 'Negation of Exile' in Israeli Culture), *Teoriyah u-Vikoret*, No. 4 (1993), pp. 23–53, and No. 5 (1994), pp. 114–32; idem, "National Colonial Theory," *Tikkun*, Vol. 14, No. 3 (April 1999), pp. 11–16; and idem, "Moreshet Rabin: Al hiloniyut, le'umiyut ve-orientalizm" (Rabin's Legacy: On Secularism, Nationalism and Orientalism), in Lev Greenberg (ed.), *Zikaron be-mahloket: Mitos, le'umiyut ve-demokratiyah* (Controversial Memory: Myth, Nationalism and Democracy) (Beer Sheva, 2000), pp. 89–107.

42   Pogrebin, *Deborah, Golda and Me.*

43   Haut, "The Presence of Women."

44   Zuckerman, *Half the Kingdom.*

45   Sara Hellman and Tamar Rapaport, "'Eleh nashim ashkenaziyot, levad, zonot shel aravim, lo ma'aminot be-elohim, velo-ohavot et Eretz Yisrael': Nashim be-shahor ve-itgur ha-seder ha-hevrati" ('These are Ashkenazi Women, Alone, Whores for Arabs, Don't Believe in God, and Don't Love the Land of Israel': Women in Black and Challenging the Social Order), *Teoriyah u-Vikoret*, No. 10 (1997), pp. 175–92.

46   Don Handelman, *Models and Mirrors: Towards an Anthropology of Public Events* (Cambridge, 1990).

47   Fagie Fein quoted in Oren, "Claiming Their Inheritance," p. 107.

48   Danielle Bernstein, "Neshot ha-kotel ve-kvutzot tfilah aherot" (Women of the Wall and Other Women's Prayer Groups), in Margalit Shilo (ed.), *Lihiyot ishah yehudiyah* (To Be a Jewish Woman) (Jerusalem, 2001), p. 190.

49   Tom Segev, *One Palestine, Complete: Jews and Arabs under the British Mandate* (London, 2000); Yifrah Zilberman, "Ha-imut shel misgad/mikdash be-Yerushalayim uve-Ayodhya" (Confrontation over Mosque/Temple in Jerusalem and in Ayodhya), in Reiter (ed.), *Ribonut ha-el*, pp. 241–68.

50   Danah Spector, "Pgishat mahzor" (Periodical Reunion) (the 70th anniversary of the tampon), *Yediot Aharonot*, 22 June 2001.

51   Danielle Storper-Perez and Harvey Goldberg, "The Kotel: Towards an Ethnographic Portrait," *Religion*, Vol. 24, No. 4 (1994), pp. 309–34.

52   Zali Gurevitz and Gideon Aran, "Never in Place: Eliade and Judaic Sacred Space," *Archives de Sciences Sociales des Religions*, Vol. 87 (July–September 1994), pp. 135–52.

53   Berkovits, "Ha-ma'amad shel har ha-bayit."

54   Reiter, "Introduction" to idem (ed.), *Ribonut ha-el.*

55   Segev, *One Palestine, Complete.*

56   Berkovits, "Ha-ma'amad shel har ha-bayit."

57   Amnon Ramon, "Me'ever la'kotel: Ha-yahas lek-har ha-bayit mi-tzad medinat Yisrael veha-tzibor ha-yehudi le-gvanav (1967–1999)" (Beyond the Wall: Attitudes of the State of Israel and Various Jewish Social Sectors towards the Temple Mount, 1967–1999), in Reiter (ed.), *Ribonut ha-el*, pp. 113–42.

58   Berkovits, "Ha-ma'amad shel har ha-bayit," pp. 184–5.

59   Ibid., pp. 195, 225.

60   Tsili Dolev-Gandelman, "The Symbolic Inscription of Zionist Ideology in the Space of Eretz Yisrael: Why the Native Israeli Is Called 'Tsabar'," in Harvey E. Goldberg (ed.), *Judaism Viewed from Within and from Without* (New York, 1987), pp. 257–84.

61   Liebman and Don-Yehiya, *Civil Religion in Israel*, esp. pp. 158–63; Maoz Azaryahu, *Pulhanei ha-medinah: Hagigot ha-atzma'ut ve-hantzahat ha-noflim, 1948–1956* (Rituals of the State: Independence Day Celebrations and Commemoration of the Fallen, 1948–1956) (Sede Boker, 1995).

62   Quoted in Storper-Perez and Goldberg, "The Kotel," pp. 311, 315, 325.

63   Yehoram Mazor, "Ha'im hashuv lehitpalel davka ba-kotel ha-ma'aravi?" (Is It Important to Pray at the Western Wall?), *B.T.L.M* (newsletter of the Reform Movement in Israel), No. 1 (July 1999), p. 6; Uri Reggev, "Ha'im la-masoret bat me'ot shanim bah nehrat ha-kotel ha-ma'aravi ba-toda'at ha-umah ein kol mashma'ut avorenu betokh klal Yisrael?" (Do We Find Meaningless, as Jews among Jews, the Centuries-Old Tradition that Inscribed the Western Wall in the Nation's Consciousness?), ibid., p. 7.

64 Oren Yiftachel, "Israeli Society and Jewish-Palestinian Reconciliation: 'Ethnocracy' and Its Territorial Contradictions," *Middle East Journal*, Vol. 51, No. 4 (1997), pp. 505–19.
65 Raz-Krakotzkin, "Galut betokh ribonut."
66 Raz-Krakotzkin, "National Colonial Theory," and "Moreshet Rabin."
67 Zilberman, "Ha-imut al misgad/mikdash."
68 Avishai Stockhammer, "Medinat Yisrael be-yovlah ve-yahasei haredim–hilonim mi-nekudat mabat haredi: Hatzavat ari'ah le-vinyanah shel hekerut hadadit ha-hiyunit kol kakh" (Israel at 50 and Relations between the Secular and the Orthodox from an Ultra-Orthodox Perspective: One Building Block towards Vital Mutual Acquaintance), *Alpayim*, No. 16 (1998), p 226.
69 Ibid., p. 232.
70 See Raz-Krakotzkin, "Moreshet Rabin."
71 Lesley Hazleton, *Israeli Women: The Reality behind the Myth* (New York, 1977), pp. 9–10.
72 Nitza Berkovitz, "Eshet hayil mi yimtza? Nashim ve-ezrahut be-Yisrael" (A Woman of Valor, Who Will Find? Women and Citizenship in Israel), *Sotziologiyah yisre'elit*, Vol. 2, No. 1 (1999), pp. 277–317.
73 See, among others, Shulamit Aloni, *Nashim ke-vnei adam* (Women as People) (Jerusalem, 1976); Philippa Strum, "Women and the Politics of Religion in Israel," *Human Rights Quarterly*, Vol. 11, No. 4 (1989), pp. 483–503.
74 Judith Baskin, "The Separation of Women in Rabbinic Judaism," in Yvonne Yazbeck Haddad and Ellison Banks Findly (eds.), *Women, Religion and Social Change* (New York, 1985), pp. 3–18.
75 See Michel Foucault, *Histoire de la sexualité*, Vol. 1, *La Volonté de savoir* (Paris, 1976); Nira Yuval-Davis, *Gender and Nation* (London, 1997).
76 Raz-Krakotzkin, "Galut betokh ribonut," *Teoriyah u-Vikoret*, No. 4 (1993), p. 41.
77 Hazleton, *Israeli Women*, especially Chap. 4, "Zionism and Manhood"; Berkovitz, "Eshet hayil"; Yosef Ahituv, "Tzni'ut bein mitos le-etos" (Modesty between Myth and Ethos), in Nahem Ilan (ed.), *Ayin tovah: Du-si'ah u-fulmus be-tarbut Yisrael* (Ayin Tovah: Dialogue and Polemics in Jewish Culture): anthology in honor of Tova Ilan (Tel Aviv, 1999), pp. 224–63.
78 Haddad and Findly (eds.), *Women, Religion, and Social Change*, p. xii; Janet Bauer, "Conclusion: The Mixed Blessings of Women's Fundamentalism, Democratic Impulses in a Patriarchal World," in Judy Brink and Joan Mencher (eds.), *Mixed Blessings: Gender and Religious Fundamentalism Cross Culturally* (New York, 1997), pp. 222–3; Sered, "Women and Religious Change," pp. 2–3.
79 Hazleton, *Israeli Women*; Berkovitz, "Eshet hayil"; Ahituv, "Tzni'ut."
80 Hazleton, *Israeli Women*, pp. 85, 46, 158–9.
81 Bauer, "Conclusion," pp. 243–4.
82 Berkovitz, "Eshet hayil."
83 Tamar Rapoport, Anat Penso and Yoni Garb, "Contribution to the Collective by Religious-Zionist Adolescent Girls," *British Journal of Sociology and Education*, Vol. 15, No. 3 (1994), pp. 375–88.
84 Pinhas Grayevsky (Ben-Tzvi), *Bnot Tziyon ve-Yerushalayim* (Daughters of Zion and Jerusalem) (Jerusalem, 2001), p. 180 (reissue of ten booklets from 1929 and 1932).
85 Yiftachel, "Israeli Society and Jewish-Palestinian Reconciliation."
86 Chava Weissler, *Voices of the Matriarchs: Listening to the Prayers of Early Modern Jewish Women* (Boston, 1998).
87 Helman and Rapoport, "Hen nashim ashkenaziyot."
88 Bernstein, "Women of the Wall."
89 Judy Plaskow, "Transforming the Nature of Community: Toward a Feminist People of Israel," in Alice Bach (ed.), *Women in the Hebrew Bible* (New York, 1999), pp. 403–18.
90 Bauer, "Conclusion."
91 Hazleton, *Israeli Women*; Bauer, "Conclusion"; Plaskow, "Transforming the Nature of Community."
92 Judy Plaskow, "Up Against the Wall," *Tikkun*, Vol. 5, No. 4 (July–August 1990), pp. 25–6.
93 Bauer, "Conclusion," p. 235.
94 Nancy Falk, in Haddad and Findly (eds.), *Women, Religion, and Social Change*, p. xv.

"Gone to Soldiers":
Feminism and the Military in Israel*

Orly Lubin

In the last decade, more and more young women have been trying to get into combat units when drafted to their obligatory term of duty with the Israel Defense Forces (IDF). In 2000 the Israeli parliament passed an amendment to the Law of Military Service, which stipulated women's right to equal choice of army professions. The more persistent of the drafted women usually became trainers of fighters in several facilities and different professions; several women even became pilot candidates (so far, only one has completed the entire training cycle for fighter pilots). This tendency has become a major issue of debate among feminists: should feminists struggle for the implementation of equal rights in the army in the form of the inclusion of women in exactly the same roles and functions of men, or is feminism about dismantling all modes of violence, the army included? Should women representatives in the parliament fight for the right of women to "be all that they can be," fighters included, or would such a struggle send the wrong message, harm the feminist goal, and finally play into the hands of those who try to satisfy women's demands at the minimal cost?

Suspicious as we all are when told that something is being done solely to promote our equality in society, I would like to turn the tables and ask the opposite question: not "do we need to be in the army," but "what does the army need *us* for?" What needs do we *really* serve, other than the (redundant) increase in labor force or the (false) appearance of equal participation in performing national duties?

Being a woman soldier, or at least having the option to become a soldier, gains women entrance into the modern nation's metanarrative and its cultural manifestations as equal, active members. On the other hand, entering the collective, that is, consigning oneself to "what it means to be a woman in this place, on this territory" means paying the price of serving the collective's needs, usually by following the models of looks, behavior and womanhood provided by these cultural manifestations. In the case of Israeli women at large, and women soldiers in particular, that would mean serving the needs of the collective's army by following the original model of the women of the Palmah, the voluntary fighting forces prior to the establishment of the State of Israel and the IDF. This study will take a close look at representations of several Palmah women and of other women whose identity and womanhood correspond to theirs, are linked to it or are derivative of it. The kind of womanhood, and the kind of national participation, offered by the prominent representations of Palmah women achieved a forceful presence in and profound impact on the understanding of "what it means to be an Israeli woman": always a soldier, and therefore part of the Israeli militaristic society, but always also providing the necessary repressions and veiling of the violence needed for the perpetuation of this militarism, in its civil form and especially in its materialization within the army.

The Ritual

"Going to the army" consists of a set of rituals: some communal, such as arguing with your peers and with army representatives about where the best place to serve is, some both collective and individual, such as deciding whether to refuse to serve on pacifist, emotional or ideological grounds, and some familial, culminating in the family trip to the enlisting point. All involve the woman soldier, as well: she, too, is accompanied to the army base; she, too, can also refuse to serve, though in her case both the decision and the process are much less complex and complicated; and she can decide to try and "improve" her term of duty by applying to serve in certain preferred units.

But by and large, the "going to the army" rituals are male-centered. At their core is the construction of male fraternity, enacted both among peers and within the family, between father and son. Father and son are a close unit within the family: they share the threat of fighting in a war, of which the women of the family are exempted. Nevertheless, they cannot disconnect their male unity from the family: the family is needed exactly because of that threat, the threat of being killed, or wounded.

Going to the army is, by definition, implicitly accepting the possibility of being killed. If you're lucky, you'll survive; but by the very act of joining one is, in effect, walking towards death. And it is here, at the juncture of life and death, at the moment of being called upon to choose death, that the woman is needed. She is there, part of the final rituals before the actual act of being drafted: the larger family circle getting together the day before; the family car driving to the army base; the crying mother and lover, saying goodbye. Her presence as mother represents and reminds of that which is broken at this very moment: the familial chain; but as the lover she is also the promise of its possible continuation. He who goes to die, who is about to lose his place in the world as a link in a continuous line of family ties, can be encouraged to do so only when there is a promise, visible to his eye in the figure of "his" woman, that it will not be lost. And so at one and the same time the woman represents the promise of not dying, the promise of familial continuation represented by the mother-woman; and the justification (and aim) of dying, that is, the conquest and preservation of territory for the (national) family imaged through the (imagined) conquest of the female body of the woman-lover.

Left behind, her womb symbolically emptied of her son-soldier and filled with her lover-soldier, the woman becomes the axis of the ritual taking place every day, every minute of the army service: the ritual of replacing the narrative of battle and death, of violence and wounds, with a narrative of continuity, of family tranquillity, of stitching the wounds of the torn body and of the torn-apart family, of returning home, and of desire. The narrative of desire, then, and the narrative of constituting a family which is its supposed culmination, are subservient to the military narrative, to the narrative of conquest, thus both reflecting and maintaining it.

A Chain of Narratives

The military narrative, which is inherently a narrative of death, is replaced, then, not only by sets of rituals which recast it by creating narratives of friendship, loyalty, mutual reliance, fraternity and heroism, but by an additional narrative — the narrative of desire. These narratives and the sets of rituals they produce have to include the woman's presence in order to "soften," socialize and accommodate the threat of dying. Thus, the set of rituals of heroism or of fraternity, for example, may include women as spectators; and the inclusion of women in the rituals pertaining to the heroic dead (the "living dead") involves their role as commemorators and carriers of legacy.[1]

In replacing the narrative of death (and the preparations for death through the life of the fraternity), the narrative of desire places the body above rather than below (ground), displaces violence (from the battlefield to the battle between the sexes, thus metaphorizing and depoliticizing violence altogether), and mutes the threat of death, of being wounded, of pain, which the violence inherent in the military narrative carries with it.

But the narrative of desire also carries with it a threat, the threat desire always poses to culture: the threat of the untamed, uncontrolled, that which can burst out at any given moment without submitting itself to the norms and dictates of cultural and social proper order. Thus, stories of desire almost never make their way into women's stories of their life, hence making their life appear orderly and normative. The story of sex life in the Palmah, or the lack thereof, is revealed as part of the unequal life of women in the Palmah as told by Netiva Ben-Yehuda in her fictional autobiographies.[2] Interestingly, desire appears constantly in one autobiography written by a woman about the era — Geula Cohen's *Underground Memoirs*. These memories are the story of an underground fighter who belongs to a peripheral group fighting the British Mandate in its own way, disobeying the dictates of the formal, hegemonic leadership of the Jewish community of the times. Cohen's autobiographical rhetoric, entirely different from the usual rhetoric to be found in women's autobiographies in general and of this era especially, is extremely focused on the body. She describes in detail bodily reactions ("That pounding of the heart, which hit me for the first time when I stood there in front of Gera [her radio instructor and commander] and would hit me twice a week in front of the transmission microphone..."; "Both hands raised upwards and my body is severed from them by dislocation and is severed from the ground underneath it as well. Two hands raised in the evening dusk up a mountain amongst mountains and the hands are mine, but I gaze at them as strangers...");[3] and she describes bodily contact, for example with a woman warden as she tries to escape from prison:

> I bend down on her to tie, pull the rope to her chest and attempt to bind — but horror! There is nothing, there is no one, there is no body to tie, there is nothing to bind: underneath me there is only a boiling twitching lump of soft and liquid meat over dry and stiff bones, which run wild and hit and cut all over the place. And before I know what's what — this boiling lump underneath me thickens with muscles and jumps forth and slides to me with mighty force and is already in front of me and is already on me, is already on top of me, and I am already underneath it, and a fisted bony hand ringing a heavy iron bunch [of keys] strikes and gets stuck in my chest....[4]

The entire book is the story of emotional, bodily reactions; of the body in action, the body in reaction to events. And these descriptions are almost always layered with passion: political passion, military passion, patriotic passion — but always also with the nuance of sexual passion. When she reads the first bulletin issued by the political dissident group Lehi (Lohamei Herut Yisrael, Fighters for the Freedom of Israel), Cohen reacts:

> The concepts — homeland, freedom, war, enemy — old acquaintances of mine, were now baptised for the first time in their lives and I tasted in them the taste of the Beginning. My ears were full with groans-cries arising both within me and outside of me at one and the same time: yes... more... good... that is it....[5]

Yet it is only in the margins of the political sphere and the social sphere that such blunt descriptions of body, bodies, desire and emotions translated into passionate bodily reactions can be written. And in their bluntness, they expose the danger they contain: the danger of loss of direction, leading to abandoning the main road, the danger of moving to the margins, desire's site of existence. The fear of losing the way, that is, the normative, accepted social route, results in repression of desire, which returns and erupts in the writings of those who are already beyond that route, who are already in the margins.

The narrative of desire, then, needs taming: it needs to be contained within a set of rules and regulations, a set that is conveniently supplied by the heterosexual romance narrative, always culminating in marriage and inclusion in the proper social order. In this order two bodies, of two distinct sexes and genders, are united by the community (in its presence, by its appointed policing authorities), and are expected to perform certain rituals and avoid others. The rituals to avoid are basically those of desire: they should be either annihilated or performed away from the public gaze.

Thus, in order to mute the violence to the male body, which is inherent to the chain of narratives resulting in those of death and desire, the military narrative has to be finally replaced with the narrative of the family — that is, in place of a narrative of breaking the familial chain, a narrative of its continuation; in place of a narrative of pain, a narrative of comfort and warmth associated with "family." The woman needs to be constantly there, ready in the background, visually and mentally forming a space and design with her female body, into which the narrative of military violence will dissolve at its critical moment.

Dual Penetration

The female body, inherently necessary for displacing the violence to the male body, also brings with it the complex and ambiguous erotics of penetration. Being penetrated is that which defines the female body and differentiates it from the male body, which is coherent, separated from the outside and secure from penetration from the outside. Thus, the presence of the woman in the army is on the one hand the ultimate protection against the threat embedded in the male fraternity: the threat of the homosexual penetration. The unit of males only — relying on each other and also literally leaning on each other, touching each other, sharing their nakedness, practicing on each other's bodies during drills and training sessions — creates a homosocial environment.[6] And if the homosocial environment breeds homoerotics, the cloudy shade of homosexuality begins to threaten the bright sky of the fraternity, and the body — the male body, the particular male body — appears to be potentially exposed to penetration and to lose its "natural" "immunity"; it can, in fact, potentially, be penetrated, that is, become "woman," since penetration is the trait of the female, and being a woman, as Freud taught us, means being castrated: not having that which is "male." Woman, therefore, is defined both by the lack (of the male sex organ) and by being the penetrated. Hence, being penetrated (as in homosexuality) means also being castrated, since it means being a woman.

The woman in the army protects the soldier from the threatening homosexual "castration" through her promise of visible, handy, available heterosexuality, and by her role of being *the* penetrated, thus "exempting" the male from being thus positioned. Yet on the other hand she is also a sad reminder of the possibility of penetration: the realization that the male body is, after all, vulnerable to penetration as well. It is vulnerable to two kinds of penetration: the erotic one, as part of possible homosexual relationships, and the penetration of the bullet.

The woman's presence, then, paradoxically, both enhances the dangerous possibility of sexual penetration and makes it ominously present, as she is the very manifestation of "penetration," and, at the same time, also calms the fear and detracts its threat, as her presence transfers the state of being penetrated to its rightful "owner," thus promising heterosexuality and setting the ground for death's opposition — the creation of a family, and the protection and safety of "home."

It is clear now that the woman needs to be both absent and present in the military sphere: since her presence raises the shadow of the haunting penetration, of castration and of death, she needs to be invisible, absent, not part of the military visual space so as not to awaken the ghosts of violence. But her presence, which raises these threats, is acutely needed to chase away these very same haunting ghosts: when visible to the eye, she is the penetrated one, veiling the man's possible castration. She needs to be there — and not there; part of the army, always part of the visual space — but always not really part of it, always also an outsider; there to help eliminate all that threatens in the army, in the fraternity, in violence — and not there so as not to arouse the very same threats through that which she signifies: the penetrated.

It is only through this dual existence (yet another stereotype of woman-hood: duality) that woman can become the connecting thread between the military space and the familial space. The female body needs to be present at the same time in both spaces: the military one and the romantic, familial one; she needs to become a dual presence: a home at the army base, a soldier who is a mother/lover, a homemaker who wears a helmet together with the guys. Only then does she become continuity itself. Only this dual body — fighting and bearing children, with the soldiers but always also back home and waiting for them to return — can make the connection between the two domains.

The promise of this connection is precisely the reason why the army needs woman in the military space: she will become the smooth surface connecting between the private and the public sphere, the space that is life and continuity and the space that is death and violence. This apparent, false continuation conceals the deep abyss, the gap, between the two spheres; it conceals the fracture, the rupture between them. It makes them appear as one, continuous space, within which the male soldier can move back and forth, to combat and back to desire, to death and back to family, to his comrades and back to his lover — a movement that erases all that differentiates between the two worlds and thus all that is frightening in the military sphere: it erases the military's one and only trait, violence.

Creating the Dual Positioning

The female body's occupation of both spheres, the military site and the space of the home, and the reinforcement, maintenance, replication and repetition of this duality, entail investing vast cultural energies of representation which will create a visual environment and a visual and literal model to be followed and repeated.

The women drafted to the Palmah sometimes had to struggle for their right to be drafted, and for the recognition of their ability to serve in the same capacities as men. Not everyone was happy with their inclusion; on the contrary. Debates about their very inclusion were carried out on all levels. Yitzhak Sadeh, chief commander of the Palmah units and the Haganah's Chief of General Staff (1945), finally decided the troops could not miss the opportunity to increase the number of soldiers given the eagerness of women to be drafted. Nevertheless, they were usually assigned the traditional roles of women, necessary in the Palmah (whose members lived in kibbutzim and participated in their regular daily routine, such as cooking). The few who did fight were pulled back after a short while, following a story about women's fragility which Netiva Ben-Yehuda exposes as a fabrication (benign or not so benign).[7] Her fictional autobiography is a clear testimony to the roles allocated to the women fighters and their humiliation as combat soldiers; and the few other testimonial anthologies or personal memoirs reveal — not necessarily with the same accusing approach chosen by Ben-Yehuda — the "real" life of women in the Palmah; in other words, their dual capacity as being placed in the domestic space, but not limited to it, and as handling arms, but not controlling them.

"Generally speaking," says Surika, Sara Shpechner Braverman — the only one of the three women members of the paratroopers' mission from Mandatory Palestine to occupied Hungary during the Second World War who came back home (Hannah Senesh and Haviva Reik were captured and killed) — in a volume of collected memoirs of Palmah women, "I saw us women participate in the war as fighters of a static war — post commanders, section commanders and Ma'aziyot [settlement commanders] — and I am not talking about the few that fought in the actual battles."[8] This oxymoron, "static war," is the major characteristic of both the memoirs and the photographs taken of Palmah women: Figure 1 shows a soldier in 1948, obviously posing for the camera; her choice of position is static, her choice of location — a phallic pole, her smiling face bending towards it. Should she choose to move, to take action, this phallic pole will give her no direction; it points only to itself, the arrows point only to the pole.

FIGURE 1
WOMAN SOLDIER (1951)

Plate no. 12 SP (1) in the M.H.T. (Michal Heiman Test) 1997
Photographer unknown (Courtesy of Michal Heiman)

The promise of a "static war" is also embedded in the 1970s photograph of three soldiers, posing for the traditional photo in uniform and with rifles, but their hold on the rifle does not endow them with control over the phallus: the flowers in the barrels make sure they won't be used (Figure 2).

FIGURE 2
THREE WOMEN SOLDIERS (1974)

Plate no. 18 in the M.H.T. (Michal Heiman Test) 1997
Photographer unknown (Courtesy of Michal Heiman)

In these two photos the woman/women are both part of the army and not; part of the fighting forces but with the phallic (pole, rifle) force stopping them from actually becoming part of the fraternity, lest they lose their ability to occupy both spheres. Even when she is on top of the phallic symbol, the urban "horse" of the urban cowboy/macho, and the caption says "Haganah dispatcher/running on motorcycle," her eyes staring into the horizon, she is yet one more model put on display, her gaze staring ahead just as it has stared a minute ago into the mirror, not forgetting the slight tilt of her Palmah "gerev" (sock) cap, static despite the potential movement inherent in the male vehicle (Figure 3). And when she is actually running, covering territory — desolate desert emptiness — and conquering the land with her own legs, the caption chosen by the editors of the booklet in which this photograph appears, reads: "The boys are coming, the boys are coming!" (Figure 4).

Roland Barthes, when describing the effect of photography, talks about the "punctum," that minor, peripheral detail, whose very presence changes the viewing, turns it into a new photograph with sublime value. It is the "element which rises from the scene, shoots out of it like an arrow, and pierces me."[9] The punctum, Barthes says, is not intentional: "from the viewpoint of reality (which is perhaps that of the Operator [the photographer]), a whole causality explains the presence of the 'detail'."[10] Putting flowers in the rifle barrel (Figure 2) is clearly an ironic self-reference, alluding to the traditional pose and its translation into the popular Hebrew song "flowers in the barrel and girls in the turret [of the tank]"; and in any case, inside a room and at the beginning of training (see their new, starched uniforms), there is no shooting — nor enemy; the road sign (Figure 1) might point to an actual site when viewed from a different perspective; and photographing the dispatcher in action, in movement (Figure 3) may result in a blurred, unclear image. So, the photographer may have an explanation for these "details." But "from the *Spectator's* viewpoint," Barthes continues, "the detail is offered by chance and for nothing."[11]

The puncturing force of the detail seems to be culture bound. The recurring phallic objects "puncture" (pun unintended) me, a woman who is already a child of the feminist revolution; the empty vast stretches of land conquered by the boys, now returning to the home-making girls, punctures only a post-Zionist woman, for whom the empty land "shoots out like an arrow" from the photograph as an unintended exposure of the Zionist myth of "a people without a land returning to a land without a people," and the static positioning is a punctum only when the photographs are reread from a perspective of visual culture. In fact, not only the punctum is culture bound; its opposite, the studium, is, finally, culture bound as well. Here is what Barthes writes about the studium:

> It [the scene of the photograph] has the extension of a field, which I perceive quite familiarly as a consequence of my knowledge, my culture; this field ... always refers to a classical body of information [historical, cultural].... Thousands of photographs consist of this field, and in these photographs I can, of course, take a kind of general interest, one that is even stirred sometimes, but in regard to them my emotion requires the rational intermediary of an ethical and political culture.[12]

The punctum, says Barthes, "will break (or punctuate) the *studium*."[13] These photos of Palmah women are regular, traditional — I've seen thousands of them — and they arouse my interest, as I understand them as part of the materials for my self-constitution, and they even arouse excitement, as they draw me into a scene I identify with. But I am also reading them — the

FIGURE 3
A HAGANAH DISPATCH RIDER ON HER MOTORCYCLE (17 MARCH 1948)

Photo by Zoltan Kluger (Courtesy of the Government Press Office)

FIGURE 4
"THE BOYS ARE COMING, THE BOYS ARE COMING!"

Photographer unknown (Courtesy of the Government Press Office)

studium — through a certain "ethical and political culture," and when so doing it is almost impossible not to notice how the shot, the framing, the angle of the camera, the positioning and staging of the woman actually create this "ethical and political culture" in the first place. By reacting to what now becomes punctum, that detail (the tilt of the hat, the arrows leading nowhere) which shoots — now — out of the photo, we realize how the visual not only reflects political culture, not only reflects that which is then burned into our memory and is now projected back onto the photo, but actually invents an imagined image which becomes an imagined female subjectivity.

"To some extent," writes Irit Rogoff in her study of visual culture, *Terra Infirma*,

> the project of visual culture has been to try and repopulate the space with all the obstacles and all the unknown images which the illusion of transparency evacuated from it. Space, as we have understood it, is always differentiated, it is always subject to the invisible boundary lines which determine inclusions and exclusions.... Clearly space is always populated with the unrecognized obstacles which never allow us actually to "see" what is out there beyond what we expect to find. To repopulate space with all of its constitutive obstacles as we learn to

recognize them and name them is to understand how hard we have to strain to see....[14]

Departing from Barthes to point to the mediation of the rational, i.e. the ethical and political culture, to trace points of puncture that transcend the rational, and to reveal a new reaction, a new reading, a new image, we now look at the photos, and at the testimonial memoirs, as exposing that which they are lacking, as including traces of that which they exclude.

Resting on the way to besieged Safed is a group of soldiers, men and women (Figure 5). But among many men, there is only one woman, as if a representative of her gender. She is very visible as the lone, single woman, sitting at the edge of the group, but her status is unclear. She is either an integral part of the group — or trailing in the back; she is either not carrying anything — or her gun, radio, backpack are well hidden behind her slim back. The one clear detail in her positioning is her hand held to her mouth, with a hint of the obligatory erotic leaf of grass between her teeth. Here is a woman soldier; she is clearly on her way to battle together with the other men. But at the same time she is the only one of her kind, only a token stand-in for her gender, and therefore inconsequential in terms of the male fraternity; she is also not totally similar to them as she is at the margins, she is not carrying anything that might help her in combat, and she still remains erotic in her posture. She is both part of the fighting army and not; she is both in the military sphere, but still a "woman" remaining also at "home" — both by virtue of her erotics and because she is the only woman actually present at the site of battle.

Such are also all the other photographs: the women are always both part of the military sphere but never entirely; both representing home, desire and family, but at the site of the male fraternity. Although they appear as "studium," being so regular and intellectually mediated (by the knowledge of the history, the organization and the myths of the Palmah, that is, its participation in both military activities and farm work at the kibbutzim which hosted them, and the traditional roles women took upon themselves in this structure), they contain that "punctum" detail, that trace of the excluded or uniqueness of the included, which when noticed — as it leaps at today's viewer — points to the duality of the representation of the Palmah women: both there and not there, both part of the army but always also part of away from it, of "back home." The excluded gun of the woman on her way to combat; the exclusion of the bullets from the rifles with the flowers, or of the wheels of the male transportation vehicle, the motorcycle, which are cut off by the frame so it can't move, all these are unrecognized details which nonetheless appear to the eye ("shoot out like arrows" to "repopulate space," in Barthes' words) as constructing the form and the character of the subjectivity constituted by the photos.

FIGURE 5
A GROUP OF SOLDIERS ON THE WAY TO BESIEGED SAFED (1948)

Source: Yiftah ahuzat ha-sufah: Sipurah shel hativat Yiftah-Palmah (Yiftah in the Grip of the Storm: The Story of the Yiftah-Palmah Brigade), published by former Brigade members (November 1970), p. 9.

When the Palmah women testify in retrospect, this duality is told mostly through that which is the ultimate representation of both penetration and home: pregnancy, and the female nurturing characteristic. "When it was my turn to work in the [kibbutz] kitchen," says Rina Tadmor Averbuch in the memoir collection, "I always made sure that Zvi Gatzub, who couldn't stand tomatoes, had some other food — 'bimkom' [replacement]. A minor thing, minor detail, and yet. A girl has this 'caring,' 'motherly sense.' And it had significance."[15] The search for significance elsewhere, other than in the battlefield, characterizes some of the memoirs but not all; time and again they complain of getting pregnant at "the wrong time." Ziona remembers:

> When I was a signaler I was trained to work on illegal immigrants' ships. But when finally I received the order to board such a ship I was already pregnant. I was devastated. I had to tell Nachum Sarig the truth about the pregnancy. My mission was canceled; I wanted to go, but … I have not participated in the wars and did not do anything special. When my friend Michal, a member of Kibbutz Ginosar just like me, told me she

participated in the operation to release the illegal immigrants at Atlit I was consumed by jealousy, I went out of my mind. And I already had a child and I'd missed out, I simply missed the important things.[16]

And Sara laments: "In 1945 I was released from service. In 1948 my heart broke — I already had a baby and I'd missed the war."[17]

Pregnancy marks the moment which is the juncture of both spheres; it is the very creation of the surface continuation between the penetration (the military sphere, the male fraternity and the threatening bullet) and the home and family lineage, as well as between being at the site of fighting and being at the site of home and nurturing. "We worked in the kitchen," tells Rochele.

> We cooked outside, and ate at the sheep-pen wing. The first two got pregnant. We knew those pregnant should be taken care of, that we should make sure they ate right. The members' food was very meager. So every morning we went to the pregnant women and asked them what they wanted to eat. One morning, I asked and they said scrambled eggs and a pickle. I prepared what they wanted and arranged it all on a tray, and just as I was about to serve them — shots were heard. All of a sudden we've been shot at. I lay down with the tray in my hand and as I was falling down I thought of the scrambled eggs. That "the pregnant" won't get their scrambled eggs.[18]

The combination of combat and nurturing is strictly balanced in one of the spreads in the reunion booklet (Figure 6): two photos are neatly laid out one alongside the other; in one the women are training for one-on-one body combat, bringing to mind the male heterosexual pornographic erotics of women touching each other, and right next to it is a photo of a woman cooking in a huge pot, for the entire battalion, presumably: the military balanced by nurturing, the erotic balanced by the motherly. As a matter of fact, in both cases, both when participating in the fighting (a signaler in action, albeit with her femininity intact [Figure 7]) and nurturing (distributing food to the forces at Kibbutz Negba, buckets in hand but also helmet on the head [Figure 8]), there is an erotic edge to the image: the food-distributor, a shadow of a smile on her face, is coming out of a dark, unmarked tunnel, with an entrance but an invisible end. This image represents both a desired haven, a comforting, nurturing, protecting womb, and a location threatening in its secrecy, the vaginal engulfing, swallowing "Dark Continent." The signaler too displays a shadow of a smile in the middle of the battle, but the shot is also wide enough to include the flora surrounding her and her hand leaning on the cylinder, the gaping, round open end of which is dark, inviting as shelter and frightening as a trap with no visible end.

But even before pregnancy, when still within the frame of military activity, the woman is both there and not there. "I've always been alongside the

FIGURE 6

WOMEN TRAINING FOR COMBAT, AND WOMEN COOKING

Source: Yiftah ahuzat ha-sufah, p. 162.

FIGURE 7
A HAGANAH MEMBER OF THE COMMUNICATION BRANCH IN ACTION
(17 MARCH 1948)

Photo by Zoltan Kluger (Courtesy of the Government Press Office)

FIGURE 8
DISTRIBUTING FOOD TO THE FORCES AT KIBBUTZ NEGBA (30 OCTOBER 1948)

Photo by Teddy Brauner (Courtesy of the Government Press Office)

events," describes/complains Yael:

> Partner to cleaning the weapons, before and after the action, to pulling
> out the weapons and to their concealment. In our battalion they did not
> take women to real actions. Maybe I did contribute something but I
> never took part in real combat. I went through life feeling it is not the
> real thing. I got married. When I brought a note from the doctor
> confirming I'm pregnant I was released from the Palmah.[19]

And when they are in the lookout itself — "Girls at the post" at Mount
Canaan (Figure 9) — the shot is so wide they appear as two tiny, smiling
figures inside the huge, protecting structure, lost inside it as they smile, almost
dissolving into its vast space, not threatening the male ownership of the vast
empty territory captured by the camera and not sharing the responsibility of
its conquest by the male soldier. Thus they altogether resemble a photo from
the family album depicting a trip to the traditional Independence Day IDF
open base exhibit, hardly in control of anything, their military function
undermined by the shadow of buildings to escape to in the background.

The duality of both being there and not being there appears in its full
clarity in a famous unstaged photograph (on the cover of *Ba-Mahaneh*, the
IDF's magazine) featuring Ziva Arbel as "The young woman with the gun," as
the caption reads, at a cease-fire in the Ben Shemen forest following the
conquest of Lod in July 1948 (Figure 10). Again, there is only this one single
woman among a large group of men, as if a representative, a symbol, of
women's presence among the male fraternity; totally exhausted, she is leaning
against a (phallic, decapitated) tree, a bandage on her forehead and the gun
on her hip signaling her participation in combat, and her bare feet and
keffiyeh-covered long hair signaling her erotic femininity. No one in the
photograph is facing the camera; one guy to the left is smiling at someone, the
guy next to him seems to be whistling to himself, and a whole group on the
right is gathered around looking at something — a map, maybe. Only Ziva
Arbel stands on her own, excluded from the group and not looking anywhere;
her slightly opened mouth is not engaged in conversation but is making an
effort to breathe, she alone, she and the gun, not part of anything, just
standing there separated from the others even by her different exhausted
appearance. Both there and not there, both a partner (bandage, gun) and
totally different and separated, both the symbol of the erotics of penetration
and the promise of heterosexuality in the midst of the ignoring male fraternity.

Otherness

But if her functions vis-à-vis the male soldier are what make woman part of
and differentiated from the military fraternity, she still needs to be marked as

FIGURE 9
MOUNT CANAAN: GIRLS AT THE POST (FEBRUARY–APRIL 1948)

הר כנען - בנות בעמדה

Source: *Ah, pigishah she-kazot … Yuval le-hakhsharat ha-tzofim 4, 1946–1996* (Ah, What a Meeting … The Fiftieth Anniversary of the Scouts No. 4 Training Group, 1941–96) (internal publication, n.d.), p. 20.

FIGURE 10
THE YOUNG WOMAN WITH THE GUN (JULY 1948)

Photo by Boris Carmi (Courtesy of Carmi's estate)

unique in her very participation in the army: to be marked as the "right" national woman, the figure to symbolize the Nation and to be the model for national female subjectivity. That cannot be achieved through her otherness to the male; she needs to be differentiated from others within the group of women, as Ziva Arbel is differentiated from all other women by being the only one at the battle, and by the gun she carries.

She is differentiated by her non-pregnancy; becoming pregnant removes her from the group of the optionally fighting women. Pregnancy is reserved to the woman who will become part of the nation — but is still outside of it: ultimately, she is the new immigrant. Here she is at the entrance to a tent (which could have been just as well an army tent), her belly thrust forward as if to emphasize this difference (Figure 11). No less striking is the otherness of the older, urban, so very Jewish bourgeois woman (Figure 12). The similarity between her hand lifted to her face and Moshe Dayan's hand lifted to his forehead, though genderly differentiated, foregrounds the otherness embedded in the little black handbag hanging on her arm, a city handbag, a mother from the city burying her kibbutznik son in the presence of he who symbolizes the national ideal of capturing and occupying territory and working the land. Here she is, older, so "other" than the other women we are expected to accept as ourselves, as our image, the woman fighter and the woman farmer, who has no belly and no handbag.

But the model of national womanhood needs also be differentiated by her bodily function, the very characteristic that would make her identical to other women. She needs to be differentiated from other possibilities of womanhood, not only through not performing the act of pregnancy, but also through the very representation of her female body. This differentiation is accomplished by separating women whose body wounds can be represented from those whose wounds are not to be represented, in order to enhance even further their function as flesh and blood — and not as representations.

By being flesh and blood, as she is in culture, woman leaves "representation" to man. He, now, can become the "living dead"; and he is not constantly confronted with the threat of the material penetration of the bullet, since the present bodily woman is corporeality itself and thus subsumes the flesh and blood which can be harmed in battle. Being his "other," she now marks him as the master of the domain of "representation." The "real," material penetration is the domain of woman; the domain of man is the represented penetration — the living dead. Man is representation of corporeality; he is the result, to follow Judith Butler, of materiality becoming culture. The corporeal body, says Butler, is repressed and excluded from culture by culture, by being signified as the unrepresented; the woman is stereotyped as being corporeality, as both outside culture and within culture.[20]

In order to maintain this order of things a woman's body will not be represented as wounded; the representation of the wounded is reserved to the

FIGURE 11
PREGNANT NEW IMMIGRANT AT THE ENTRANCE TO HER TENT, 1 JANUARY 1949

Photographer unknown (Courtesy of the Government Press Office)

FIGURE 12
FUNERAL OF RO'I ROTBERG IN NAHAL OZ

Photo by Moshe Eitan (Fuchs); from *Ba-Mahaneh*, 30 April 1956
(Courtesy of Military [IDF] and Defense Establishment Archives)

male soldier as he becomes a living dead. The "right" female body has to remain within the domain of materiality. Thus, a representation of a wounded female body is the mark of the "other," the other nationality, where representing womanhood does not affect "our" females' materiality nor their ability to become the symbol of the nation when in a domestic, presumably nonmilitary, context.

It is the Palestinian woman's body, then, which, when represented wounded, becomes an "other" and marks the Jewish woman soldier as that which she constructs herself, and is culturally constructed, to be: the nationally "correct" femaleness. This "other" is the torso of Na'ima Mahmud — headless, legless, and uterus-less after being penetrated by a gas grenade thrown by an Israeli soldier standing a few meters away (Figure 13). The representation of the penetrated female body is being displaced onto the other; thus, the Israeli woman soldier is kept marked as "corporeal" rather than "represented," and material penetration becomes twice removed from the male soldier's body, which maintains its power to become a representation rather than corporeality when wounded, when penetrated. The Palestinian woman, then, functions in the already familiar dual capacity, except now she is constructed as a subject rather than an object which will function in its duality as the otherness necessary for the Israeli female subject to differentiate and thus constitute herself as the "right" national subject. She, the Palestinian, is both the other — the representation of bodily wound — but also a model to be imitated by the Jewish newcomer, thus becoming the tool with which the "new" Jewish woman can differentiate herself from the "old" (i.e. diasporic) Jewish woman; and that is achieved not only by putting distance between the new, working-the-land woman fighter and the urban, bourgeois woman, but also by performing as a native.

Here again is Ziva Arbel, and again on the cover of *Ba-Mahaneh* (Figure 14); the caption, which reads "Who is jealous of the pitcher?" became the title of a song, inspired by the photo, written by Avraham Halfy and Mordechai Zeira, the words of which are easily imagined. In the photo Arbel performs nativeness: the *keffiyeh*, the pitcher, drinking water directly from the pitcher as the "natives" do. But this is not a representation of nativeness as an origin, but as performance; and as such, it also exposes itself as performance, as a performative self-constitution, since it contains also traces of the excluded, the erased, the repressed: that which is perceived as the "true" native. In order to appear natural one needs to look like — to imitate, to perform — the natural, but this necessary imitation then becomes the punctum that exposes it as imitation.

This punctum "shoots" out of the photo when it is compared with another — the imitated original performance: that of the Palestinian woman (Figure 15). This photograph was taken by Hanna Safieh in Bethlehem in the 1940s; and although the similarity between the two performances is clear to the eye, so is the difference: while Arbel drinks directly from the jar, the Palestinian woman holds it at a distance, away from her body, separate from herself, not an extension of herself and not making her one with the symbolic "regional" object, as does the imitating Arbel. The power relations between the two "identical" women, power relations that keep the Israeli woman higher up in the hierarchy and therefore her nativeness unquestioned, is maintained through the

FIGURE 13
NA'IMA MAHMUD, 1988

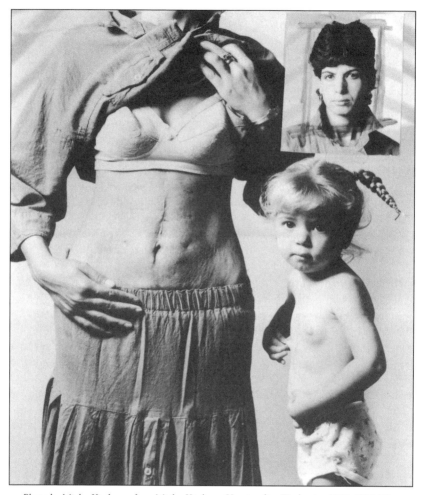

Photo by Micha Kirshner; from Micha Kirshner, *Ha-yisraelim: Tatzlumim, 1979–1997* (The
Israelis: Photographs, 1979–1997) (Or Yehuda: Hed Arzi, 1997), p. 93
(Courtesy of the photographer)

distribution of the visual of nativeness: while Arbel's photo became one of the
icons of Palmah women, and thus the model Israeli woman, the other photo was
exposed publicly to Jewish spectators only in 2001 by an Israeli Jewish woman,
Rona Sela, in an Israeli museum exhibit rereading the visual context of Zionist
culture. This exclusion over a long period of time of the visual of "being native"
maintained the ethos of the nativeness of the newcomer.

FIGURE 14
"WHO IS JEALOUS OF THE PITCHER?" (JULY 1948)

Photo by Boris Carmi (Courtesy of Carmi's estate)

FIGURE 15
BETHLEHEM, THE 1940s

Photo by Hanna Safieh (Courtesy of Raffi Safieh)

Finally, then, the complex role of the woman soldier is exposed as a performative act similar to the performativity of that which she is structured to protect: the military male fraternity. In his staged photographs Adi Nes exposes the hidden homoeroticism of this fraternity, and its "neutral natural" standing as performative. Himself imitating famous homoerotic and homosexual photographs while using as his subject uniformed models, Nes focuses on the elements that create homoerotics, but he also exposes both the male soldier and his fraternity, and the homoerotic undercurrent, as performative. It is especially clear in one photograph in which a "wounded" soldier lies in the arms of his brother-in-arms, who paints the wounds on the recumbent body, with the palette itself clearly visible (Figure 16).[21] Thus it is not only womanhood or heterosexuality or the use thereof in the narrative of militarism that is performative, but also the narrative of military fraternity and its practices.

But even with the presence in the scene of visual culture of such products as Nes's photos, these other performative acts of self-constitution as the "real," "good" Israeli woman, modeled as they are in accordance with the

FIGURE 16
ADI NES, UNTITLED, 1995

(Courtesy of Dvir Gallery, Tel Aviv)

representation of Palmah women, still dominate the scene of the construction of Israeli womanhood as part of the metanarrative of the military aspect of Israeliness, which is to this day the main defining feature of Israeli nationality as much as daily civil life.[22] These apparatuses of displacement, based on the stereotype of female duality, perpetuate the complex and contradictory, but finally destructive, role of the female body in the construction of the necessary conditions for war — and of war itself. Active refusal to fulfill this role, or an active exposure of its performativity and thus its imaginary inventedness, through cutting the Gordian knot of the dual function of the female body, are the only modes of relieving the woman's body from the cycle of affirmation, enforcement and maintenance of male military rule and violence.

NOTES

*   My special thanks to Professor Hannah Naveh for her enlightening comments, help and friendship, and to the Porter Institute for Poetics and Semiotics at Tel Aviv University, and to its director, Professor Ziva Ben-Porat, for their support.

1   Both the concept of the heroic dead as the "living dead" and the feminine role associated with it were researched extensively in Hebrew literature. See Hannah Hever, "Hay ha-hay ve-met ha-mat" (Alive is the Living and Dead is the Dead), *Siman Kri'a*, No. 19 (March 1986), pp. 188–92; Dan Miron, *Mul ha-ah ha-shotek: Iyunim be-shirat milhemet ha-atzma'ut* (Facing the Silent Brother: Essays on the Poetry of the War of Independence) (Tel Aviv and Jerusalem, 1992); Hannah Naveh, "Al ha-ovdan, al ha-shkhol ve-al ha-evel ba-havayah ha-yisre'elit" (On Loss, Bereavement and Mourning in the Israeli Experience), *Alpayim*, No. 16 (1998), pp. 85–120; Hannah Hever, "Gender, Body, and the National Subject: Israeli Women's Poetry in the War of Independence," in Edna Lomsky-Feder and Eyal Ben-Avi (eds.), *The Military and Militarism in Israeli Society* (New York, 1999), pp. 225–60. Michael Gluzman, "Ha-estetikah shel ha-guf ha-merutash: Al tarbut ha-mavet be-'Hu halakh ba-sadot'" (The Esthetics of the Smashed Body: On Culture and Death in "He Walked in the Fields"), *Sadan*, Vol. 5 (2001), pp. 347–77.

2   See, for example, Netiva Ben-Yehuda, *Bein ha-sfirot: Roman al hathalat ha-milhamah* (1948 — Between the Calendars: A Novel) (Jerusalem, 1981), pp. 340–9.

3   Geula Cohen, *Sipurah shel lohemet* (Underground Memoirs) (Tel Aviv, 1995), pp. 128, 249. All translations are mine.

4   Ibid., p. 214.

5   Ibid., p. 13.

6   "Homosocial" refers to the notion of socialization and sexual identity development in relationships that exclude — or seem to exclude — women. According to Eva Kosovsky Sedgwick, "in any male-dominated society, there is a special relationship between male homosocial (including homosexual) desire and the structures for maintaining and transmitting patriarchal power: a relationship founded on an inherent and potentially active structural congruence." See her *Between Men* (New York, 1985), p. 25. For elaboration in Jewish and Israeli culture, see Daniel Boyarin, *Unheroic Conduct: The Rise of Heterosexuality and the Invention of the Jewish Man* (Berkeley, 1997); Michael Gluzman, "Ha-kmihah le-heteroseksualiyut: Tziyonut ve-miniyut be 'Altneuland'" (The Yearning for Heterosexuality: Zionisma and Sexuality in "Altneuland"), *Teoriyah u-Vikoret*, No. 11 (Winter 1997), pp. 145; Yosef Raz, "Ha-guf ha-tzva'i: Masokhizm gavri ve-yahasim homoerotiim ba-kolno'a ha-yisre'eli" (The Military Body: Male Masochism and Homoerotic relationships in Israeli Cinema), ibid., No. 18 (Spring 2001), pp. 11–46.

7   Ben-Yehuda, *Bein ha-sfirot*, pp. 317–21.

8   Aya Gozes-Saburai, *Sapri li, sapri li: Haverot Palmah mesaprot* (Tell Me, Tell Me: Stories of Palmah Women) (Tel Aviv, 1993), p. 56.

9   Roland Barthes, *Camera Lucida*, trans. Richard Howard (London, 1984), p. 26.

10   Ibid., p. 42.

11   Ibid.

12   Ibid., pp. 25–6.

13   Ibid., p. 26.

14   Irit Rogoff, *Terra Infirma: Geography's Visual Culture* (London and New York, 2000), p. 35.

15   Gozes-Saburai, *Sapri li, sapri li*, p. 27.

16   Ibid., pp. 15–16.

17   Ibid., p. 19.

18   Ibid., pp. 115–16.

19   Ibid., p. 64.

20   Judith Butler, *Bodies That Matter: On the Discursive Limits of "Sex"* (New York, 1993).

21   I thank Professor Donald Mengay and Channing Sanchez for teaching me this aspect of homosexual photography, and pointing to the specifics of Nes's work of imitation.

22   For the militarization of the civilian sphere, see the extensive work done by the members of "New Profile: Movement for the Civil-ization of Israeli Society", at www.newprofile.org.

Index

1948 War of Independence 150
1967 Six Day War 39, 142–3, 148–50

Aal-Far'un 6, 13
Aaronsohn, Sarah xv
Abna al-Balad (Sons of Our Country) 27, 29
Abu Baker, Khawla xiii
Abu T'umi, Khaled 15
Abu-Ghanam 20–21
Abu-Lughod, Lila 3, 6
Abu-Zeid 4–5
Adar, Shaul 1
advertising 118–23
Ahmed, Leila 87
al-Aref, Aref 8, 11, 13
al-Fanar Organization 17, 23–4, 26, 29
aliyah x
al-Jamal, Mufti Sheikh Muhammad 25
Aloni, Shulamit 33, 115
al-Qassem 27
al-Wazir, Intisar 28
Arabism
  as an approach to social theory 1–2
Arab *see also* Palestinians
  demographics 51–3
  familism amongst 51–3
  Hadash (Arab–Jewish Progressive
    Democratic Party) 115
  Israeli Bureau for Arab Affairs 18
  relations with the Jews 48–50
Aran, Gideon 145
'Asa'ahsa, Nura 15

Barak, Aharon 137
Barak, Ehud 58
Barthes, Roland 173, 175–6
Bar-Zvi, Sason 13–14
Baskin, Judith 151–2
Bedouin 11, 15
  crimes of honor within 11
Ben Rafael, Eliezer 66
Ben-Yehuda, Netiva 166, 170
Berkovits, Shmuel 138
Blu, Greenberg, Rebbetzen 128
Borkovitz, Nitza 153–4
Bussel, Joseph 66
Butler, Judith 184

Canada 40–42
capitalism
  capitalist-patriarchal ideology 110

impact on the structure of families 57–8
in Palestinian society 9
career opportunities xii
Carp, Yehudit 24
Chazan, Naomi 130
childcare xii–xiii, 99–100
  attitude of Palestinians towards 99–104
  within a Kibbutz (*mitzvah*) 65–7, 69–83
civil religion 140
civil society 19
cognitive map 134
Cohen, Geula 166–7
collectivity xii
commemoration xv
communism xii, 29
consciousness raising 157
constitutional revolution 58, 136–8
crimes of honor 1–33
  characterization of those committing 9
  connection to law in Bedouin society 11
  countries where they take place 17–18
  Druze involvement in 17, 30
  economic basis for 1, 7–9
  in Jordan 18–19
  in Lebanon 19
  legal character and repercussions of 3–4,
    9–11, 18, 22–5
  Palestinian views of 25–9
  psychological analysis of 15, 32–3
  ritual character of murder 15–17
  role of close marriage 22
  role of Israeli state politics/patriarchy
    18–25, 32
  role of the police 19–21, 24
  role of vengeance 13–14

Dayan, Arye 26
Dayan, Moshe 146, 184
decolonization 154–8
democracy
  as part of ethnocracy 148–9
  contradictions within 49
  influence of changes to 136–7
demographic changes within 38, 40–42, 51
  of Arab Citizens of Israel 51
  of Christian Arab Citizens of Israel 52
  demographic competition 48
  of different countries Israel, the US,
    Canada and Japan 40–42
  of different religious groups 40–42
  of Druze Arab Citizens of Israel 53

of Jewish Citizens of Israel 53–5
of Muslim Arab Citizens of Israel 52
Denin, Ezra 18
Deri, Aryeh 136
diaspora
    Jewish 48, 128, 148, 158
discourse
    collectivist 136
    public 110
    secular-enlightenment 133–40
domestic violence 56, 93–4, 103–4 *see also*
    crimes of honor and violence
Druk, Rachel xv
Druze 17
    Druze Religious Court 43
    involvement in crimes of honor 17, 30
    Shari'a court 26
Dumon, Wilfred 57
Durkheim, Emile 48

economics
    of domestic politics xi, 39–40
    of families 55–8
    inheritance law 7–9
    Ministry of Education 91, 146
    post-industrialism xii
    role of capitalism in producing gender bias
        xii, 9, 57–8, 110
    support given to crimes of honor 1, 7–9
education xii, 156
    compulsory education law 53, 91
    of Palestinian women 9, 89–90
    of murderers 27, 29
    problems of university education for
        women 99–100
    representation of women in 111
    role in changing values 103
    within a Kibbutz 65–7, 77, 79
Egypt 105
Eliezer, Rabbi 151
Elon, Ari 140
Elon, Menahem 140
employment *see* labor
epistemology 110, 157
ethnicity
    ethnocracy 148–58
    ethno-religious groups xii, 50, 57
Europe
    as source of migration 68

Falk, Smadar, 126
families
    economics of 55–8
    neomodern 54–5
    postmodern 55

relation to the military 165, 168
    Ultra-Orthodox 53–4
familism xii, 38–58 *see also* marriage
    among Christian Arab Citizens of Israel 52
    among Druze Arab Citizens of Israel 53
    among Jewish Citizens of Israel 53–4
    among Muslim Arab Citizens of Israel 52
    among Palestinian Arab Citizens of Israel
        51–2
    anti-familism of the Kibbutz 66
    as basis of identity 39, 49
    effect of diminishing fertility on 38
    effect of postmodern families 38
    individualization of 38
    as Jewish national asset 47–9
    as Palestinian national asset 49–50
    role of marriage in 38
    sororicide and filiacide *see* crimes of honor
    in state building 39
Feige, Michael xv
feminist
    radical 154–9
    representation of 122
    revolution within the Kibbutz 65, 68,
        70–76
    second wave of 110
    within Orthodox Judaism xiv–xv, 127–60
femininity
    as mother xii
    representations of xii, 112 *see also*
        representation of women
fertility 38–42
    contraception 46
Fogiel-Bijaoui, Sylvie xii–xiii
fundamentalism
    Islamic 106

Ga'on, Rabbi Sa'adya 147
Gadir, Sheikh Hussein 23
Getz, Rabbi Yehudah 129–31, 134, 137
Ginat, Joseph 2, 17, 20, 24–5, 31
Goddard, Victoria 6
Goldberg, Harvey 144
Granqvist, Hilma 7
Gulf War 117
    media policy towards women in 117–18
Gurevitz, Zali 145

Ha'aretz 28
Habasha, Ibtisam 26
Haberman, Bonna 137
Habib, Shafik 24
Hadash (Arab–Jewish Progressive
    Democratic Party) 115
Haddad, Yvonne 153

Haider, Aziz 28
Halabi, Nur el–Din 26
Hasan, Manar xi
Haskalah xvi
Haut, Rivka 128–9, 131, 133
Hazelton, Lesley 151, 153
Heffer, Haim 150
Helman, Sarah 141, 157
Herzog, Hanna xv, 116
Herzog, Yitzak 131
historiography xv
Hoffman, Anat 130
homosociality xiv, 168–9
honor (*hamula*) xi, 1–33, 51–2 *see also* crimes
    of honor
    definition 3–7
    different senses of 4–5
    difference in the standards applied to men
        and women 5–6
human rights groups
    silence on crimes of 'honor' 26
Hungary 170
Huri, Samira 26

Ibrahim, Nora 9
identity
    familism as the basis of 39, 49
    state 120
    of women 68, 123
Ighbariya, Raja 29
immigration 120
individualization 38
    limits to 39–43
inheritance law
    connection to pre-Islamic custom 8
    hamula 7
    role in perpetuating patriarchy 7–9
Intifada 24, 116–17, 140
    Al-Aqsa 58, 142
    representation of women as involved in
        116–17
Iraq 105
Israeli
    attitude towards Palestinian society 18–25,
        32
    Bureau for Arab Affairs 18
    declaration of independence 148
    demographics of 40–42, 53–5
    economic description of 39–40
    Government Advisor on Arab Affairs
        21–2, 24
    history of 47
    Knesset 26, 136, 138–9, 142
    Ministry of Defense 146
    Ministry of Education 91, 146

Ministry of Religions 129, 131, 136, 146–7
    Ministry of Welfare 21
    state involvement/complicity in crimes of
        honor 18–25, 32
Israeli Defense Force 15, 53
    enrollment of women 164
Israeli–Palestinian conflict 121
Israeli Woman's Network (IWN) 137

Jaskow, Rahel 156–7
Japan 40–42
Jewish
    demographic make-up of Israeli 53–5
    diaspora 48, 128, 148, 158
    enlightenment 133, 135
    familism amongst Israeli 53–4
    feminists 127
    First International Conference of Jewish
        Feminists 127
    Hadash (Arab–Jewish Progressive
        Democratic Party) 115
    involvement in crimes of honor 30
    Judaism *see* Reform Judaism, Orthodox
        Judaism and Ultra-Orthodox
    Rabbinical courts 43, 54
Jordan 18–19

Kana'an, Ikhlas 5, 26, 30–31
Kazaz, Nisim 22
Kehat, Hannah 128
kibbutz xii, 63–83, 176
    anti-familism amongst 66
    attempted sexual equality within 67
    Beit Hashita 63, 67–72
    changes in status of 64
    childcare within (*mitzvah*) 65–7, 69–83
    early history of 66–70
    education within 65–7, 77, 79
    feminine revolution within 65, 68, 70–76
    gender differences in the perception of
        67–8, 78
    Gilgal 63, 73, 77–83
    ideological basis of 66
    masculine revolution xii–xiii, 65, 76–82
    periodization of Kibbutz history xii–xiii,
        64–83
Klausner, Joseph 146
Kol al-Arab 27
Kolech (religious woman's forum) 128
Koran 17
Kressel, Gideon 2, 10, 15, 17, 19–20
Kuhn, Thomas 126
Kurdistan 17

labor xiii, 50–51, 54

employment of Young Palestinian women
    in Israel 85–108
  gendered judgment of professions 100
  history of gender make-up in the labor
    force 40
  unemployment 51
  work versus career 86
Lapid, Herut 1
Law of the Protection of Holy Sites 130, 147
Law of Return 148
Lebanon 105
  crimes of honor within 19
  occupation of 117
  movement to withdrawal from 115
legal system
  civil rights 138
  Compulsory Education Law 53, 91
  constitutional revolution 40, 58, 136–8
  division of traditional law and customary
    law 12
  Druze Religious Court 43
  Law of Military Service 164
  on marriage 43–4, 85, 87–105
  Rabbinical courts 43, 54
  relating to crimes of honor 3–4, 9–11, 18,
    22–5
  religious law 43–50, 53, 57
  response to 'Women of the Wall' 130–33,
    136–9, 147, 154
  role of religious laws 48
  Shari'a rule 26, 28, 44
  tribal court system 11–14
Leibovitch, Yeshayahu 145
Lieblich, Amie xii–xiii
Likud Party 115
Lustick, Ian 22

marriage
  attitudes of Palestinians 85, 87–105
  changing patterns of 39–43
  connection to familism 38
  cross religious comparison of attitudes on
    divorce 44–6, 88–9
  different types of marriage 47
  Druze Religious Court 43
  laws relating to 43–4, 85, 87–105
  managing change in demands on 98
  premarital relationships 96–7
  as a psychosocial developmental stage 87
  Rabbinical Court 43, 54
Marxism 157
media
  absence of women from 111–12
  advertising 118–20
  bias against 'Woman of the Wall' 129–30, 143

feminization of 122
  internationally 112
  Jerusalem Post 130
  policy of 117
  possible change in 115–16, 121–3
  relative appearance of men/women 112
  representation of politics 114–17
  representation of sport 114
  representations of 'first ladies' 113–14
  representations of women 110–24
  sexual representation of women 113
  Woman's Tefillah Network (WTN) 128, 130
Melman, Billie xv
memory
  collective 120
  familial and communal 147
Meretz Party 115, 130
Mi'ari, Muhammed 26–7
military xiii–xiv, 123–4, 164–91
  dependence on gendered narrative xiv–xv,
    166–8
  example of the Palmah women 165–6, 70
  Freudian analysis of 168–9
  homosociality within 168–9
  Israeli Defense Force 15, 53, 165
  Law of Military Service 164
  Ministry of Defence 146
  narratives within 166–8
  ritual within 165–6, 168
Mintz-Aberson, Esther xv
Mizrahi 120
modernity 140, 157
  difference from Judaism 157–8
Mohammed 87
Mujrabi, Amira 31
multiculturalism xi, 33
murder xi, 1 see also crimes of honor

narratives
  analysis 67–73, 77–82, 101
  difficulties of narrative approach 82
  dominant xvi, 145
Netanyahu, Benjamin 115
Netanyahu, Sarah 113
Nj'idat, Salah 21, 29
Nora, Pierre 147

Oren, Susan 141
Orientalism 1–2, 32
  analysis of the orientalist social analyst 1
  within Israeli society 18
Orthodox Judaism xiv, 48, 120, 127–60
  as Catholic 136
  conservative movement 48, 131, 154
  feminism within xiv–xv, 127–60

Halakah 129, 131–3, 137, 139
Jewish Orthodox Feminist Alliance 128
  relation to secularism 135, 149–50
  security status of religious sites 142–3
  Woman's *Tefillah* Network (WTN) 128, 130
  Women of the Wall group (WoW) *see* Woman of the Wall
  women's prayer groups (WTG) 127–9, 131–2, 139
Othering 110, 185
Ottoman Empire 155

pacifism 165
Pakistan 17
Palestinians xiii
  academics 93–4, 106
  attitude to childcare 99–104
  changing career options for 92, 104
  changing social role of woman 86, 92
  consequences of divorce for 89
  crimes of honor within *see* crimes of honor
  employment of Young Palestinian women in Israel 85–108
  exclusion from the Israeli discourse 148
  familism as assets of 49–50
  history of paid labor for women 90–92
  interpersonal relationships 93–105
  in the Occupied Territories xiii, 18
  Supreme Monitoring Committee 26
  violence xv, 1–33, 93–4, 103–4
  women's self perception 86
Palgi, Michal 77
Paolei Zion party xv
Parush, Iris xvi
Peace Now 120
Peli, Pnina 128
Peres 113
Plaskow, Judith 158–9
Pogrebin, Letty 140–41
pornography 178
  comparison with advertising 119
postmodern xii, 38
privatization xiii
Progressive List for Peace 26
public sphere xi, 111
  secularization of 135

Rabin, Leah 113
Raday, Frances 137
Rafael, Ben 70–71, 78
Rapaport, Tamar 141, 147
Raz-Krakotzkin 148, 158
Reform Judaism Movement 48, 129–31, 134, 148, 154

Regev, Mati 20–21, 26
religion
  civil 140
  connection to nationalism 47, 140, 145, 150
  cross-religious attitudes on divorce 44–6, 88–9
  demographic of different religious groups 40–42
  Law xii, 43–50, 53, 57
  Ministry of Religions 129, 131, 136, 146–7
  municipal religious councils 139
  political bodies xiv
  Rabbinical courts 43, 54
  religious/secular cleavage 155
  as scapegoat for inequality 140–53
  secular feminism compared to religious feminism 154–8
religious feminism 128–60 *see also* Women of the Wall
  as corrective to ethnocratic bias 154–8
representation of women
  in advertising 118
  changes facilitated by new technology 121
  cross-cultural Jewish/Palestinian comparison of the media 116
  epistemological issues related to 110–11, 157
  involved in honor murder 15–17
  masculinization of 121–2, 176
  as Madonna or whore 120–21
  in the media xiii–xiv, 110–24
  physical representation xiv, 6, 9–11
  physicality 114
  possible change in 115–16, 121–3
  as sexual objects 113, 118–21, 169–91
  as victims 112–13
  as wife/mother 112, 114–15, 118, 120–21, 123, 165–6, 173
  within the military 165–6, 168
  in Women of the Wall 129–30, 135–40
Rivlin, Lilly 141
Rogoff, Irit 175
Rojanski, Rachel xv
Rosenfeld, Henry 22

Sadik, Walid 27–8
Safieh, Hanna 187
secularism xiv, 120, 149–150, 158
  connection to Orthodox 135, 149–50
  secular feminism compared to religious feminism 154–8
  secularization of the public sphere 135
Sela, Rona 188
Sered, Susan 139

sex industry 113, 119, 178
sexuality xiv
  as the basis of murder 3, 25–8, 31, 45–6
  changes in attitudes towards sex 94–5
  homoeroticism 190
  homosexual impulses in the military 168
  representation of women as sexual objects
      113, 118–21, 169–91
  representation of 113, 118–22
  required suppression of 3, 25–8, 31, 45–6
  sexual performativity xiv
  within the narrative of the military
      168–70, 173–91
Shakdiel, Leah xiv
Shalev, Carmel 43
Shani (Israeli Women Against the
  Occupation) 141
Sharon, Ariel 115, 142
Shas Party 136
Shepher, Joseph 71
Simon, Akiva Ernst 134, 136
social ecology 144
socialism, decline of 136
state xi
Stockhammer, Avishai 149–50
Storper-Perez, Danielle 144
stratification xi, xiii
subjectivity xiv, 177–8
Suleiman the Magnificent 145
symbolic
  annihilation 111, 120
  borders 141
  frontier 110
Syria 105

Talmon-Garder, Yonina 71
Tandi 26
Tariq, Um 8
territorial politics 155
Thirty Years War 136
Tiger, Lionel 71
Torah 145, 152, 156
  women's access to 127–32
Turkey 17
Turki, Fawaz 16
Tydor Baumel, Judith xv

Ultra-Orthodox (Haredi) 53–4, 131–2,
  134–5, 137, 139, 143, 146–9
  families of, 53–4
Um Jihab see al-Wazir, Intisar
United Kingdom
  Balfour Declaration 149
  British Mandate 90, 94, 145–6, 149,
      166–7, 170

Queen Victoria 155
United States
  American Jewish Congress 131
  anti-Vietnam movement 115
  demographics of 40–42
  experience of Orthodox Jews 139
  influence on feminism in Israel 127–8,
      130–31, 134
  perceived influence of 129

veterans 120
violence against women 113, 119, 124 see also
  crimes of honor
  against the Woman of the Wall 129, 131
  depoliticization of 166
  domestic 56, 93–4, 103–4
  feminist attitude towards 164

war
  1948 War of Independence 150
  1967 Six Day War 39, 142–3, 148–50
welfare policy 55–6
Western norms
  influence of 95, 103–6
Western Wall
  as ethnocratic site 149
  Committee for the Wall 146
  history of 145–6
  legal consideration of the status of 147
  political significance of the Wall 142–5
  in relation to Women of the Wall 126–60
Women in Black 117, 141
Women of the Wall 126–60 see also Western
  Wall
  connection to peace movement 140–41
  connection to secularizing influence
      135–6, 138–40
  Group 'Herstory' of 127–33
  inappropriateness of religious/secular
      explanations for 133–40
  International Committee for Women of
      the Wall 130
  international connections 127–8, 130–31,
      134, 156
  legal response to 130–33, 136–9, 147, 154
  media bias against 129–30, 143
  opportunity for change 154–8
  perception of 129–30, 135–40
  as Protestant Jews 134–5, 137
  and radical feminism 127
  second stage of 137
  state bias against 129
  violence against 129, 131
  women's prayer groups 127–9, 131–2
women's organizations 26

silence on crimes of 'honor' 26

Yaniv, Orly 117
Yiftachel, Oren 148
Yishuv (pre-state Jewish settlement) xv
Yohanna, Rabbi 151

Zebeidat, Ikhlas, 11
Zini, Levy 142–3
Zionism 48, 145–6
  decline of 136
  hegemonic narrative of 135
  Paolei Zion party xv

Other Title in the Series

Israeli Identity
In Search of a Successor to the Pioneer, Tsabar and Settler

Lilly Weissbrod

'This book undertakes a challenging task: to trace the changes in Israeli social identity over the past 100 years. The changes are related to the changes in the territorial borders of the country, real or desired, and to the ideology that justified them at different points in time. It requires a courageous and experienced sociologist to undertake such a momentous task, yet Dr Weissbrod's interesting work proves that it is indeed possible. In a thoroughly researched and well-argued book she takes the reader through major stages in the development of Israeli society and the identity formation of its people. Though the book is professionally sound, it is written in a user-friendly style, thus making it interesting reading not only for expert sociologists and middle-eastern scholars ... undergraduate and graduate students, as well as the educated lay reader, will be able to appreciate Dr Weissbrod's analysis.'
Dr Yael Enoch, Head of Sociology Section,
Open University, *Ramat Aviv*

272 pages 2003
0 7146 5376 4 cloth
Israeli History, Politics and Society Series No. 26

FRANK CASS PUBLISHERS
Crown House, 47 Chase Side, Southgate, London N14 5BP
Tel: +44 (0)20 8920 2100 Fax: +44 (0)20 8447 8548 E-mail: info@frankcass.com
NORTH AMERICA
920 NE 58th Avenue Suite 300, Portland, OR 97213-3786 USA
Tel: 800 944 6190 Fax: 503 280 8832 E-mail: cass@isbs.com
Website: www.frankcass.com